The Abortion Papers
Ireland: VOLUME 2

To Anne
Best wishes
Sinéad x

Catherine Conlon.

Happy Reading!

Anne, I do hope you enjoy
the read. Thanks for
supporting it as a project.

Aideen x

Attic

Image: Alice Maher 'The History of Tears' (2001)

The Abortion Papers Ireland: VOLUME 2

EDITED BY:

Aideen Quilty, Sinéad Kennedy
& Catherine Conlon

First published in 2015 by Attic Press
Attic Press is an imprint of Cork University Press
Youngline Industrial Estate
Pouladuff Road
Togher
Cork T12 HT6V, Ireland

British Library Cataloguing in Publication Data

ISBN: 978-1-78205-172-5

Printed by CPI, UK
Typeset by Burns Design

www.corkuniversitypress.com

CONTENTS

Above and Beyond the Silence

AILBHE SMYTH

Tell us, they say, about women and abortion in Ireland.

I'M NOT SURE THAT I CAN ANY MORE, or at least not in any straight-forward way. There are several reasons for this, as always personal as much as political. I'm not sure which is the most complicated, and in any case (in my case), the reasons are peculiarly resistant to partition. One way and another, I suspect it's to do with the passage of time, the transmutations of generations and, above all, with how abortion is framed and dealt with in Ireland.[1]

But it's not in Ireland, abortion, that's the whole point. If it were, we wouldn't be here having to write about it. Again. Or think about it, or not much, or not so endlessly. It's Byzantine, this business of abortion, convoluted, complex beyond all reason and necessity, harrowing, tortuous. Also wounding, sometimes grotesque.[2]

As I'm writing this, keeping an ear to the ground, I hear a bishop speak. He says, *inter alia,* that lesbians and gay men who have children may be care-givers, but they 'are not parents'. When asked about his views on a woman having an abortion after she has been raped, the bishop says women who become pregnant through rape should not 'destroy a life in order to get back at the rapist'.[3] That these models of logic aroused more satirical and caustic comment than ire is proof of the rapid and steep decline of the power of the Catholic Church in Ireland over the past twenty years. The bishop's intervention in a secular debate is seen as contentious and out of step with contemporary morality and behaviour. It is counter-cultural. Irish people are no longer cowed or obsequious in the face of episcopal intimidation. And we're certainly not obedient. Mostly, we don't believe the bishop, and definitely we don't do what the bishop says.

To be fair (although I'm under no obligation, given our history of subjugation by the Catholic clergy), the next day, other bishops and priests rushed *en masse* to dissociate themselves from their fellow bishop's remarks, and he had to apologise for any hurt he 'might' have caused, which is more of a damage limitation exercise than an apology. Mind you (I'm still being fair), it wasn't the abortion remarks the hastening clergy were detaching themselves from, just the comments about the parental credentials of lesbians and gay men, considered as potentially damaging to the Catholic Church in light of the upcoming marriage equality referendum. So a strategic partial rebuke then. Nothing to do with truth.

All the same, and it's a change that changes so much, after generations of feminism, we know a lot more now about the truths of women's lives, and we're talking about them, not *sub rosa* and *entre nous*, but out loud and in public. Raising our voices in protest, challenging the suppression of the truth about the realities of our lives.

> I grew up knowing nothing. No one ever told me the 'facts of life', and I'm not sure when I even knew there were facts I didn't know. Until quite a ripe age, sex and reproduction remained largely a mystery. In my convent school when I was about fourteen or fifteen, a nun told us in all seriousness that if we met boys (and we did, to be sure), we should keep our berets and gloves on at all times. For me, and for so many women of my generation and the generations before me, you had to learn on the job. Trial and error. The consequences of the errors were always left to us, the women, to bear. These were the wages of sin, because sex (outside marriage) and sin were synonymous. Hence the Magdalen laundries, followed, in so many cases, by the lonely boat to England and lifelong damage. I was lucky not to get pregnant. It wasn't because I was well informed and well equipped. Au contraire. I was just lucky, that's all.

The silence surrounding abortion has been deafening, only ruptured every decade or so by a dreadful human tragedy – the loss of a woman's life or the awful public drama of court cases taken to wrest from the state the right to an abortion here in this country. It has a been a silence where women cannot talk of their experiences, and where even to fight for women's right to abortion has meant being branded as a kind of pariah. To be known as a pro-choice activist has been a consistent guarantee, throughout my adult life, of consignment by mute consensus to the social and political outlands. This is changing now, especially for younger women, but it has by no means entirely disappeared.[4]

In Ireland, the very word 'abortion' is unspeakable, shunned as too shocking, shameful, stark – and true. Not only is abortion exiled so that it doesn't happen here, *hic et nunc*, and our hands clean, our consciences clear; it has been banished from the discursive hubs of our society, including academe, the media, and the Dáil, and effectively paraphrased out of conceptual existence.[5] We have to break that silence. We have to end deceitful and damaging equivocation. We have to call a spade a spade, and an abortion an abortion.

What would happen if one woman told the truth about her life?
(Rukeyser, 2005)

If we had abortion right here and now, we'd be talking about it differently, in a matter-of-fact way, as neither more nor less momentous than other events and experiences in the life of a woman. Because that's what abortion is: a matter of fact and a quotidian reality. Every day twelve women leave this country and go abroad, mainly to England, to have an abortion. It's about time Ireland faced up to that fair and square. Persistent denial and problem-exportation is not only a disavowal of women's human rights, it is profoundly dishonest.

If we had abortion here, we'd be talking about it if and when we needed or wanted to, and not to satisfy the relentless probing of (certain) media for 'true life' abortion dramas. It's an irony, that: all over the media if you're an extreme case, but better shut up if you've had a unexceptional abortion, or taken the abortion pill, for the good and simple reason that you don't want to have a baby. You might want to later, or you might not, but not now anyway. No drama, no dilemma. Just a decision: '*Women have abortions every day. It's just one choice*'.[6]

The thing is that abortion shouldn't be an 'issue' at all. Having your appendix out or your varicose veins removed are not 'issues' (except perhaps in medical research and practice. I don't know anything about that.). You don't see documentaries or read books or blog posts about people's experiences of these routine medical procedures. They are unsensational and non-spectacular, not matters of public debate, argument and intense scrutiny. Morality doesn't come into play. They're not about right or wrong, but rather taken for granted as everyday necessities or choices ('election', to be precise, as in 'elective surgery'). The law doesn't come into it. To be sure, medical practice is regulated, but procedures are not subject to detailed enumeration, regulation or surveillance by the forces of law and order. Abortion is the extremely rare, if not unique, exception.[7] In Ireland anyway.

The plain fact of the matter is that abortion is not everywhere a 'dilemma for the nation', not everywhere controversial and divisive, not everywhere so profoundly stigmatised and silenced. Other facts follow from this: abortion is one of the most commonly carried out medical procedures,[8] and, where it is legal, it is also one of the safest.[9] Even for women from, although not 'in', Ireland. Of course, what the Irish abortion rate is I can't say, because abortion technically doesn't exist here, medically, legally or statistically, unless a woman's life is in danger or she is suicidal.[10] Even in these dreadful situations, the law is so restrictive and punitive, as well as baffling and intractable, that it continues to have a 'chilling' effect on the medical profession (see *A, B and C v. Ireland* (2010) ECHR 2032).

• • •

'Ciunas! Ciunas! I can't hear myself speak!' my mother used to say
(there were six of us, an unruly mob).

Inside my head, there's a cacophony of facts and stories, sedimented over decades of struggle for the right to control our bodies and our reproductive lives. I try to sort it all out for myself, because I want to honour them, all these women denied the right to freely decide for themselves, because that matters, because their lives matter.

I think about the bitterly fought decennial referendums,[11] wrenching infinitesimal gains for women's freedom.[12]

The Constitutional cases, in Irish and international courts, challenging the Eighth Amendment to the Constitution and the law, or lack of law, that follows from it.

The many women batted about from court to court in individual cases, their lives, their griefs, their hurts rawly exposed, judged, rarely remedied. Some we know by name, others only by a letter – strange alphabet of human woe and the frigid impartiality of the law.

The thousands upon thousands of women who have been forced to travel abroad to access abortion – a constant stream, every day, every week, every year, from all over the country.[13]

The women and the couples forced to carry a pregnancy to full term despite there being a fatal foetal anomaly. The cruelty of that. The enduring pain.

I think too of the thousands and thousands of women over the years who wanted to but could not travel for an abortion: migrant women without the necessary papers, or facing uncertain exit and re-entry permits; disabled women or women too ill to travel; women whose family or work commitments mean they can't travel; women who haven't got the money to travel; women who can't tell their partners or families. There is any number of reasons, and all of them mean denial of a basic human right to access the health services we need, specifically abortion.[14] We'll never know how many women had to go ahead with an unwanted pregnancy because they had no choice. We'll never know their names or their stories, but they're there.

I think of the devastating case of Ms Y, a young asylum seeker who discovered not long after she arrived here that she was pregnant as a result of rape in her home country. She repeatedly requested an abortion during the first several months of her pregnancy, but this was refused although she was suicidal. Eventually, Ms Y was forced to have a caesarean section at twenty-four weeks.[15]

I think most of all of the women who did not survive. The women whose deaths occurred because they were refused an abortion. We know the names and stories of some of these women, but certainly not all.[16]

Their deaths make me very sad.

They also make me very angry with a society, a system, a state that places so little value on the life of a woman, that treats her – us – with such contempt. I know Ireland is not unique in this regard. I hold no candle for Irish 'exceptionalism'. But it's the place I grew up in and the place I know more viscerally than anywhere else. I know its savagery and inhumanity, the scars it leaves on bodies and lives, and I know how it tries to bury, hide and deny.

I detest those life-denying silences and their legacy of torment and distress. I repudiate utterly the power of the silencers.[17]

En filigrane, the chorus of my life as a woman, I hear the voices of all those women denied, voices in the wilderness, voices at the edge of my consciousness, *sotto voce,* haunting, uncomprehending.

Why did they have to suffer, why did some have to die?[18]

> *What would happen if one woman told the truth about her life? The world would split open.* (Rukeyser, 2005)

We have started to speak plainly, raising our voices loud and clear above and beyond the silence, about the facts that matter and the truths and realities of our lives.

We will not be exiled, outlawed, ignored, scorned, dismissed or discounted. We are unfaltering in our opposition and unflinching in our resistance.

We will not stop until we are free, free to make our own decisions about our bodies and our lives. We will not stop until the hypocrisy is ended and the truth can be told. We will not stop until women can have abortions in Ireland.

> *[...], it's a shame to say*
> *that as long as we have the capacity*
> *to bear children, Ireland is not a safe place for us;*
> *women, rise up, this country hates us*
> *it's long past time we changed it*
> *enough is way too much this time.*
> (Clancy, 2014).

Dublin, May 2015

ACKNOWLEDGEMENTS

THE EDITORS WOULD LIKE TO THANK Ailbhe Smyth for her enthusiasm, facilitation and encouragement for this project. Ailbhe is a strong presence across this volume not least because of her own activism and academic work. As a feminist she has changed knowledge production in profound and imaginative ways, making it possible for generations of feminists to exchange across academic and activist boundaries.

We would also like to thank each of the contributors for their commitment to this project over its lengthy period of gestation and to Cork University Press, and Maria O'Donovan in particular, for their enthusiasm, investment and direction in this project.

Elizabeth Crean's diligent editorial assistance and her encouragement for the project was hugely valued and appreciated by us as was the extensive work done by Paula McGarry in assembling the bibliography.

We are grateful to Niall Behan, Chief Executive of the Irish Family Planning Association, for permission to use their legal timeline on abortion in Ireland and to the National Women's Council of Ireland, especially director Orla O'Connor, for support in hosting the Abortion Papers Symposium in June 2013, from which this volume emerged. Finally, we owe our gratitude to Alice Maher for so kindly making her wonderful image available to us for the cover.

AIDEEN QUILTY, SINÉAD KENNEDY
AND CATHERINE CONLON

May 2015

NOTES ON CONTRIBUTORS

IVANA BACIK is the Reid Professor of Criminal Law at Trinity College Dublin, and a barrister. She is a Labour Party Senator for Dublin University (elected 2007 and re-elected 2011). Ivana has written extensively on criminal law, criminology, human rights and related matters, and has a record of campaigning on civil liberties and feminist issues. Her publications include *Kicking and Screaming: dragging Ireland into the twenty-first century* (O'Brien Press, 2004).

URSULA BARRY is a Senior Lecturer with the School of Social Policy, Social Work and Social Justice, University College Dublin, specialising in gender, equality and public policy and long-time writer and activist on reproductive injustice in Ireland. She contributed a chapter to the original *Abortion Papers*; and edited, and contributed to *Where Are We Now: new feminist perspectives on women in contemporary Ireland* (New Island Publishers, 2008). She is the Irish representative on EU Research Network on Gender Equality and Employment (ENEGE.eu). Ursula also presented a paper on 'Women and Austerity in Ireland' to the International Association for Feminist Economics (IAFFE) Annual Conference in Barcelona in 2013. With Pauline Conroy co-author of 'Ireland in Crisis: Women, Austerity and Inequality' in Jill Rubery and Maria Karamessini (eds), *Women and Austerity: the economic crisis and the future for gender equality* (Routledge, 2014).

CATHERINE CONLON is an Assistant Professor in Social Policy at the School of Social Work and Social Policy, Trinity College Dublin. Her principal areas of interest are: gender, sexuality and reproductive health; intergenerational relations and sexual socialisation. She is co-author with Evelyn Mahon and Lucy Dillon of *Women and Crisis Pregnancy* (The Stationery Office, Dublin, 1998). Her current research explores parents' accounts of communicating with their children aged four to nine years about the body, relationships and sexualities.

PAULINE CONROY is a social scientist and has been writing and active on questions of reproductive rights since the 1960s in London. She published *Ireland: rape and incest not grounds for abortion* with the Center for Women Policy Studies in 2012 and *The Deadly Solution to* *an Irish Problem: backstreet abortion*, with Brian O'Reilly, in 1983 during the campaign against the Eighth Amendment to the Constitution. She was secretary to the Dún Laoghaire branch of the campaign – the only constituency to vote 'No'. Pauline has been an external expert with the Commission to Inquire into Child Abuse and a lay member of the Mental Health Tribunals. She recently worked with a collective on 'Women to Blame: 40 years of struggles for women's reproductive rights' – an exhibition which opened in Temple Bar in November 2014.

LEAH CULHANE is a feminist academic and social activist. She is currently completing her PhD at the University of Manchester, where she is part of an ERC-funded project entitled 'Understanding Institutional Change: A Gender Perspective'. She holds a master's degree in Equality Studies from the School of Social Justice, UCD and a BA in Communication Studies from Dublin City University. Her broad research interests lie in the area of social change, gender and public policy.

CLARE DALY is the independent socialist TD for Dublin North where she served on the Council for thirteen years. Clare was elected to the Dáil in February 2011. As president of the students' union in DCU, she was a leading member of the campaign for abortion information and the battle against SPUC in the 1990s. In 2012 Clare was the first TD in the history of the state to introduce pro-choice legislation to the Houses of the Oireachtas. The bill intended to provide access to abortion where there is 'real and substantial risk to the life' of the pregnant woman, in line with the X case.

CATHIE DOHERTY is a feminist whose activism focuses on the use of electronic communication for community-building. A founding member of the Abortion Rights Campaign (ARC), she is an editor and contributor at the ARC blog, www.abortionrightscampaign.ie

RUTH FLETCHER is Senior Lecturer in Medical Law at Queen Mary University of London. She has published and lectured widely on issues of reproductive rights, health care law and legal theory. Ruth contributed to a submission to the European Court of Human Rights in *A, B and C v. Ireland* and gave evidence to the Joint Committee on Health and Children as they considered the Protection of Life During Pregnancy Act 2013.

GORETTI HORGAN is a lecturer in Social Policy at the University of Ulster, a member of the Institute for Research in Social Sciences and Deputy Director of ARK's Policy Unit. She is also a director and former chair of the Northern Ireland Anti-Poverty Network. A socialist and trade unionist, she has been active in the pro-choice movement in Ireland for over thirty years. A member of the first Women's Right to Choose Group in Dublin, she was National Organiser of the campaign against the anti-abortion amendment to the Irish Constitution, 1981–83. Since moving to Northern Ireland in 1986, she has been working to extend the 1967 Abortion Act to the region. She is a founder of Alliance for Choice (NI), set up in 1996 to try to use the thirtieth anniversary of the act to promote its extension.

SINÉAD KENNEDY is a Marxist and feminist activist and teaches in the School of English, Theatre and Media Studies at Maynooth University. She has written on feminism, popular culture, Irish and European politics and is currently completing a book on Marxism, feminism and neoliberalism. She is a founding member of Action on X, now Action for Choice, which campaigns for access to free, safe and legal abortion in Ireland, North and South and is currently secretary of the Coalition to Repeal the Eighth Amendment.

RONIT LENTIN is a retired Associate Professor of Sociology, Trinity College Dublin, where she specialised in race critical theory, and gender, race and conflict and founded the MPhil in Race, Ethnicity, Conflict. She has published extensively on race, racism and gender in Ireland, Israel-Palestine, and gender and the Holocaust. Among her books are: *Women and the Politics of Military Confrontation: Palestinian and Israeli gendered narratives of dislocation*, with Nahla Abdo (Indiana University Press, 2002), *Racism and Antiracism in Ireland* (Beyond the Pale, 2002), and *After Optimism: Ireland, racism and globalisation* (Metroeireann Publications, 2006), both with Robbie McVeigh, *Race and State*, with Alana Lentin (Cambridge Scholars Press, 2006), *Thinking Palestine* (Zed Books, 2008), *Co-Memory and Melancholia: Israelis memorialising the Palestinian nakba* (Manchester University Press, 2010), and *Migrant Activism and Integration from Below in Ireland*, with Elena Moreo (Palgrave Macmillan, 2012).

STEPHANIE LORD is an activist, writer and feminist from Drogheda. She has been involved in a number of campaigns on sexual health and reproductive rights. Stephanie graduated with an honours degree in Law (UCD), and also holds an honours diploma in Housing and Community Studies and an MSc in Equality Studies from the School of Social Justice, University College Dublin.

SANDRA McAVOY teaches on Women's Studies postgraduate and adult and continuing education programmes in University College Cork. Her research interests include the history of sexuality and the history and politics of reproductive rights. Recent publications include 'Vindicating women's rights in a foetocentric state: the longest Irish journey', in Noreen Giffney and Margrit Shildrick (eds), *Theory on the Edge* (Palgrave Macmillan, 2013) and a co-edited volume, Jennifer Redmond, Sonja Tiernan, Sandra McAvoy and Mary McAuliffe (eds), *Sexual Politics in Modern Irish History* (Irish Academic Press, 2015).

ANTHEA McTEIRNAN is a journalist with *The Irish Times*. She is the former chair of the Irish Family Planning Association and a member of the National Women's Council's advisory group on reproductive rights, the Abortion Rights Campaign and the Repeal the Eighth Campaign. She worked with the late Michael Solomons on his biographical polemic *Pro Life? the Irish question* (Lilliput Press, 1992). She is also the mother of two sons.

LIA MILLS writes novels, short stories, essays, reviews and an occasional blog. Her most recent novel, *Fallen* (Penguin, 2014) is set during the early years of the First World War and the Easter Rising. She teaches aspects of writing, most recently at the Irish Writers' Centre and at University College Dublin, where she was previously a Teaching and Research Fellow at the Women's Education, Research and Resource Centre with a particular focus on the work of Irish women writers. She lives in Dublin (www.liamills.com).

JO MURPHY-LAWLESS is a sociologist, lecturing in the School of Nursing and Midwifery, Trinity College Dublin since 2005. She has published widely on childbirth and new motherhood in Ireland and internationally. She served on the editorial board of international journal *Reproductive Health Matters* from 1996–2003 and is a member of the

EU-wide COST research network, 'Childbirth Cultures, Contexts and Consequences'. She set up the Birth Project Group as a joint effort for the School with the University of Edinburgh, Napier University and the Birth Resource Centre Edinburgh.

JANET Ní SHUILLEABHÁIN has been a sex education and reproductive rights activist for the last twenty-six years, having been a teen during the X case. After her own abortion she has worked to help others with information and support when they have travelled to the UK. She is a member of the Abortion Rights Campaign working to end the stigma that surrounds abortion and towards free, safe and legal abortion in Ireland. She lives in Dublin with her two children and has recently returned to full-time education, pursuing a degree in Communication Studies in Dublin City University.

ORLA O'CONNOR is Director of the National Women's Council of Ireland. She holds a master's degree in European social policy from NUIM and a degree in social science from UCD. Orla has worked in senior management in non-governmental organisations in Ireland for over fifteen years. Previously the Head of Policy of NWCI, she has led campaigns on a wide range of women's rights issues, including social welfare and pension reform, reproductive rights and the introduction of quality and affordable childcare. Orla has also worked in local community-based projects developing services for the unemployed, lone parents and young people.

PEADAR O'GRADY is a socialist and human rights activist who is a member of the Socialist Workers Party, People Before Profit, Transgender Equality Network Ireland and Doctors for Choice. He works as a consultant child psychiatrist in the Irish health service.

ANNE QUESNEY is a feminist and abortion rights advocate and activist. She has worked as Director of Abortion Rights and Head of Advocacy for Marie Stopes International, as well as on a number of sexual reproductive health and rights projects and reports. She has served as Chair and still volunteers for the Abortion Support Network. She recently wrote her MSc dissertation on women's voices in contemporary Ireland, of which this article is an extract, and worked closely with the Abortion Rights Campaign to organise a public 'speak out' in Dublin in September

2013, in collaboration with BPAS and Catholics for Choice and with other pro-choice organisations in Europe.

AIDEEN QUILTY teaches in the School of Social Policy, Social Work and Social Justice, UCD and is Director of their Women's Studies Outreach Programme. As a feminist educator she seeks to engage students at undergraduate and graduate levels in critical debate on social issues including reproductive epistemologies, policies and politics. Her research combines feminist and spatial theories and practices with the aim of articulating place pedagogies for community-based higher education and disenfranchised groups including the LGBTQ community.

SINÉAD REDMOND is a feminist, abortion rights activist, and maternity rights activist. She is a mother, was a founding member of the Abortion Rights Campaign (ARC), and is currently a committee member of the Association for Improvements in the Maternity Services (AIMS) Ireland, www.aimsireland.ie.

ANN ROSSITER, a long-standing Irish feminist who has been involved in pro-choice work for many years, is from Bruree, Co. Limerick and has lived in London for nearly half a century. She was a member of the Irish Women's Abortion Support Group (IWASG) 1980–2000 helping Irish abortion seekers with information, finance and accommodation. Currently, she is a member of the London Irish Feminist Network and of the performance art group, speaking of IMELDA (Ireland Making England the Legal Destination for Abortion). Her writings include *The Other Irish Journey, a survey of Northern Irish women attending British abortion clinics, 2000/2001* (Marie Stopes International, 2001) and *Ireland's Hidden Diaspora: the abortion trail and the making of a London-Irish underground* (Iasc, 2009).

LESLIE SHERLOCK is a gender and sexuality educator, activist and researcher. She recently completed her PhD in Trinity College Dublin's Children's Research Centre, using a queer and feminist perspective to examine narratives of good and inclusive practice in sexuality education from professionals in Ireland and Sweden. Leslie's activist and educational interests include sex education, trans* experiences, sexual health, feminism, hetero/cis-normativity, queerness and empowerment. She has been an engaged activist for trans* rights in Ireland since 2006.

Leslie regularly lectures on university courses and delivers training on gender, sexuality and sex education to colleges, workplaces and community groups. Since 2009, Leslie has served on the board of directors of the Irish Family Planning Association (IFPA), and served as Chairperson of this organisation.

AILBHE SMYTH was the founding head of Women's Studies/WERRC at UCD, and has been active in feminist, LGBT, and radical politics for a long time. She has researched and written extensively about women, sexuality and reproduction as well as feminism, politics and culture in contemporary Ireland. She was the editor of the first volume of *The Abortion Papers Ireland* (Attic Press, 1993). Ailbhe is a founding member of Action on X / Action for Choice, of Feminist Open Forum, and is Convenor of the Coalition to Repeal the Eighth Amendment.

LISA SMYTH is a Senior Lecturer in Sociology at Queen's University Belfast. Her research interests focus on gender inequalities in contexts of reproductive and family life. Her recent book, *The Demands of Motherhood: agents, roles and recognition* (Palgrave Macmillan, 2012), provides an analysis of the strains experienced and coping strategies adopted by women as they occupy this contested social role. Her previous book, *Abortion and Nation: the politics of reproduction in contemporary Ireland* (Ashgate, 2005), analysed the citizenship consequences of a gendered politics of national identity, as it has played out through a focus on abortion law. She has also published papers on the social politics of breastfeeding, abortion, sex education and motherhood, and is currently working on how fear and resentment shape maternal action in response to political change in Belfast.

MAEVE TAYLOR is Senior Policy and Advocacy Officer with the Irish Family Planning Association (IFPA). She has a BCL from University College Dublin and an LLM in human rights law from Queen's University Belfast. She previously worked for many years with the feminist human rights and development NGO, Banúlacht.

ABORTION IN IRELAND:
A LEGAL TIMELINE [19]

2015

MAY 2015: A private member's bill to repeal article 40.3.3 (the Eighth Amendment) of the Irish Constitution is put before the Dáil. The bill is rejected.

APRIL 2015: In its reply to the List of Issues of the United Nations Committee on Economic, Social and Cultural Rights (CESCR), ahead of the committee's third periodic review of Ireland in June, the government states that it 'does not intend to propose any amendments' to the Protection of Life During Pregnancy Act or to article 40.3.3 of the Constitution.

FEBRUARY 2015: A private member's bill to legislate for abortion in cases of fatal foetal anomaly is put before the Dáil. The bill is rejected (104 TDs vote against the bill and 20 TDs vote in favour).

2014

DECEMBER 2014: A private member's bill to repeal article 40.3.3 (the Eighth Amendment) of the Irish Constitution is put before the Dáil. The bill is rejected.

SEPTEMBER 2014: A guidance document for the Protection of Life During Pregnancy Act 2013 is published. The guidance document appears to be more restrictive than the act. For example, the document states: 'The purpose of this Act is to restate the general prohibition on abortion in Ireland while regulating access to lawful termination of pregnancy in accordance with the X case and the judgement in the European Court of Human Rights in the *A, B and C v. Ireland* case.' This language is not part of the act.

AUGUST 2014: Concerns are raised about the adequacy of the Protection of Life During Pregnancy Act 2013 after a young migrant woman, known as Ms Y, who was pregnant as a result of rape, sought an abortion on grounds of suicide under the 2013 Act but was subsequently delivered of her baby by caesarean section.

JULY 2014: During the fourth periodic review of the state under the International Covenant on Civil and Political Rights (ICCPR), the UN Human Rights Committee criticised Ireland's abortion laws and urged legislative and constitutional change to bring these laws in line with human rights standards.

The UN body expressed concern at restrictive provisions of the Protection of Life During Pregnancy Act and criticised the discriminatory impact of Irish abortion law. The state admitted that only those women and girls with resources can exercise their right to travel to another country for an abortion. The state also admitted that the public has never been given the opportunity to vote for less restrictive laws on abortion.

In his concluding remarks, committee chair and former UN Special Rapporteur on Torture, Nigel Rodley, stated that 'recognition of the primary right to life of the woman, who is an existing human being, has to prevail over that of the unborn child' and expressed disbelief in a system where 'priority would be given to the latter rather than the former'. Mr Rodley also described women in Ireland pregnant as a result of rape and denied access to an abortion as being 'treated as vessels and nothing more'.

The committee's concluding observations called on the state to 'revise its legislation on abortion, including its Constitution, to provide for additional exceptions in cases of rape, incest, serious risk to the health of the mother, or fatal foetal abnormality'.

JANUARY 2014: On 1 January, the Protection of Life During Pregnancy Act is brought into operation by a commencement order. The act retains the criminalisation of abortion in Ireland and permits abortion only where there is a risk to the life of a pregnant woman.

The act provides that two doctors must confirm that there is a physical threat to the life of the pregnant woman. In medical emergencies, however, one doctor may make the decision. Where the threat arises because of risk of suicide, three doctors – a woman's obstetrician and two psychiatrists – must agree that her life is at risk.

The act includes a review procedure to cover situations where there is disagreement as to whether a risk to life exists. The pregnant woman has a right to address the review committee.

A medical practitioner, nurse or midwife who has a conscientious objection must make arrangements for the transfer of care of the pregnant woman concerned to another practitioner. The right to conscientious objection does not override the duty to provide care in emergency cases.

The act states that 'it shall be an offence to intentionally destroy unborn human life'. A person found guilty is liable to a maximum fourteen-year sentence.

The act defines 'unborn' as 'commencing after implantation in the womb of a woman'.

Regulations are introduced by ministerial order in relation to certification of procedures under the act and their notification to the minister for health, as well as application for a review of a decision that a particular case does not fall within the act.

2013

NOVEMBER 2013: The United Nations Committee Against Torture and Human Rights Committee highlight Ireland's abortion law in advance of their reviews of the state's compliance with the Convention Against Torture and the International Covenant on Civil and Political Rights.

JULY 2013: President Michael D. Higgins signs the Protection of Life During Pregnancy Act into law. The act is intended to implement the 1992 judgement of the Supreme Court in the X case and the 2010 European Court of Human Rights in the case of *A, B and C v. Ireland* and provide for lawful access to abortion where a pregnant woman's life is at risk. Twenty-five public hospitals are listed as appropriate institutions where a termination can be carried out.

MAY 2013: On 17, 20 and 21 May the Oireachtas Health Committee holds a second series of public hearings into the Heads of the Protection of Life During Pregnancy Bill 2013 – i.e. the general scheme of the legislation that is intended to implement the judgement of the European Court of Human Rights in *A, B and C v. Ireland.* Experts from the medical, psychiatric, legal and medical ethics fields are heard.

JANUARY 2013: On 8, 9 and 10 January the Oireachtas Health Committee holds public hearings into the report of the expert group established to advise the government on the implementation of *A, B and C v. Ireland*. Experts from the medical and legal fields and representatives of advocacy organisations are heard.

2012

DECEMBER 2012: The government announces plans to introduce a combination of legislation and guidelines to implement the judgement in the case of *A, B and C v. Ireland*.

DECEMBER 2012: The Council of Europe issues its most strongly worded response to the Irish government in relation to the judgement of the European Court of Human Rights in the case of *A, B and C v. Ireland* and urges the government to expedite the implementation of the judgement.

NOVEMBER 2012: The report of the expert group, appointed by the government to advise on options for the implementation of the European Court of Human Rights judgement in the case of *A, B and C v. Ireland*, is published. The report is limited to the narrow grounds of the court's finding of a violation of the European Convention on Human Rights. The report makes recommendations in relation to the implementation of the 1992 Supreme Court ruling in the X case. The expert group report makes clear that such implementation requires that appropriate and accessible services be put in place. The report expresses doubt that any option short of legislation will give effect to the right to an abortion where there is risk to a woman's life to the satisfaction of the European Court of Human Rights.

NOVEMBER 2012: A private member's bill to implement the X case is put before the Dáil. The bill is rejected (101 TDs vote against the bill and 27 TDs vote in favour).

OCTOBER 2012: Savita Halappanavar dies in Galway University Hospital in circumstances where she was refused a termination during inevitable miscarriage because a foetal heartbeat was detectable. The report into her death found over emphasis on the need not to intervene until the foetal heart stopped, together with under emphasis on managing the risk of infection and sepsis.

APRIL 2012: A private member's bill to implement the X case is put before the Dáil. The Bill is rejected (110 TDs vote against the bill, and 20 TDs vote in favour).

MARCH 2012: The Committee of Ministers of Europe, the body that monitors the implementation of rulings of the European Court of Human Rights, expresses concern at the government's delay in implementing the judgement in *A, B and C v. Ireland* and at the lack of any interim measures in place to ensure that a woman in the position of Applicant C would have access to the right to a termination of her pregnancy.

JANUARY 2012: The government submits an action report to the Council of Europe outlining the terms of reference for the expert group to advise on implementation of *A, B and C v. Ireland* and listing its members. The action report states that the expert group will complete its report within six months.

2011

SEPTEMBER 2011: The Committee of Ministers of the Council of Europe, the body that monitors the implementation of the rulings of the European Court of Human Rights, underlines the importance of putting in place substantive measures to implement the Court's judgement in *A, B and C v. Ireland.*

JUNE 2011: The government submits an action plan to the Council of Europe stating that an expert group will be established to advise on the implementation of the judgement of the European Court of Human Rights in *A, B and C v. Ireland.*

2010

In the case of *A, B and C v. Ireland,* the Grand Chamber of the European Court of Human Rights unanimously rules that Ireland's failure to implement the existing constitutional right to a lawful abortion when a woman's life is at risk violates Applicant C's rights under article 8 of the European Convention on Human Rights. The court also ruled that the three women challenging Ireland's ban on abortion did not have an effective remedy available to them under the Irish legal system in theory or in practice. The three women lodged their complaint with the European Court of Human Rights in August 2005 and an oral hearing of the case was heard before the Grand Chamber of seventeen Judges on 9 December 2009. The women, known as A, B and C to protect their confidentiality, argued that Ireland had breached their human rights under Articles 2 (Right to Life), 3 (Prohibition of Torture), 8 (Right to Respect for Family and Private Life) and 14 (Prohibition of Discrimination) of the European Convention on Human Rights.

Michelle Harte, who became pregnant while receiving treatment for cancer, is forced to travel to the UK for an abortion whilst severely ill. Although her doctors had advised her to terminate the pregnancy because of the risk to her health, Cork University Hospital refused to authorise an abortion on the basis that her life was not under 'immediate threat'. Michelle Harte died from cancer in 2011.

2007

A seventeen-year-old known as Miss D, who is in the care of the state, discovers she has an anencephalic pregnancy and wishes to terminate the pregnancy. Although it seems that the Health Service Executive (HSE) tries 'to shoehorn her case into the grounds set out in the X case', Miss D refuses to say she is suicidal. The Health Service Executive writes to the Gardaí to request that they arrest Miss D if she attempts to leave the country. The HSE also requests that the Passport Office refuse to issue her with a passport. Miss D goes to the High Court to force the Health Service Executive to allow her to travel to obtain an abortion. In the High Court Mr Justice McKechnie rules that she has a right to travel.

2006

The European Court of Human Rights (ECHR) rules *D v. Ireland* inadmissible because the case did not go through the Irish courts. The Irish government relies on the argument that in the applicant's particular circumstances, she could have been legally entitled to an abortion in Ireland should she have gone through the Irish courts system. The applicant, known as D, argued that Ireland's ban on abortion in the case of fatal foetal abnormalities violated articles 1, 3, 8, 13, 14 and 20 of the European Convention on Human Rights.

2002

Irish voters reject the Twenty-fifth Amendment of the Constitution (Protection of Human Life in Pregnancy) Bill 2002 which would remove the threat of suicide as a ground for abortion and increase the penalties for helping a woman have an abortion. Voter turnout is 42.89 per cent of total electorate. 50.42 per cent vote against. 49.58 per cent vote in favour.

2001

The Department of Health and Children establishes the Crisis Pregnancy Agency to prepare and implement a strategy to address the issue of crisis pregnancy in Ireland as recommended by the All-Party Oireachtas Committee on the Constitution's Fifth Progress Report on Abortion.

The strategy is to provide for:

- a reduction in the number of crisis pregnancies by the provision of education, advice and contraceptive services;

- a reduction in the number of women with crisis pregnancies who opt for abortion by offering services and supports which make other options more attractive;

- the provision of counselling and medical services after crisis pregnancy.

2000

The All-Party Oireachtas Committee on the Constitution, chaired by Deputy Brian Lenihan, publishes its Fifth Progress Report: Abortion. The 700-page report is a political assessment of the issues raised in the Green Paper on Abortion, submissions received and hearings conducted. The views of women who have had abortions are not heard. The committee fails to reach a political consensus on the substantive legal issues of abortion but agrees on a strategy to reduce the number of crisis pregnancies. The report further recommends the establishment of a dedicated agency under the Department of Health and Children to implement the strategy. The report is sent to a cabinet subcommittee chaired by the Minister for Health and Children, Micheál Martin, for consideration.

1999

The cabinet committee chaired by Brian Cowen, Minister for Health and Children, publishes a Green Paper on Abortion prepared by an interdepartmental working group. The Green Paper aims to set out the issues surrounding abortion, provide a brief analysis and to consider possible options available. It is a discussion document and not a policy document.

1997

A thirteen-year-old girl, known as Miss C, is raped and becomes pregnant. The Eastern Health Board takes C into its care and in accordance with the girl's wishes, obtains orders from the District Court to take C abroad for an abortion. C's parents challenge these orders in the High Court case *A and B v. Eastern Health Board.* District Court Judge Mary Fahy and Mr Justice Geoghegan rule that as Miss C is likely to take her own life if forced to continue with the pregnancy, she is entitled to an abortion in Ireland by virtue of the Supreme Court judgement in the 1992 X case.

1996

The Constitution Review Group recommends the introduction of legislation covering matters such as the definition of 'unborn', protection for appropriate medical intervention, certification of 'real and substantial risk to the life of the mother' and a time limit on lawful abortion.

1995

The Regulation of Information (Services outside the State for the Termination of Pregnancies) Act 1995 is enacted. The act allows doctors, advisory agencies and individual counsellors to give information on abortion services abroad should a woman request it. However, the act requires any information on abortion services be provided along with information on parenting and adoption and may only be given in the context of one-to-one counselling. The act also prohibits service providers (including doctors) from making an appointment for a termination abroad on behalf of their client. Advisory agencies, doctors and counsellors that do not provide information on abortion services abroad but do engage in pregnancy counselling are not subject to the provisions of the act.

1992

As a result of the X case judgement and the issues relating to travelling and information on abortion, the government puts forward three possible amendments to the Constitution in a referendum.

The three amendments include:

- The freedom to travel outside the state for an abortion – **passed**

- The freedom to obtain or make available information on abortion services outside the state, subject to conditions – **passed**

- To roll back the X case judgement in order to remove suicide as a grounds for abortion in Ireland – **rejected**

In the case of *Open Door and Well Woman v. Ireland*, the European Court of Human Rights rules that Ireland violated article 10 of the European Convention on Human Rights guaranteeing freedom of expression. The court finds that the Irish courts' injunction against Open Door and Well Woman from receiving or imparting information on abortion services legally available in other countries is disproportionate and creates a risk to the health of women seeking abortions outside the state.

The Supreme Court rules in *Attorney General v. X* that a fourteen-year-old girl, known as X, pregnant as a result of rape, faces a real and substantial risk to her life due to threat of suicide and this threat can only be averted by the termination of her pregnancy. Therefore, X is entitled to an abortion in Ireland under the provision of article 40.3.3 of the Constitution that requires the state to have 'due regard to the equal right to life of the mother'.

The court does not consider that abortion can be permitted only where the risk is of immediate or inevitable death of the pregnant woman, as this would insufficiently protect her right to life.

The law is now clear that termination of pregnancy should be considered a medical treatment whether the risk to the life of a pregnant woman arises on physical or mental health grounds. Risk to life does not have to be a virtual certainty. But risk to physical or mental health alone is not sufficient.

1991

Upon the request of the Irish High Court in relation to the 1989 case to prevent student groups distributing information on abortion services in the UK, the European Court of Justice rules in *SPUC v. Grogan* that abortion could constitute a service under the Treaty of Rome (Treaty of the European Economic Community) and therefore a member state could not prohibit the distribution of information by agencies having a commercial relationship with foreign abortion clinics.

However, the court also rules that since the student groups have no direct links with abortion services outside of Ireland, they cannot claim the protection of European Community law.

1983

Referendum on the Eighth Amendment of the Constitution (article 40.3.3) is passed after a bitterly contested campaign. 53.67 per cent of the electorate voted, with 841,233 votes in favour and 416,136 against. Article 40.3.3 of the Constitution is inserted to read: 'The State acknowledges the right to life of the unborn and, with due regard to the equal right to life of the mother, guarantees in its laws to respect, and, as far as practicable, by its laws to defend and vindicate that right.'

Sheila Hodgers, who was pregnant and suffering from breast cancer, dies in Our Lady of Lourdes Hospital in Drogheda two days after delivering her pregnancy two months premature. Her baby dies almost immediately after birth. Sheila Hodgers' cancer treatment had been stopped by the hospital, which claimed it would harm the pregnancy. She had also been denied an x-ray and pain relief.

1861

The 1861 Offences Against the Person Act is passed, which criminalises women who 'procure a miscarriage'. The act also makes it a crime to assist a woman to 'procure a miscarriage'. The punishment in both cases is life imprisonment. The act also criminalises anyone who knowingly supplies the means to 'procure a miscarriage'. These criminal laws remain on the Irish statute books and are interpreted to criminalise abortion in all circumstances. Subsequent amendments to the Constitution and court cases have interpreted further the dimensions of abortion, however, the 1861 act remains the basis of criminal law on abortion in Ireland.

EDITORS' INTRODUCTION

THE ORIGINAL *Abortion Papers Ireland* was published in 1992, the year of the X case, and a year that proved to be a defining moment in the struggle for abortion rights in Ireland. It was a significant moment because it transformed the nature of the abortion debate in Ireland by clarifying precisely the argument on which the whole debate about abortion rests: should the rights of a foetus be given priority over the mental and physical wellbeing of a pregnant woman? In February 1992 Irish people were forced to answer this question and when faced with the reality of the situation they overwhelmingly stood with the pregnant woman. More than twenty years later this second volume of *The Abortion Papers Ireland* returns to discover a radically different place in terms of social and political attitudes yet remarkably similar in terms of the regulation and control of women's bodies. Writing in the first volume of *The Abortion Papers Ireland*, editor Ailbhe Smyth argued that '[w]omen in Ireland are living in a police state ... the reproductive activities of women in Ireland are being subjected to a process of "regulation, discipline and control" ... in accordance with state policy and laws' (1992b, p. 138). In 2012 these policies and laws would result in the tragic death of a young pregnant woman, Savita Halappanavar, after being repeatedly denied an abortion. Indeed, Savita Halappanavar is omnipresent throughout this entire volume. Her death turned the international spotlight on Ireland's shameful and restrictive abortion regime, provoking national outrage and protest and reigniting and reinvigorating abortion rights activism in Ireland and beyond.

The majority of the pieces in this volume were conceived and written in 2013 and early 2014 but one of the challenges facing both the contributors and us as editors in producing a volume like this has been the fluctuating nature of abortion politics in Ireland. The second volume of *The Abortion Papers Ireland* began as the symposium convened in June 2013. Since then, we have seen the introduction of restrictive abortion legislation with the Protection of Life During Pregnancy (PLDP) Act 2013. The purpose of this legislation was to give effect to the 1992 Supreme Court judgement in the X case, which allows for abortion where there is a risk to the life of the pregnant woman, including the risk of suicide. This should have been an important and historic moment in the struggle for abortion rights in Ireland – the introduction of limited abortion rights for the first time in the history of the Irish state. It was not. Instead of introducing legislation to give effect to a woman's right to abortion, the impetus behind the legislation was to restrict women's access to abortion and to retain and enforce the criminalisation of abortion in Ireland. The act requires that three doctors – the pregnant woman's obstetrician and two psychiatrists – certify that her life is at risk from suicide. If there is disagreement as to whether a risk to life from suicide exists, the pregnant woman has a right to address the review committee (a further three doctors). The problems with this act became terrifyingly clear in the summer of 2014 as we prepared the final draft of this manuscript. Ms Y, a young migrant woman, probably living in Ireland's notorious direct provision system, and who was pregnant as a result of rape attempted to access an abortion. Instead of allowing the woman access to a legal abortion in Ireland under the PLDP Act, as she repeatedly requested, she was forced to continue her pregnancy and gave birth by caesarean section at twenty-five weeks after she had threatened suicide and had refused food and fluids for several days. In late December 2014 another deeply distressing case of a pregnant woman who had been declared clinically brain dead was referred to the High Court (*PP v. HSE*). The court ruled that the woman should be taken off life support. To the dismay and profound concern of many, the court reached its decision not on the basis that this was a vindication of the woman's right to dignity, but primarily on the basis that the court deemed it to be in the 'best interests' of the foetus.

Since the death of Savita Halappanavar Ireland's restrictive abortion regime has come under increasing international scrutiny, with leading international human rights bodies taking Ireland to task over its long-standing failure to legislate for abortion in line with international human rights standards and conventions. Most recently in July 2014, the United Nations Human Rights Commission in its Fourth Periodic Review of Ireland's implementation of the International Covenant on Civil and Political Rights took the Irish government sharply to task, criticising the 'discriminatory impact' of the state's reliance on women travelling to another country to access abortion services. It noted that its 'highly restrictive' abortion laws fail to meet human rights standards and expressed concern at the continuing criminalisation of women and their doctors. In widely publicised critical remarks the committee chair and former UN Special Rapporteur on Torture, Nigel Rodley, stated that the 'recognition of the primary right to life of the woman, who is an existing human being, has to prevail over that of the unborn child' and expressed disbelief in a system where 'priority would be given to the latter rather than the former' and described women who became pregnant as a result of rape and denied access to an abortion as 'treated as vessels and nothing more'.

Despite the continuing list of women being subjected to cruel, abusive and degrading treatment at the hands of the Irish state and its institutions, Irish women have experienced precious little change in the twenty-two years since the publication of the first volume of *The Abortion Papers Ireland*. While opinion poll after opinion poll reveals extensive support across Ireland for more liberal abortion legislation, there remains little or no political will to act. For the political establishment abortion is a matter of deep moral consequence and any attempt at change cannot be prompted by the mere facts of a particular hard case but only after the careful consideration of abstract moral and legal principles. The purpose of any new legislation must be to keep the floodgates of choice firmly closed.

There are multiple analytic frames or interrogative lenses through which we might consider historic and contemporary discourses and practices in relation to abortion: socio-political, legal, medical, moral, philosophical. Reflecting this reality, it was the explicit intention of the editors of *The Abortion Papers Ireland: Volume 2* to identify and include contributions spanning the various sectors involved in shaping and contesting the terms of the abortion debate in Ireland and beyond. We purposively selected a breadth of contributors reflecting different backgrounds, approaches and voices. This decision to curate the range of pieces spanning academic, activist, NGO, political, media and literary spheres was key. The intersection of activist voices with those from the academy and formal political sphere alongside writers and those from the NGO sector give this publication a distinct flavour and form. Robyn Wiegman reminds us that in the history of academic feminism there has been an unwavering commitment to knowledge production as the scene of political struggle, one that wagers the relationship between what and how we know as being crucial to knowing what to do, or, as she specifically argues, 'knowing how to use knowledge to exact justice from the contemporary world' (2012, p. 85). This relationship between knowledge and action as it relates to the development of the abortion debate in Ireland is strongly represented in this collection.

As noted above, the twenty-five pieces contained in this second volume build on the Abortion Papers Symposium, which sought to prompt discussion on feminist and woman-centred activism and research in relation to abortion in Ireland during the period 1992 to 2013. As the genesis for this edited collection, the symposium was designed around a series of panels comprising activists and researchers and sought to prompt thinking, action and research on abortion during the twenty-one years between the X case and the death of Savita Halappanavar. The symposium format was designed to provide the maximum opportunity for discussion between panellists and symposium participants to ensure a critical space in which personal narratives, creative responses, activist insights and intellectual reflections would come into conversation. These resulting complex conversations sit at the core of how it is we seek to make sense of, challenge and offer insights into the complexities of the abortion regime in Ireland: they raise questions of purpose, policy and practice, questions which relate to this place of Ireland and its abortion stories.

As the convenors of this second volume we have been in the very privileged position of receiving people's thoughts, ideas, questions, analysis, emotions and frustrations in relation to the abortion regime in Ireland and beyond. The voices represented are intellectually interdisciplinary. They are also stylistically intertextual, spanning a range of forms including reflection, research paper, academic essay, literary creations and journalism. The resulting diversity is, we believe, one of the key strengths of the volume. The logic behind the presentation of the twenty-five contributions as a stream of pieces, defying thematic groupings and any suggestion of a hierarchy of voices, was deliberate. We sought to present each piece as both stand-alone and potentially in conversation with any number of other pieces within the collection. Within this interdisciplinary and intertextual edition, reflecting on the very particular subject of abortion, you can expect to encounter some overlap as multiple contributors reference particular events and experiences across the Irish abortion landscape. Again, this was intentional. Such repetition creates the conditions through which a variety of different analytic lenses, intellectual traditions and genres come into direct conversation. We believe such repetition reinforces 'the capacity that allows a looking through the windows of the actual toward alternative realities' (Greene, 2009, p. 138). We might therefore read these multiple, divergent and simultaneously overlapping conversations as part of a complex spatial ecology of abortion in which we operate and through which we might take account of 'not merely knowledge, content, conceptions and acquisitions, but also ontology, or values and beliefs, uncertainty and complexity' (Savin-Baden, 2008, p. 16).

Incorporating both first- and second-hand narrative accounts alongside personal reflective voices, this volume highlights the centrality of the personal within the political, so critical within the feminist movement. This feminist sensibility is evident throughout the volume, as it was in the first volume over twenty years ago. Indeed, this personal intervention into the political and intellectual sphere, evident in this collection, reflects an increasing acknowledgment that 'our knowledge of the world is always mediated and interpreted from a particular stance and an available language, and that we should own up to this in explicit ways' (Cousin, 2010, p. 10). The contributors to this edited collection have sought to do just that as they have given voice to their divergent and diverse subjective positions, ideological underpinnings, activist histories, intentions and aspirations.

In arranging this volume of papers we editors considered the diverse places, perspectives and positions the contributions represent and this determined our role as one of 'curation' rather than thematic ordering. Some connections we saw across the volume are traced here but readers are invited to engage with the pieces separately and together in an ordering of their own discovery, as there is much to discover in each and in the whole.

KNOWINGS

Janet Ní Shuilleabháin breaks ground to tell her story of the journey she made to Britain seeking abortion. Alongside her own story she narrates her continuing journey: advocating for and supporting Irish women who continue to need abortions. The ebb and flow of Janet's story from the evocative detailed memories of the trip, the women she journeyed with, the clinic, care and challenges she encountered and her returning, is powerful and compelling. The personal weaves with the political as Janet's journey extends to support other women needing to travel for abortions and political advocacy to legalise abortion in Ireland. The story's layers remind us how Irish women who have had abortions encounter prevailing discourses of judgement that at once silence them and demand justification but also demonstrates how empowering it is for a woman to hold sight of the solid ground on which her decision to have an abortion is made. Lia Mills' story of surviving rape and encountering the prospect of pregnancy and the certainty of needing abortion is another courageous space for reflection in this collection. Contrasting the imagined unwanted pregnancy with the wanted pregnancy that happened for Lia, as for Janet, Lia asserts the 'minute by minute, day by day, year on year' commitment this constitutes and asks who is it that carries through on the absolutist positions adopted by 'pundits, politicians and experts'.

ACTIVISMS

Ann Rossiter's 'flash fiction' story provides a glimpse of the experience of being an activist who supports Irish women seeking abortion by hosting them while in London for the procedure as she and colleagues in the Irish Women's Abortion Support Group did and the current Abortion Support Network now do. Ruth Fletcher locates this form of activism by ESCORT in Liverpool within the framework of reproductive justice, illustrating how such civic feminism addresses critical deficits in abortion care services. Such activism is constitutive of feminism in action, affirming and supporting the resilience and creativity of Irish women who succeed in accessing abortion in Britain. Supplementing activists' accounts with those of women who have travelled for abortion, Anne Quesney's contribution joins Ruth Fletcher's to demonstrate how the legacy of organisations such as ESCORT and IWASG is being continued by a new generation of young feminist activists in the Abortion Support Network (ASN), supporting Irish women seeking abortion within a civic feminist model.

Maeve Taylor characterises the Irish Family Planning Association's (IFPA) activism through efforts to support women who seek to travel for abortion within Irish legal regulations as working at the intersection of abortion law and abortion stigma. Such stigmatisation dissuades community-based health professionals from supporting women seeking abortion and ruptures the continuum of care that usually prevails across medical services, another critical deficit. The IFPA supports women with complex support needs, especially asylum-seeking women, by forging partnerships with voluntary organisations that fill the gaps, the authors writing on IWASG, ESCORT and ASN portray. Orla O'Connor outlines activism by the National Women's Council of Ireland (NWCI) in the form of policy development, engaging with human rights monitoring bodies and campaigning for abortion. The mandate given by the NWCI's 180 diverse member organisations for a pro-choice position is demonstrated as rooted in principles of gender equality, women's human rights and social inclusion.

Portraying new iterations of civic feminism, Cathie Doherty and Sinéad Redmond write as young Irish women being moved to advocate for reproductive rights by efforts of an anti-choice organisation to shame and silence women for having an abortion. This new generation of activists put social media to work to forge connections across the island and connected with the global movement for safe and legal abortion in a rally in September 2012 to celebrate their awakened solidarity with women seeking abortion. And then the harsh cruelty of Ireland's abortion regime showed itself again as we all awoke to the news of the death of Savita Halappanavar one morning in November 2012. Their successor generation felt the full force of devastation just as previous generations had when names of other women who lost their lives were announced, details of women hauled before Irish courts revealed or as they battled campaigns to insert anti-woman clauses into the constitution. The Abortion Rights Campaign is a new iteration of generations of activism. A generation with much to gain from connections forged across gener-ations with seasoned activists delighted to have new energy to harness old outrage.

EXCAVATIONS

Some contributors excavate women's place in key institutions to illuminate how this created the conditions for women's reproductive autonomy to be circumscribed. Covering six decades from the 1930s to the 1980s, Pauline Conroy portrays how women were 'relegated from comrades and citizens' active in fighting for the independent state into 'silent and subordinated service' that actively excluded women's participation in shaping policy and laws of the state. Interlocking legal instruments restrictively circumscribing women's production and reproduction were implemented, excluding women from many spheres of employment and banning publication, provision or use of abortion and contraceptive-related services. Pauline demonstrates how this 'bundle of anti-woman laws' foreshadows the constitutional ban on abortion. Women's activism particularly during the 1970s including constitutional challenges in the courts, establishing services supporting women parenting alone or surviving domestic violence and campaigns for legal and social rights constituted alternative forms of citizenship. However, the insertion of an anti-abortion amendment into the Constitution in the early 1980s re-asserted the position of a state that gives effect to women's exclusion by circumscribing their participation, rights and wellbeing.

Sandra McAvoy's detailed and careful consideration of how the Catholic Church has developed its position on reproductive rights and sought to assert its influence on the formation of Irish social policy and legislation illuminates forms of 'dystopia' that effect the exclusion of women and women's perspectives. Abstract theological arguments without concern for women's lives and wellbeing are developed by Church authorities from a position of detachment from the lives of women, who in contrast engage directly with conceiving, carrying, sustaining, nurturing and rearing children. Key events and actors in Irish political history who designated a special position to the Catholic Church created conditions for that legacy to hold particular influence long after formal structures had been altered. The evolving forms by which these abstract positions have influenced both framing and voting on laws circumscribing women's reproductive autonomy are revealed in Sandra's original analysis. Goretti Horgan complements Sandra's analysis from the twenty-six-county Irish state with an account of the 'holy alliance' of evangelical Protestanism and fundamental Catholicism successfully proscribing policy discourse on abortion in the six counties of Northern Ireland. Close analysis of anti-abortion activism, debates by elected representatives and indicators of public opinion generate a compelling argument by Goretti that the hegemony opposing abortion has stifled the forms of support for women seeking abortion evident in the Republic through protests on cases such as Savita Halappanavar.

Lisa Smyth engages a notion of 'honour code' as bundles of norms defining the moral character of a collectivity to consider whether the development represented by the, albeit highly limited, provision for legal termination of pregnancy in Ireland contained in the Protection of Life During Pregnancy Act 2013 represents a step towards a 'moral revolution'. Shifting gender norms de-emphasising difference ruptured the key woman-mother premise, individual women's fates cast doubt on the norm of moral certainty governing the ban on abortion internally in Ireland and attracted international critical attention, raising questions about Ireland's status as a moral actor by external norms. Lisa contends that the pursuit of national honour through an absolutist ban on abortion is mutating to become a collective sense of shame constitutive of a moral revolution. Such an external perspective condemning Ireland's treatment of women in pregnancy is highlighted by Anthea McTeirnan in the form of anomalies between Ireland's espoused position in relation to UN Human Rights' provisions and Ireland's prohibition on abortion. Ireland's accession to the UN human rights Council for the first time in 2012 happened within days of the death of Savita Halappanavar. A UN Committee decision in 2014 that the Irish state fails to meet its obligations to protect women's rights under the International Covenant on Civil and Political Rights due to Irish abortion laws underlines Anthea's arguments.

Aideen Quilty employs a spatial frame to consider abortion in relation to place and in the places of the Irish education system, particularly schools. The significance of place for Irish women seeking abortion who have to re-locate to a place where access is legally permitted, however temporarily, such that abortion has no place in national discourse is considered for its effect on women's subjectivity. While the subject of abortion and the lack of debate surrounding it in Irish schools is taken as illustrative of how the 'religiously infused power–knowledge nexus' operates, she also identifies potential for challenge to that power. Catherine Conlon situates the pregnant body as a crucial resource for knowledge capable of illuminating dominant ideologies governing women's pregnant subjectivity. A woman's narrative of concealing pregnancy in contemporary Ireland is posited in her analysis as demonstrating agency, power and personal enrichment in contrast to the pathologising discourses attaching to dominant framings of concealed pregnancy.

RE-FRAMINGS

Discourses framing abortion and reproductive rights by those advocating for abortion services for women are considered by contributors who draw attention to how the positions taken by advocates shape the conditions under which women can materially access services and imbue actions women take to resolve a pregnancy with meaning. Leah Culhane interrogates positions centring on 'choice', 'rights' and 'medical necessity' with reference to principles of respect, resources and power. Leah argues that advocacy groups should hold sight of broader reproductive justice principles when framing arguments and not allow concerns for political expediency cause them to take positions closer to prevailing ideological discourses. This position respects the integrity of all women in deciding on abortion, addresses gendered division of responsibility for repro-duction and childcare at social level and recognises how sites of inequality including in economic, racial and sexual relations differentially shape access to abortion.

Leah Culhane's abstract consideration of principles is complemented by Leslie Sherlock's discussion of how 'norms and privileges create exclusions'. Reflecting on the 'heroines of our movement', referring to women who have come to public awareness because the prohibition on abortion refused them life-saving treatment or brought them before the courts, Leslie illustrates how women's diverse status shapes differential access, treatment and recognition. Harnessing lessons learned from the most distressing of sources will generate a movement founded on prin-ciples of reproductive justice that holds sight of diversity and difference as it advocates for abortion access. Ronit Lentin's location of Savita Halappanavar's story within a recent history of casting migrant m/others' birthing practices as threatening the integrity of the Irish nation illustrates Leslie's entreaty well. Connections are drawn between the Irish state's efforts to assert a racial state through a constitutional referendum to deprive migrant children of entitlement to citizenship and efforts to legally regulate reproduction. Ronit portrays how migrant women are rendered devoid of state protection and a 'pregnant migrant' devoid of legal status as an effect of intersections of sexuality, gender, race, class and legal status.

Foetal rights discourses deriving out of foetal imagery technology giving way to foetal embodiment are, Ursula Barry argues, being forged alongside the disembodiment of women. Considering how these discourses have featured in Ireland and other contexts, the Canadian position vesting a strong position of bodily integrity in women is contrasted with the position represented by article 40.3.3 of the Irish Constitution vesting equivalence between the right to life of the woman and the foetus. The Irish position is characterised as a hostile deconstruction of bodily integrity based on the unequal distribution of reproductive justice. Ursula Barry identifies how the effect of article 40.3.3 continues to evolve as foetal imagery and the power of foetal rights ideology overshadows women's very bodily integrity and embodiment, another dimension of status to consider. Reinforcing Ursula Barry's emphasis on embodiment, Jo Murphy-Lawless argues that women's embodied truths of maternal mortality has been obliterated by practices of 'under-reporting' with the effect of obscuring shortcomings in maternity services. In a context where the official narrative of Irish maternity services is of international best practice in avoiding maternal mortality, it is the bodies of women that become the truth-tellers.

LAWS, REGULATIONS AND PUNISHMENTS

This volume continues to consider the nature, scope and effect of the legal regime governing abortion in Ireland intended to be accessible to readers new to the topic and informative for readers already knowledgeable about the Irish context. Stephanie Lord brings us back to consider how the insertion of article 40.3.3 has impacted on women's lives while Ireland's abortion rate persists despite this development. Drawing on recently available state papers, arguments made at the time are revisited in light of what has transpired to demonstrate how both those opposing and some supporters of the amendment did foresee the crises the amendment generated for women. Ivana Bacik considers how abortion has been regulated in Ireland since it first appeared on the statute books against the backdrop of Ireland's persisting abortion rate as Lord does, but also taking into account evolving public opinion that has moved closer to supporting legalisation of abortion in Ireland in recent years. Court hearings in national and supra-national courts are analysed by Bacik, including positions put forward by the Irish government to give effect to the legal provisions as well as judgements themselves. Insights generated from infrastructure initiated by the Irish government to consider legal reform in the area including a Constitution Review Group and Oireachtas Health Committee hearings illustrate how the effect of Irish abortion law in practice contributes to the impetus for change, albeit at a tortuously slow pace.

Sinéad Kennedy draws attention to how formations of class, power and control all play out in a regime that even today constitutes pregnant women as nothing more than vessels and women's bodies as 'ideological battlefields'. Considering how a young migrant woman was treated when she sought protection for her life under the 2013 Protection of Life During Pregnancy Act, Sinéad illustrates the case not just for repeal of article 40.3.3 of the Constitution but also the dismantling of the architecture of support erected in its wake in order that we extend bodily autonomy to all in our Republic. Child psychiatrist Peadar O'Grady hones in on the penalty of fourteen years imprisonment contained within the Protection of Life During Pregnancy Act 2013 for undergoing an abortion procedure in Ireland, to argue how a measure shown to be highly ineffective in other jurisdictions will show its greatest effect in constraining communication between women and their doctors. Clare Daly, an elected representative in the Dáil (Irish parliament) describes her activism in moving a private member's bill to give effect to the recognition of the, albeit highly limited, right to abortion iden-tified in the X case judgement. Though defeated, the bill represented the first time that abortion was 'proactively discussed in the Dáil without a tragedy provoking it'. As was inevitable, that tragedy soon followed with the loss of Savita Halappanavar's life in an Irish maternity hospital.

CONTINUITIES AND CHANGE

Within these analyses we see continuity in the highly restrictive regulation of women's fertile bodies in the Irish context just as the *Abortion Papers Ireland*: Volume 1 portrayed. But we also catch glimpses of change, suggesting women's persistent personal and collective struggles are eroding the absolutist position. Whether this has the potential for the 'moral revolution' Lisa Smyth hopefully imagines in this volume remains to be seen. What it does bear witness to is how women's continued need for abortion is supported by actions, activisms, articulations and analyses on the part of individuals and collectives committed to effecting change towards greater reproductive justice for all in Ireland.

1

My Story

JANET Ní SHUILLEABHÁIN

IN FEBRUARY 2014 Janet Ní Shuilleabháin assumed the curatorship of the @Ireland Twitter account. Janet used her turn at the helm to give her account of the abortion she had in her youth, and how the experience has affected her life since. Below are those tweets.

- So I am going to talk about that for the next little while, figured I'd give people a heads up as it may be triggering for some.

- I only have one regret about my decision to have an abortion and that is I had to travel. My partner at the time was very supportive.

- When the X case was happening in 1992 I was in 6th year. While the nuns were trying to get us to wear foetus feet pins.

- My sympathies lay with Ms X who was pregnant and did not want to be. She was only 3 years younger than I was.

- So a few years later when I ended up pregnant due to contraception failing (no contraception is 100%) I knew what I wanted.

- If I had continued with the pregnancy, I knew I would not end up putting it up for adoption, family ties are that strong.

- I was working at the time and wanted to go on to 3rd level education, I wanted to be able to provide well for my children when I had them.

- We had to go for counselling to get information and then make the arrangements and book flights.

- My first time ever on an airplane was to travel to the UK for my abortion, far from the glamorous way flying was portrayed.

- Every time I see an airplane seat buckle it reminds me of that journey and how I had all day 'morning sickness'.

- Having an abortion was my choice. I respect the choices of other women. I am not ashamed of my choice. So why be silent about it.

- I am not alone in my choice. We know that at least 150,000 women have taken that same journey to the UK to have an abortion.

- The mid morning flight. The pale serious women on it were easy to spot. There were 3 other women travelling on the same plane as me that day.

- One of whom I got talking to when we got on the train at the airport. Turned out she lived in the same area I did.

- She also had her partner with her. We talked about everything but why we were travelling.

- When we got to the first clinic, another young woman saw her and rushed to her and they cried loudly sobbing clutching each other.

- Turns out they were cousins and neither knew the other was pregnant and travelling to have an abortion.

- I had a scan and had blood work done. Saw a counsellor and a dr. Then left to spend the night in a B&B.

- I remember all the floors of the waiting rooms, the B&B, the corridors clinics and wards so clearly.

- The next day we travelled to the clinic, there were protesters outside. They shouted at us in English and Irish.

- 'Tá grá ag an Dia tusa agus a léanbh.' Unforgettable.

- Léanbh? I was 11 weeks pregnant.

- We had to tell so many lies about travelling. It was a supposed romantic weekend away.

- We had to have our story straight for when we got back. What we did, what we saw. So many lies.

- I knew people would ask me questions and I had to be able to smile about travelling, when it was what I had to do to get my life back.

- I was put under a general anaesthetic. I had no concerns about that as I had one when I had my tonsils out at age 7.

- When I woke up I knew I wasn't pregnant any more as I was lying completely flat on my stomach.

- I cried from relief and sadness that the first time I had been pregnant it wasn't a happy event. It was a time of stress and worry.

- Most of that stress would have been minimized if I didn't have to travel to a different country.

- Recently @Doctors4Choice have said that more Irish women have had abortions than have had their tonsils out.

- I guess I am one of the rare overlapping ones who have had both procedures.

- I spent that night in the clinic being checked on by nurses and crying a lot. I no longer had to hold it together. I had got to the UK.

- I had overcome all the difficulties, the booking of flights, the getting the money, the getting information, the currency exchange.

- I had done it. I had managed to have an abortion and not be pregnant any more.

- The 3rd night was spent in the B&B and I knew I had to get all of my crying over and done with before I got home.

- As I shared my bedroom with my 3 younger sisters.

- It was like the time over there in that strange place was another universe and I would leave it all behind when I got on the plane home.

- This was also back before mobile phones, there was only the house phone, so there was no way to talk to my partner about it.

- I remember the rush of relief and elation when I got off the plane in Dublin Airport. I was home I was safe. I was no longer pregnant.

- I would not have the children I have today who I love so much, if I had not ended that pregnancy.

- I got on with my life, not telling anyone. It was hard, esp walking past pro life protesters at the GPO.

- When I went to college I got elected a WRO, women's rights officer.

- I ended up dealing with young women in crisis pregnancy situations. I would refer them to Cura or the IFPA.

- If they made the same decision I did, I tried to be supportive. Sharing my experience, letting them know what would happen.

- I would ring and try sort out grants and accommodation for them the same way @AbortionSupport does today.

- I even had married women who had children come into the college to find me for information, as their family dr was pro life.

- The @AbortionSupport helps women from Ireland every day with information, money and somewhere to stay when they travel to the UK.

- The @AbortionSupport is a small charity run on grants and donations by volunteers.

- Some people ask why not adoption. Adoption solves the question of an unwanted child not an unwanted pregnancy.

- Some of the young women went mid week to the UK and would then stay up the weekend to recover in digs and rented houses.

- I would bring my fellow students paracetamol tissues and listen to them, when they got home.

- To this day some of them still get in touch via email when that time of the year comes around.

- Some of them are now married with kids and their husbands don't even know they had an abortion.

- There are so many of us who have had an abortion, but the shame and stigma has kept us silenced far too long.

- That silence causes suffering for ourselves and for others who are travelling, estimated 12 women a day from Ireland.

- My godmother was a single parent. Cherish did wonderful work to end the stigma around being an unmarried mother.

- Women who choose to continue the pregnancy have my utmost admiration, respect and support.

- Some of my fellow students did choose to do that and came back after taking a year off to have the child.

- They were very cute babies and I baby-sat some of them.

- I have lost track over the years of the number of women I have helped. It's easily over 60.

- And over the years many more women shared their stories with me. Each one was an honour as it's not easily told.

- When I was pregnant with my first-born I was giddy and happy when I went for my booking in appointment at the hospital.

- I gave a full and honest medical history. I believe that doing so is important.

- I got a very hostile reception when I answered the question of have you been pregnant before, honestly.

- I was told I should pray to god for forgiveness and hopefully this child would be ok and survive.

- Needless to say when I encountered that midwife again I asked to see someone else.

- When I got into my 2nd trimester, I was now finally more pregnant then I had been before.

- My pregnancy went well and what mixed feelings had remained with me were washed away when my son was born.

- I was finally a mother. I was a parent, on my terms and at a time of my choosing.

- Nearly 3 years later I had my second booking in appointment. Again I got a less than friendly response when giving my medical history.

- I looked the midwife in the eye and told her if she could not be professional then she should fetch someone else.

- Then I had my daughter and I was overjoyed as my family was complete.

- I only ever wanted two kids. I was lucky to get one of each.

- I still remained an activist, sharing information on contraception, where to get the morning after pill and referring people to the IFPA.

- I do believe that an ounce of prevention is better than a pound of cure.

- I wrote about abortion and the silence on my blog. 2005 I wrote this piece, Someone you know has had an abortion. http://sharrowshadow.wordpress.com/2005/08/16/taken-from-humanities/

- So when a certain group rolled out posters all over the country, I was furious.

- More shaming, more stigma, more lies. Having an abortion did not tear my life apart. I felt that having an abortion saved my life.

- It made me able to have the life I chose. I made my decision, I made my choice, it gave me back control over my body, my life, my future.

- So I heard about a meeting before the Rally which was planned outside Leinster House.

- It was strange and empowering to be in a room full of unapologetic pro choice people.

- I got involved with the Irish Choice Network and out of that the Abortion Rights Campaign was formed. @freesafelegal

- I was at the meeting that the campaign name was announced. It was slightly surreal.

- Abortion had been such a taboo word, but with the protests and the Vigils after Savita's tragic death that taboo was broken.

- The word abortion was finally being used. It was no longer the 'Substantive Issue'.

- At that meeting I for the first time publicly say to a group of people that I had an abortion.

- I wrote about that experience here http://sharrowshadow.word press.com/2013/01/22/blog-for-choice-day-i-had-an-abortion.

- For the last year I have been working with the abortion rights campaign, working on admin work and being a spokesperson.

- I attended a speak-out which @freesafelegal organised, where women shared their stories of having an abortion.

- Women who have travelled to the UK or Holland or Spain and some who used the abortion pill here in Ireland.

- We shared our stories, hugged, cried, laughed, broke the silence.

- The feeling of solidarity was huge. We looked at each other with a feeling of not being alone or isolated any longer.

- I have spoken about the fact I have had an abortion to @PennyRed when she was over.

- I mentioned it when I was on @newstalk to discuss the @bpas1968 notice about how they look after women.

- I spoke about how having a daughter & how if contraception fails & she chooses to have an abortion I don't want her to have to travel.

- When I was on #thehenhouse yesterday with @barbrascully Thank you for having me on.

- I believe that we should have the right to an abortion when a woman's health is in danger not just life.

- I believe we should have the right to an abortion in the cases of fatal foetal abnormalities. No woman should be a walking coffin.

- I believe we should have the right to abortion in the cases of rape or incest.

- I believe that we should have the abortion pill legalised, to give women the right to choice.

- I believe that abortion should be decriminalised, no woman or dr should face 14 years in jail.

- I agree with Minister Shatter that while the 8th amendment is in place women are not truly equal citizens.

- I believe that I have to be careful about only using the word women when talking abortion rights cos Transmen may need an abortion.

- So that is my story, that is my journey that is why I am #prochoice and am part of the abortion rights campaign. @freesafelegal

- I would like to think that pregnant people will have the healthcare they need here when we #repealthe8th repealthe8th.ie

- The last 12 months have been huge for me personally and for many others who have had an abortion we are no longer silent.

- So I am done for now, it's been a hell of an hour. I will answer some questions.

2

Dúirt bean liom …
A woman told me …

Punishing the productive
and the reproductive

PAULINE CONROY

THE HISTORY OF IRISH WOMEN'S STRUGGLE for reproductive rights remains to a great extent unwritten. Yet it is difficult to go forward without having some insight into the past, and in particular the period from the 1920s to the 1980s. This chapter argues that the current impasse on abortion in the twenty-first century dates back to the difficulty of unravelling a bundle of anti-women laws passed shortly after the foundation of the state. Between 1926 and 1937 in the first years of the life of the state, the gains of the women's movement (McCoole, 2004) – the suffragettes, the Irish Women Workers' Union, the Irish Women's Franchise League, women members of the Citizen Army, Cumann na mBan, Inighinidhe na hÉireann, the election of the first woman cabinet minister in Western Europe, Constance Markievicz – were systematically stripped from the body of the newly emerging Irish Free State.

Why were women so harshly treated? (Cullen Owens, 2005, pp. 264–279; Knirk, 2006). Was it a punishment for the intractable opposition of the first raft of elected women deputies who argued against the signing of the Treaty to establish the Irish Free State? Perhaps if the women deputies had been a bit more constitutionally cunning or astute, they might have attracted less subsequent venom from all sides of the Dáil. This is the view of Margaret MacCurtain (1978). Examining the debates of the time, she found that the Republican women in the Treaty debate expressed a political ideology that had not moved with the times. 'Had they been more constitutionally agile in the Treaty debate they might well have held the balance of power between the two sides', she wrote of the six anti-Treaty women. Those bitter exchanges left a lasting mark on the subsequent second-class treatment of women by political parties. Most of the elected women argued that they were speaking for or on behalf of their now dead family members, or were speaking directly as their dead kin would have wanted them to speak. They stressed the suffering of those left behind as widows, sisters and mothers rather than their own intrinsic rights (McArdle, 1937).

Following the War of Independence, Constance Markievicz refused with other elected women to recognise the Treaty which, in her opinion, provided for dominion status for Ireland (Conroy, 2013). She argued:

> It is the capitalist interests in England and Ireland that are pushing the Treaty to block the march of the working people in England and Ireland. (McArdle, 1937, p. 630)

The Censorship of Films Act of 1923 was the first step in defining state-public morality. Bearing in mind that films were then silent, Section 7 stated that a film could be banned from showing because it was:

> unfit for general exhibition in public by reason of its being indecent, obscene or blasphemous or because the exhibition thereof in public would tend to inculcate principles contrary to public morality or would be otherwise subversive of public morality.

The protection of public morality continued shortly afterwards in a controversy over the stained glass panels commissioned from stained glass artist, Harry Clarke, by the government to hang in the Geneva offices of the new International Labour Organisation. The panels were rejected and were never hung in Geneva. The panels allegedly contained scantily dressed females and sensuous images. With the Juries (Amendment) Act in 1926, women were quickly relegated from comrades and citizens to a caste of silent and subordinated servants. In the course of the juries Bill debate, justice minister Kevin O'Higgins (Cumann na nGaedheal) stated:

> This section has been inserted in order to get rid of the unwilling woman juror. In this country the number of women who desire to serve on juries is very small, and in practice the insertion of women's names in the Jury Book leads to nothing but trouble ... (Dáil Éireann, 1924, vol. 6, p. 1665).

In her interesting review of women's protests against the Juries Act, Valiulis (1992, p. 56) shows that 'undaunted by the sneers, the jibes and the derision, they pressed their claim with force and vigour not only for jury service but for full citizenship'. It took the challenge to the act half a century later by Máirín de Burca and Mary Anderson for the Juries Act to be found inconsistent with the Constitution and for it to be reformed in 1976.

The Censorship of Publications Bill 1928 was enacted in 1929. Section 17, which deals with birth control and abortion, says:

(1) It shall not be lawful for any person, otherwise than under and in accordance with a permit in writing granted to him under this section –

   (a) to print or publish or cause or procure to be printed or published, or

   (b) to sell or expose, offer, or keep for sale, or

   (c) to distribute, offer or keep for distribution, any book or periodical publication which advocates or which might reasonably be supposed to advocate the unnatural prevention of conception or the procurement of abortion or miscarriage or any method, treatment, or appliance to be used for the purpose of such prevention or such procurement.

The then Cumann na nGaedheal minister for justice, Deputy James Fitzgerald-Kenney, was adamant that absolutely no discussion on contraception or abortion would take place in Ireland under any circumstance. He would undoubtedly have been aware that Marie Stopes had opened one of the first birth control clinics in London in 1921 offering free contraceptive advice to any married woman (Eaton and Warnick, 1977, p. 13; Sanger, 1971, p. 171; Hartmann, 1987, p. 94). Referring to section 17, he stated:

> That section has been attacked by persons who say that this question may be treated as a social question, and that its merits or demerits should be argued out. That is a proposition to which we cannot and will not assent. In our views on this matter we are perfectly clear and perfectly definite. We will not allow, as far as it lies with us to prevent it, the free discussion of this question which entails on one side of it advocacy. We have made up our minds that it is wrong. That conclusion is for us unalterable. We consider it to be a matter of grave importance. We have decided, call it dogmatically if you like – and I believe almost all persons in this country are in agreement with us – that that question shall not be freely and openly discussed. That question shall not be advocated in any book or in any periodical which circulates in this country. (Dáil Éireann, 18 October 1928, vol. 26, p. 608)

Having banned any free thinking or discussion on the subjects of contraception and abortion, the legislature moved on to matters which might tempt its citizens to engage in any sexual relations. This was the matter of dancing. Minister for Justice James, Ruttledge TD, presented a new bill on dancing to the Seanad in 1934 saying that:

> This Bill is made necessary because of the increase in dancing throughout the country and, consequently, of the increase in the number of dance halls. (Seanad Éireann, 12 December 1934, vol. 19, p. 792)

The Act was in no way seen as a revenue-raising exercise, rather as a method of social and sexual control. Dancing was duly regulated by the state in 1935 (O'Connor, 2013). The period 1934–1937 was marked by sharp exchanges concerning the bills to control and restrict women's position in the workforce by Minister Seán Lemass's Conditions of

Employment Bill, 1935 and women's reproductive rights by the Criminal Law Amendment Bill of 1934. Both of these laws led into the debate on the new Draft Constitution in 1936 which was adopted in 1937. The Conditions of Employment Act, 1936 allowed the minister to restrict access to any employments deemed unsuitable for women. Lemass commented on the bill saying:

> There is no doubt that there are certain classes of work on which it is undesirable that women should be employed and for which they are not suited ... it is very definitely the case that processes which were done by men and could only be done by men, can now be carried on by women, because these processes have been mechanised. (Dáil Éireann, Questions, 17 May 1935, vol. 56, p. 1282)

Section 16 (1) (a) and (b) of the act allowed the minister to prohibit *the employment of female workers to do such form of industrial work or fix a proportion which the number of female workers employed by any employer to do such form of industrial work may bear to the number of other workers so employed.* This expressed a view common in Europe at the time, though Lemass may have viewed it pragmatically since it responded to the concerns of some trade unionists at losing their jobs to women (Horgan,1999, p. 86).

This drastic provision remained in place for forty-one years until the passage of the Employment Equality Act of 1977. Not just industrial workers were affected. Married women primary school teachers were barred from work in 1932 followed by a bar on married women in the civil service. These bars effectively denied women the right to a full pension on retirement and opportunities for promotion to higher and managerial positions in the public service.

The Criminal Law Amendment Act, 1935 combined prohibitions on brothel keeping (§ 13) and contraception (§ 17) in the same act, rendering them falsely, but deliberately equivalent in law. Section 17 criminalised the importation, sale and distribution of contraceptives but not their manufacture or usage. The section of the bill which raised the age of sexual consent for young girls had been apparently inspired by the Carrigan Committee – an early but secret enquiry into the sexual abuse of minors and which was never published. Senator Kathleen Clarke opposed the criminalisation of contraceptives. The senator's views were influenced by the time she spent in America between 1901 and 1907 (Seanad Éireann, 6 February 1935, vol. 19, p. 1248). The penalty for selling contraceptives was a fine and/or six months in prison and confiscation of the contraceptives.

If this was insufficient to subordinate women, there were finally those sections of the Draft Constitution which related to women's place in the home (Coogan, 1993, pp. 494–7). The views of Minister Seán Lemass and Taoiseach de Valera were not convergent. De Valera envisaged the Constitution as providing protection for rural mothers of families (ár mháithreacha clainne) in particular from the burden of physical labour in agriculture of the time.[20] There are a variety of interpretations as to the inspiration for his views (Clear, 1995, p. 180). Lemass on the other hand wanted all women and not just mothers, removed from industry and if feasible from the workforce as well.

There was organised opposition to the employment measures from, among others, Louie Bennett and the Irish Women Workers' Union in a tentative manner (Jones, 1988), university women and individual women in the Oireachtas such as Kathleen Clarke (Clancy, 1990, pp. 206–32). Kathleen Clarke was committed to equality for women. She supported the right of unmarried mothers to seek maintenance from the fathers of their children and to raising the age of consent in the case of indecent and sexual assault. She opposed restrictions on women's employment in the Conditions of Employment Bill and her demand for equal pay was radical at that time.

The Criminal Law (Amendment) Act came into effect in February 1935 and the first prosecution in Dublin took place in 1936. Mr K., a Jewish shopkeeper, was to his astonishment prosecuted for keeping prohibited goods, selling, keeping for sale and attempting to import prohibited goods. The contraceptives were seized. He was convicted on all counts, fined £200 which was the equivalent of a year's wages, and sentenced to six months in prison with hard labour. In the event that he did not pay the fines quickly he was sentenced to further imprisonment of thirteen months. He appealed.

Women's production and reproduction were thus restrictively circumscribed and controlled by interlocking legal instruments. Central in this process was to convince women, to have them internalise the view, that they had a 'natural vocation as housewives and mothers', a process lucidly described by Inglis (1998). It was to take another forty, in some cases more than fifty years and into the present day for this basket of legislation to be unravelled and undermined by successive waves of feminism.

UNDERGROUND AND OVERGROUND: THE 1940s

With the outbreak of the Second World War travel between Ireland and England was restricted. From 1939 to 1946 travel to the UK required a travel permit obtained by applying to a Garda station (Commission on Emigration and Other Population Problems (1954) Report). This hampered movement across the Common Travel Area between Ireland and England including pregnant women seeking to hide a pregnancy by giving birth in the UK. The situation contributed to generating a thriving market in back street abortion, which was very visible through prosecutions of women and men engaged in abortion provision that were prominently reported in papers like *The Irish Times*. The more than fifty investigations and prosecutions for abortion ranged from country women assisting a poor neighbour to procure an abortion, through to illegal and dangerous commercial enterprises located on Merrion Square or Parkgate Street (Jackson & O'Brien, 1983; Conroy Jackson, 1986). In 1949, perhaps due to the proliferation of infanticide cases, a special law was introduced entitled The Infanticide Act, 1949 so that recently pregnant mothers could be charged with infanticide instead of homicide in certain specific instances. Interestingly, the Catholic Church was quite indifferent to the question of infanticide despite its commitment to human life as sacred, compared with its intensive lobbying against abortion and adoption (Maguire, 2009, p. 182)

In 1942, the Censorship of Publications Act was used to ban a book entitled *Abortion: Right or Wrong* by Dorothy Thurtle. Thurtle was from the famous left-wing Labour Party Lansbury family and was a council member in East London with a special interest in access to contraception for working-class women. In 1946 a revised Censorship of Publications Act was enacted reproducing again the absolute ban on publications of any kind advocating the use of contraception and abortion. Attempts to improve the maternal and infant health services by Minister for Health Noel Browne TD and member of the Clann na Poblachta party began in 1948 (Kennedy, 2002, p. 59). Both the Catholic Church and the Irish Medical Association opposed his scheme;

on the one hand because it was free and on the other hand it would allow doctors a greater range of interventions with pregnant mothers. Faced with the insertion of the Catholic Church into the legislative process, Dr Browne resigned (Dáil Éireann, 12 April 1951, vol. 125).

How was fertility controlled then?

- There were Magdalene laundries for those who got caught pregnant with an illegitimate child.

- There was infanticide and many prosecutions for it (Rattigan, 2012).

- There was birth concealment (Conlon, 2006).

- Some went to England, gave birth there and handed over their child for adoption to Catholic societies.

- Others gave birth in Ireland and took themselves and their child off to England never to return (Rossiter, 2009).

- Some gave birth and – if young – passed their child off as their mother's latest child.

- Some gave birth in Ireland and their children were placed in industrial schools (Commission, 2009, Vol. IV, p. 215) or for adoption (Milotte, 2011).

- There was back street abortion (Conroy Jackson, 1986).

THE OFFENSIVE OF THE 1960s AND 1970s

During the late sixties and seventies a new wave of feminist groups, associations and activists appeared in communities, workplaces and on the streets. Demands for repeal of the contraception laws were loud and included significant legal challenges. The year 2013 was the fortieth anniversary of the 1973 Supreme Court case in which the brave Mrs Mary McGee from County Louth successfully defended her right to privacy, as a married woman, in importing contraceptives into Ireland (Jackson, 1993, p. 133; IFPA, 2013). In its judgement, the Supreme Court noted that her husband was a fisherman; they lived in a mobile home, already had four children and she suffered from the risk of thrombosis. The fifty-page judgement in the case tested the consistency of section 17 of the Criminal Law Amendment Act, 1935 with the Constitution. The judgement, to the surprise of many, clearly articulated an unenumerated social right to privacy. It took until 1979 for that positive decision to be converted into a law allowing contraception to married women only and until 1994 for contraception to be legalised without distinction of marital status.

New counter agencies emerged such as the Irish Family Planning Association, and the Well Woman clinics, defiant breaking of the laws in the form of a 'Contraception Train' to Belfast and meetings on contraception rights mobilised by such organisations as Irish Women United. The ban on contraception was already beginning to be undermined by the discovery and then marketing of an oral contraceptive pill in 1961 in the UK which was subsequently prescribed in Ireland (FPA, 2010). It could not be banned as it had wider therapeutic uses. Its appearance was not unrelated to the publication of a papal encyclical called *Humanae Vitae* on birth regulation by the Vatican in 1968 (Paul VI, 1968) in which all forms of unnatural prevention of conception were outlawed.

Abortion in a restricted form was already legal in England and Wales and in 1967 almost 10,000 women had abortions there. This was partly due to the effects of the favourable judgement in the case of the prosecution of Dr Aleck Bourne in 1939 who had carried out an abortion on a fourteen-year-old pregnant rape victim who had been assaulted by a group of soldiers. It was in 1967 that the UK Abortion Act was introduced, expanding hugely the grounds on which a termination was permitted in law. It came into effect in April 1968. By the end of that year sixty-four women from the Republic of Ireland and thirty-six women from Northern Ireland with Irish addresses had a pregnancy terminated in England and Wales (Walsh, 1975, p. 144). In other words, Irish women went abroad for an abortion at the rate of one every three days as far back as 1968. By 1971, women were leaving Ireland and Northern Ireland at the rate of twenty-three a week. The annual numbers for Ireland rose to 1,500 in 1975, to 6,600 in 2001 (Clements and Ingham, 2007, p. 9), falling back to 3,900 in 2012 (Department of Health, 2013, p. 54).

A review of the status of women in Irish society was undertaken to set a new agenda for women, particularly in relation to pay and employment opportunities. Its final report recommended that 'information and expert advice on family planning should be available through medical and appropriate channels to families throughout the country' (Commission on Emigration and Other Population Problems (1954) Report). The seventies was a period of women's movement, of direct action, of coalitions and alliances, of pickets and campaigns, new magazines, posters and leaflets (Connolly and O'Toole, 2005, pp. 22–64) that began to regain the rights that the women of the 1920s and 1930s had hoped to be realised on independence. Organisations such as Cherish, AIM and ADAPT mushroomed to articulate for rights for unmarried mothers (Conroy, 1997), for victims of domestic violence and for family law reform. The 1976 Family Home Protection Act exemplifies a resulting reform. It prevented a spouse from selling or mortgaging the family home without the agreement of the other spouse, as frequently happened.

THE BACKLASH OF THE 1980s

In the heady atmosphere of the 1970s few had a notion of the counter movement to reproductive rights in preparation in Ireland and overseas. In the words of American writer Susan Faludi (1992), an 'undeclared war against women' was about to break out. With the onset of global economic crisis and heightened tension in Northern Ireland, the government of Garrett FitzGerald of Fine Gael made a pre-election promise to hold a referendum to insert a new so-called pro-life clause into the Constitution in 1981. Once in power they were trapped with that commitment. The McGee judgement loomed heavily on anti-abortion campaigners' agenda. According to Gwynn Morgan '... opponents of abortion considered it at least possible that the Court, having discerned a right to contraception in an open area of the Constitution, might find a right to abortion in the same source' (2001, p. 24). To describe the decision to proceed with a referendum to amend the Constitution as a bombshell for campaigners for women's rights is an underestimation of the incredulity and horror with which the announcement was greeted (Arnold and Kirby, 1982). Abortion had not been, and was not then, a priority of the many women's campaigns of the 1960s and 1970s.

William Binchy, a well-known pro-life campaigner, expressed his reservations about the effectiveness of a constitutional amendment prior to its announcement:

> ... It should be appreciated that such an amendment would give no guarantee to the protection of unborn life ... what one might find is that those who are pro-life would have brought on their heads a nasty emotive battle ... with their cause having been constantly branded as anti-women, uncaring, doctrinaire and sectarian
>
> (Binchy, 1982, p. 109)

There followed two fraught and despairing years of campaigning in every constituency in Ireland against what was to become the Eighth Amendment to the Constitution. Women's groups and men, who up to then had no experience of campaigning on abortion, little contact with the legal intricacies of a constitutional referendum, or campaigning on a geographical constituency basis, had to quickly and clumsily come to terms with a highly abstract debate on the foetus, the embryo, the moment of conception and related theological concepts (Conroy, 2012). Women's rights were on the defensive. In a vile and venomous atmosphere of denunciation and hatred, women and men opposed to the amendment, including Oireachtas members, were accused of being murderers, criminals and hell-bound. It was like the civil war. The country divided into opposed camps as the greatest threat to infant life in Ireland was declared to be pregnant mothers – potential killers of their offspring.

The referendum was carried by a large majority in 1983. Just one constituency – Dun Laoghaire – voted No. In the aftermath, many activists quietly left the country for Australia, the US and the UK and women seeking an abortion crept quietly and ever more desperately to England. Far from ending the matter, unbeknownst to most campaigners, there were to be a further four referendums on the subject and several High Court, European Court of Human Rights of the Council of Europe and European Court of Justice of the European Union cases, arbitrating on the contents of the womb (Sterling, 1997).

On a high after the referendum victory, anti-abortion campaigners canvassed for prosecutions against organisations providing abortion advice or information, such as students unions and the Well Woman clinics. These prolonged, tortuous and very expensive court cases invariably ended up in overseas tribunals in Luxembourg (EU) or Strasbourg (Council of Europe) calling into question Ireland's obligations under international treaties to allow free movement of persons across Europe and access to information on abortion services in other European countries. So great has been the number of cases related to abortion that an extensive legal literature has now developed about and in Ireland.

New referendums were required in which the Irish electorate voted in favour of the right to access information on abortion services in other countries. With the preparations for a new European treaty underway in 1989, the anti-abortion campaigners targeted this treaty to put a stop to the use of international courts which they viewed as treacherously undermining the operation of the Eighth Amendment to the Irish Constitution. This daring plan was hatched in secret and discovered almost by accident in 1992. But that is another story.

CONCLUSION

A comprehensive array of laws in the sphere of employment, citizenship and fertility control were adopted by the Oireachtas and the founding fathers of the state in the 1920s and 1930s which fixed the subordinated status of women in Ireland for the subsequent five decades and more. It was not that Ireland was backward and so excluded women. Women were excluded from the outset from the founding institutions of the state and so the state became backward. The path of reform in reproductive choices did not work in Ireland in that decades passed with no response to the legitimate right of women to control their fertility even in the face of backstreet abortion, high infant and maternal mortality rates and infanticide over the decades.

A part of the war for and against the reproductive rights of women in Ireland has been, and continues to be, fought offshore. In a more Europeanised and global world, this is not surprising. However, the incremental gains from this process are indeed miniscule. There are now enough enquiries, committees, commissions, expert group reports and studies to paper a library on the subject of abortion in and outside of Ireland. Yet it remains a crime to publish a leaflet advocating abortion even in the restricted instances of rape, incest, child pregnancy and where the foetus has no chance of survival outside the womb or progressing to term. The termination of pregnancy in Ireland has now been constitutionalised and internationalised, forcing what might have been a private and tragic moment in a woman's life into an act of exile and evasion.

3

The Catholic Church and Fertility Control in Ireland: the making of a dystopian regime

SANDRA McAVOY

IN JULY 2014, Ireland's abortion law was criticised by a UN committee that identified it as one of several areas in which the Irish state fails in its obligation to protect women's rights under the International Covenant on Civil and Political Rights. Committee chairman, Sir Nigel Rodley, spoke frankly about the Irish prohibition on abortion that means a woman pregnant as a result of rape is treated as 'a vessel and nothing more' and he named the historical influence of the Catholic Church, 'the institutional belief system', as a factor inhibiting Ireland's compliance (Cahill, 2014). The Roman Catholic Church's immutable anti-abortion and anti-contraception position is at odds with the human-rights based codes that underlie a number of United Nations and European human-rights conventions the Irish state has signed up to: codes that reflect twenty-first-century thinking on women's status, reproductive rights and fundamental protections for their lives and health.[21] The extent of that Church's political power, its disregard for women's health, its insensitivity or indifference to their wellbeing, their needs and experiences, were made clear during twentieth-century campaigns against contraception and a continuing opposition to abortion.

A Criminal Law (Amendment) Act, passed in 1935, reflected Catholic teaching when it criminalised the importing and sale of contraceptives. It did not ban their use but effectively introduced a prohibition by making them inaccessible. During the 1970s, social and moral concerns raised by the Church delayed access to effective methods of birth control. Nevertheless, contraceptives became available through a small number of family planning clinics and increasing numbers of women were prescribed the contraceptive pill, although it was only legally available as a medical treatment and not for fertility control. It was 1979 before a Health (Family Planning) Act enabled married couples to request contraceptives, including condoms, on prescription – though provision was made for doctors to refuse to provide this service on conscientious grounds. It was 1993 before condoms became freely available, without an age limit, from commercial outlets and vending machines (Hug, 1999, pp. 109–140). Although there was no demand for legal change, and abortion was already prohibited in criminal law, a constitutional ban (Bunreacht na hÉireann, article 40.3.3) was introduced in 1983 following a divisive campaign.[22] Only in 2013 was legislation introduced on a woman's right to a termination when her life is in danger although, as discussed below, the constitutionality of that right was established as long ago as 1992. Even taking account of divorce and same-sex marriage, it is difficult to name other social or political issues on which the Catholic hierarchy has been as vocal over so many years as it has been in opposing women's right to control their fertility.

CONTRACEPTION

The Catholic Church equally prohibits contraception, abortion and sterilisation even, as Pope Paul VI's 1968 encyclical letter *Humanae Vitae* (Paul VI, 1968, para. 11) stated, 'when the intention is to safeguard or promote individual, family or social well-being'. Contraception is, however, one issue on which the 'faithful' in Ireland have weighed up the practical and moral issues for themselves, as do many thousands of women who travel outside the jurisdiction for abortions.[23] Though a majority has quietly chosen not to comply with its teaching, the Church puts no energy into campaigning against contraception or sterilisation and focuses on abortion instead. Looking back to the early 1970s, however, it is interesting to see parallels between arguments defining contraception as evil, immoral, and a threat to society and those made against abortion from the 1980s to the present. First, it is useful to ask why the Catholic Church has intervened with such confidence of success.

The Catholic Church's 'special position'

The Irish Free State Constitution of 1922 prohibited discrimination on religious grounds. In 1937, it was replaced by a new Constitution that reflected the majoritarian thinking of that era and of the Fianna Fáil government that was in power: the same government, led by Éamon de Valera, that banned the importing and sale of contraceptives in 1935. Importantly, it established the 'special position of the Holy Catholic Apostolic and Roman Church as the guardian of the Faith professed by the great majority of the citizens' (Bunreacht na hÉireann, 1937, article 44.1.2) and merely 'recognised' a limited list of other faiths that 'existed' at the foundation of the state (article 44.1.3). By the 1970s this 'special position' was recognised as discriminatory, problematic in relations with Northern Ireland, and out of step with post-Vatican II Catholic teaching.[24] The article on the position of the Church was repealed in a 1972 referendum but this did not mean that either the Church or Irish politicians relinquished the idea that legislation on issues of conscience should reflect majoritarian, Catholic thinking or that the Catholic hierarchy drew back from the political arena.

Contraception as a rights issue

A 1968 international human rights conference in Tehran raised concerns about accelerating population growth and highlighted the relationship between responsible fertility control and serving a greater good. Relating population control and human rights, it concluded that: '... couples have a basic human right to decide freely and responsibly on the number and spacing of their children and a right to adequate education and information in this respect ...' (National Archives of Ireland). When the Tehran statement was issued, the 1935 ban was still in force in Ireland. *Humanae Vitae* had not yet been published and during the late 1960s hopes had grown that the report of a papal commission on birth control (that included five women) might moderate the Church's anti-contraception teaching (Fuller, 2004, pp. 195–200). As early as 1965, *The Irish Times* published a carefully constructed article that examined all methods of birth control without advocating any. It dared suggest that 'in the question of contraception, human feelings and emotion should be given as much consideration as pure reason. A dry intellectual approach is likely to reach dry inhuman conclusions' (Anonymous (a), 1965). On the Church's position that artificial birth control methods were against 'natural law', it asserted that medical practice involved 'bending or turning natural processes to more humanly acceptable results' and pointed to the 'use of insulin in diabetes', 'streptomycin in tuberculosis ... the use of insecticides, fertilizers, aircraft, any civilised process you care to mention' (Anonymous (a), 1965).

In March 1968 an *Irish Times* feature suggested that, regardless of the prohibition, increasing numbers of women in Ireland were using the contraceptive pill. It quoted one pharmaceutical company's estimate that 12,000 Irish women were prescribed it annually (Maher, 1968). An anonymous gynaecologist suggested that one-fifth of his patients practised coitus interruptus or used the contraceptive pill, two-fifths 'had no married life at all – intercourse once or twice a month', while others were 'struggling along with the Rhythm Method'. He believed 'very few' practitioners would deny the contraceptive pill 'to any woman who asks for it' but emphasised that it was prescribed for medical reasons, such as 'menstrual disorders' and 'marital stress'. He added that the 'biggest reason for stress is fertility control' (Maher, 1968). Stress was also cited by Dr Karl Mullen of the Mater Hospital, Dublin, who suggested couples had good reason to be anxious about the 30–40 per cent failure rate of the rhythm method, the only method other than abstention approved by Rome. A survey on marital relations was quoted which found that anxiety about a further pregnancy 'dominates ... marital relations at all times' (Maher, 1968). The Fertility Guidance Company (later the Irish Family Planning Association) opened in Dublin in 1969. Founding member Dr Michael Solomons pointed out that at that time a majority of Irish people accepted that 'unnatural' contraception was sinful but growing numbers wanted advice on effective family planning (Solomons, 1992, pp. 28–30). In 1972 a clinic at the Rotunda Hospital began prescribing the contraceptive pill but referred patients to the Fertility Guidance Company if they preferred a diaphragm or coil (Hug, 1999, p. 91).

Fuller points out that there was confusion as well as disappointment when, in 1968, *Humanae Vitae* repeated the Church's condemnation of contraception (Fuller, 2004, pp. 199–200). She identifies a number of factors that opened up an increasingly secularised and liberal discourse on fertility control and morality in Ireland in the late 1960s and early 1970s, including relaxation of press censorship from 1967,[25] an increasingly educated laity, a vocal women's movement and a more confident Labour Party (Fuller, 2004, pp. 201–206). In March 1971, when Labour's parliamentary party voted to seek repeal of the 1935 legislation, for example, Dr Noel Browne TD was clear on women's and children's rights, arguing that:

> The right of a mother to decide whether or not she should have a child and the right of a child to be born into a home in which it would know care and love and had some chance of growing up a reasonably happy individual, was one of the most important things in society. (Anonymous (c)) [26]

In January that year the Vatican condemned the UN International Children's Emergency Fund (UNICEF) and the government of the United States of America as pro-birth control and called on Catholic bishops to speak out against artificial birth control (Anonymous (b), 1971). In March 1971, the Irish Catholic bishops issued a joint statement suggesting that contraception, divorce and abortion involved 'issues of grave import for society as a whole, which go far beyond purely private morality or religious belief'. It reminded politicians that the majority of their voters were Catholic and 'confidently hoped' their deliberations on civil law would reflect this (National Archives of Ireland (b) and Horgan (a), 1971). In the same month, a pastoral letter by the Catholic Archbishop of Dublin, John Charles McQuaid, asserted that every 'contraceptive act' was 'always wrong in itself'. Thus, he argued, to claim '… a right to contraception, on the part of an individual, be he Christian or non-Christian or atheist, or on the part of a minority or a majority, is to speak of a right that cannot even exist'. McQuaid referred to 'confusion among the faithful' when they heard terms like '*planned* or *responsible* parenthood' used about contraception (Anonymous (d)). He claimed that 'the natural use of marriage is planned and is responsible' and added:

> But, if by *planned* is meant the spacing of births by contraception, then that use of marriage is not in agreement with the law of God.

It is not *planned* according to the rational nature of man as such. It is not responsible, for it is not a deliberate act that, by its agreement within the law of God, assists man to reach his final end. (Anonymous (d))

McQuaid constructed opposition to contraception as a defence of public morality:

Given the proneness of our human nature to evil, given the enticement of bodily satisfaction, given the widespread modern incitement to unchastity, it must be evident that an access, hitherto unlawful, to contraceptive devices will prove a most certain occasion of sin, especially to immature persons. The public consequences of immorality that must follow for our whole society are only too clearly seen in other countries. (Anonymous (d))

In this, he reflected an extreme anxiety that had been twinned with theological opposition to contraception since the first efforts of English radicals to popularise birth control in the 1820s: that removing fear of pregnancy would result in such levels of promiscuity that the social fabric of the state might disintegrate (McAvoy, 2014). Many Protestant churches shared concerns about promiscuity but separated them from moral issues around family planning by married couples. Within marriage, they accepted that moral decisions might be weighted by concerns about the health of a wife, the effects of uncontrolled fertility on existing children and the intrinsic good in a mutually satisfying sexual intimacy that enhanced marital relationships. The May 1971 Church of Ireland Synod passed a motion calling for legal change (Horgan (b), 1971).

1971 was a crucial year for both kick-starting campaigns on contraception and solidifying opposition. Evidence in state files indicates that in the first half of the year the Fianna Fáil government of Jack Lynch considered legislating on the issue. Information was collected on the availability of contraceptives in nine countries, including Italy, Spain and Portugal, where it appeared they were widely available – regardless of the legal position – and it was suggested that local bishops in these states made no political interventions (National Archives of Ireland (c)). Other developments included an unsuccessful attempt by Senators Mary Robinson, Trevor West and John Horgan to introduce a private member's Bill to legalise contraceptives. Dublin feminists protested in and outside churches against the bishops' statements and the Irish Women's Liberation Movement (IWLM) grabbed media attention with its 'contraceptives train' demonstration, when members illegally imported contraceptives from Belfast and waved them at customs officers in Dublin. In a statement issued that day, the IWLM claimed that 26,000 women used the pill and that by failing to enforce the 1935 act, the government had, 'by default', 'upheld the constitutional rights of men and women' to exercise 'freedom of conscience and the right to control one's life' (Hug, 1999, pp. 89–90 and Coughlan, 1971).

Most importantly, Mrs Mary McGee, a mother of four, who suffered from toxaemia during her pregnancies and had a stroke during one, initiated a High Court challenge to the 1935 ban after customs officials seized a postal packet containing a spermicidal jelly. Her case ended with a Supreme Court ruling, in December 1973, that married couples had a constitutional right to make a private decision to limit the size of their families and were entitled to 'reasonable access' to contraceptives. It was a decision focused on a right to import contraceptives; however, it did not establish a right to sell them and clarifying legislation was required (*McGee v. Attorney General and Revenue Commissioners 1971 and 1974*).

A month before the McGee decision the Catholic hierarchy published a remarkable statement. It emphasised that contraception was morally wrong, that consequences of legalisation would be increased 'marital infidelity', pregnancy outside marriage, abortion and venereal disease rates, and that young people would access them. It went on, however, to suggest some separation between Church and state might be possible:

> It does not follow, of course, that the State is bound to prohibit the importation and sale of contraceptives. There are many things which the Catholic Church holds to be morally wrong and no one has ever suggested, least of all the Church herself, that they should be prohibited by the State. (Anonymous (e))

When a Fine Gael–Labour coalition, under conservative Catholic Taoiseach Liam Cosgrave, attempted to legislate for the McGee case in 1974, the influence of concern about promiscuity was clear. The bill proposed tight regulation of both imports and sales. Authorised importers would supply chemists or licensed outlets. Advertising and display of contraceptives would be banned and only married couples would be permitted to buy them (Control of Importation, Sale and Manufacture of Contraceptives Bill, 1974).

Hug (1999, pp. 106–107) points out that only two TDs cited *Humanae Vitae* during debates on the legislation and that, of these, Oliver J. Flannagan, denounced the bill as an attack on the family and as 'raising the sluice gates on every kind of immorality'.[27] Sixty-one TDs supported the bill but seventy-five opposed it. Even with draconian restrictions it was doomed when a conscience vote was allowed. It was difficult for Catholic deputies to stand against the Church and even the Taoiseach voted against.

The stance of the Church had successfully moved the political focus away from the needs even of women like Mrs McGee, effectively defining them as secondary. It had reinforced in the public consciousness a relationship between contraception and sin, family fracture, disease and social problems. It had relieved conservative TDs of the need to struggle with the complex weightings of moral, health, social, and individual rights. In 1979, however, restricted access to contraception – only for married couples and on prescription – was conceded in a Health (Family Planning) Act that involved restrictions similar to those proposed in 1974. Anxieties that contraception encouraged promiscuity continued to influence public policy for more than a decade but a 1985 Amendment Act – narrowly passed in the face of opposition by the bishops – reflected sexual practice in Ireland and permitted health and family-planning professionals and chemists to supply non-medical contraceptives to over-18s without prescriptions (Hug, 1999, pp. 118–21). In the early 1990s, ironically, fears about AIDS created conditions in which it was clear that the common good was better served by broadening access. In 1992 the age limit was reduced to seventeen and in 1993 it was removed, as were restrictions on outlets for condoms (Hug, 1999, pp. 122–31).

ABORTION: A POLITICAL PROJECT

On his Irish visit, in 1979, Pope John Paul II referred to the Vatican Council's definition of abortion as an 'abominable crime' and called on the country to defend the 'sacredness of all human life from conception to death' (Anonymous (g), 1983). In the early 1980s the hierarchy became involved in a campaign that succeeded in inserting what was considered an unchallengeable prohibition on abortion in the Irish Constitution in 1983. The wording of this constitutional amendment equated the life of a woman to that of an embryo or foetus:

> The State acknowledges the right to life of the unborn and, with due regard to the equal right to life of the mother, guarantees in its laws to respect and, as far as practical, by its law to defend and vindicate that right. (Bunreacht na hÉireann, article 40.3.3)

Campaigning in support of the amendment, spokesmen for the Catholic bishops argued that abortion was never necessary, even to save the life of a woman (Boland, 1982). Representatives of the Protestant and Jewish traditions took a more nuanced position. Some agreed that there were circumstances when the moral position was not clear-cut and suggested abortion should be a legislative rather than a constitutional matter (Arnold and Kirby, 1982, pp. 61–73 and Anonymous (h), 1983). The outspoken Catholic Bishop of Kerry, Dr Kevin McNamara, was one of those who defended an absolute prohibition. He condemned the willingness of Protestant clergy to consider 'abortion in case of rape or incest, where the child was likely to be seriously deformed or where it was thought necessary to safeguard the life of the mother' and argued that addressing what he called 'hard cases' and taking account of 'compassionate considerations' would be the thin end of the wedge and 'easy abortion would then soon arrive' (Anonymous (f), 1983). His statements emphasise how devoid the Church was – and remains – of concern, understanding of, or respect for, pregnant women. They also highlight an oft-repeated mantra, that allowing abortion in any circum-stances will bring 'abortion on demand', an argument equivalent to the prediction that legalising contraceptives, even for married couples, would bring unbridled promiscuity and social disintegration.

The Archbishops' imperviousness to 'hard cases' was also reflected in a 1994 Catholic Press and Information Office (CPIO) pamphlet that underlined the political importance of closing minds to women's suffering during discussion of abortion because awareness of it had facilitated the passing of the British 1967 abortion legislation:

> Campaigns of this kind appeal constantly to moral values and emotions already deep-seated in the community, such as tolerance, compassion, sympathy, avoidance of sectarianism or discrimination, liberation of the victims from repressive or oppressive legislation, etc. As well as making the cause seem progressive and morally good, this has the effect of diverting attention from the fundamental issue, which is the right of the unborn human being to life. (CPIO, 1994, p. 19)

It would be difficult to construct a more woman-indifferent and foeto-centric statement. The 'hard cases' section of the pamphlet also deals with rape, assuring the faithful that 'it is only in extremely rare cases, in fact, that conception does result from rape' but that 'intervention to remove the semen and prevent fertilisation is morally right'. It implies that a rape survivor should be deprived of further choices, however, by asserting that if a woman is made pregnant, 'it would be no service to her, nor to truth and justice, to destroy the new life within her on the plea of allaying her anguish' (CPIO, 1994, p. 19).

CATHOLIC TEACHING ON ABORTION

A passage in Pope John Paul II's 1995 encyclical *Evangelium Vitae* demonstrates how absent women are from the Church's consideration:

> All human beings from their mothers' womb belong to God, who searches them and knows them, who forms them and knits them together with his own hands, who gazes on them when they are tiny shapeless embryos and already sees in them the adults of tomorrow whose days are numbered and whose vocation is even now written in the 'book of life' ... (John Paul II, 1995, para. 61)

They are lines with no acknowledgement of woman's agency during pregnancy or that an embryo, foetus and, ultimately, developing baby depends on her body for sustenance. They deny even that the child she carries so intimately is hers. They side-step scientific knowledge about stages of development and focus instead on a supernatural power that 'forms and knits' human beings.[28] Interestingly, they appear in a paragraph of the encyclical that begins by admitting that 'the texts of Sacred

Scripture never address the question of deliberate abortion and so do not directly and specifically condemn it' (John Paul II, 1995, para. 61).

Constructions of a 'divine law' and a 'natural law' in which abortion is deemed intrinsically evil emanate from a hierarchy of celibate churchmen, as do denunciations of contraception. They are men who eschew close relationships with, or sexual knowledge of, women and have at best second-hand understandings of pregnancy and abortion. Yet, they claim authority to frame a moral code on fertility control and abortion that deprives women of power over their bodies. The catechism developed by this hierarchy excludes the possibility of an ethics that is sensitive to women's experiences, roles and rights. Instead, it emphasises that its teaching on abortion is unchallengeable and infallible – though it admits that that teaching was established in an era when women were considered the chattels of men:

> Since the first century the Church has affirmed the moral evil of every procured abortion. This teaching has not changed and remains unchangeable. Direct abortion, that is to say, abortion willed either as an end or a means, is gravely contrary to the moral law. (Catechism of the Catholic Church, para. 2271)

If they are rooted in first-century thinking on women's bodies, it is hardly surprising that clergy speaking on abortion reflect outdated and emotionally circumscribed understandings of twenty-first-century women's status, roles and autonomy.

The catechism also provides that, in the eyes of the Church, 'the rights of a person' apply and must be 'respected and protected absolutely from the moment of conception' and that abortion is a 'grave offence', with those involved punished by excommunication (Catechism of the Catholic Church, paras. 2270–4). In fact, the present absolute prohibition on abortion, from conception, only dates from 1869 when Pope Pius IX deemed abortion at any stage an excommunicable offence. Until then, a complex of alternative positions existed (Noonan, 1970, pp. 28–36 and pp. 43–5). Why do the leaders of the Church conceal this? Are they as ignorant of how privileging the 'unborn' can result in the mental and physical abuse of women and girls as they claimed to be of the meaning and impact of clerical sexual abuse?

SUPREME COURT INTERPRETATION OF ARTICLE 40.3.3 PERMITS ABORTION

The assumption was that the wording of the 1983 constitutional amendment outlawed abortion in any circumstances but, in 1992, in what became known as the X case judgement, the Supreme Court interpreted it as permitting abortion when there was a 'real and substantial' risk to the life of a woman, in this case a suicidal fourteen-year-old. The ruling made abortion in cases of suicide risk a constitutional right (Supreme Court, 1992). Two attempts were made to roll back that judgement in referenda in 1992 and 2002. The people rejected both. One development, in 2002, was the political pragmatism of the Catholic bishops who supported the failed referendum proposal because it would have removed suicide risk as a ground for abortion, although it would also have placed restrictive legislation on abortion to save women's lives in the constitution and it proposed protecting the 'unborn' from implantation in the womb rather than from conception (Irish Bishops' Conference Statement, 2001).

Legislation clarifying women's reproductive rights had still not been introduced by 2008, when three women, forced to travel to Britain because they were unable to access abortion services in Ireland, took cases to the European Court of Human Rights (ECHR). In 2010, that court ruled that Ireland must provide 'effective and accessible procedures' by which women can access their constitutional right to a lawful abortion in Ireland if their lives are at 'real and substantial' risk (ECHR judgement, 2010, paras 263–4). There had been little movement on the ECHR ruling when news broke of the death of a young Indian woman, Savita Halappanavar, in a Galway hospital in 2012.

CHURCH OPPOSITION TO LEGISLATION

In a February 2013 interview with the journal *Catholic Voice* Cardinal Raymond Burke, then president of the Apostolic Signatura, the Vatican's highest Canon Law tribunal, commented on Ms Halappanavar's death:

> Even though, if the reports are correct, Savita Halappanavar requested an abortion, her request would not have made it right for the law to permit such an act which is always and everywhere wrong. (Murphy, 2013)

The comments appeared at a moment when, galvanised by international and national censure following the death of Ms Halappanavar, Irish politicians at last prepared to act on the 2010 ECHR ruling. Cardinal Burke merely restated the Church's immutable position when he went on to refer to abortion as 'among the gravest of manifest sins', and made clear that this was so even when a woman is undergoing a prolonged and health-threatening inevitable miscarriage, as in Savita Halappanavar's case (Murphy, 2013). Few situations – except, of course, its position on contraception – could make clearer the Church's disregard for women, their experiences during pregnancy, the emergencies that might arise, or their experience of mothering.

Catholic clergy and believers are entitled to respect for their personal moral positions and choices. When state law imposes a Catholic ideology that impacts negatively on the health, lives and well-being of those who do not accept the Church's authority, imposes 'psychologically and physically arduous' journeys on women forced to travel, and has a 'chilling effect' on medical practitioners' relationships with patients, then that state fails to meet human rights standards and fails to protect women citizens (ECHR judgement, 2010, paras 239, 254, and 267–8). While discussion in 2012–13 focused largely on legislation to save women's lives, the truth about the inequity arising from the 1983 constitutional ban on abortion was spelled out plainly in the Dáil by a non-Catholic minister for justice, Alan Shatter:

> … the right of pregnant women to have their health protected is, under our constitutional framework, a qualified right. This will remain the position. This is a republic in which we proclaim the equality of all our citizens but the reality is that some citizens are more equal than others. (*Dáil Debates*, 27 November 2012)

In effect, the Irish state continues to deny pregnant women a moral status equal to men's and this impacts on their health, social and political rights.

Cardinal Burke had no inhibitions about hammering home a further message that he must have known would be conveyed to Irish Catholic politicians. He warned that, under canon law, those who broke ranks and supported abortion legislation should be denied communion:

... as long as he continues to support legislation which fosters abortion or other intrinsic evils, then he should be refused Holy Communion. In my own experience, when I have informed Catholic politicians who were supporting anti-life or anti-family legislation not to approach to receive Holy Communion, they have understood and have followed the discipline of the Church as it is set forth in Canon 915. (Murphy, 2013)

Taoiseach Enda Kenny may have spoken with his Catholic conscience intact when he asserted, in the Dáil, in June 2013, that he was 'a Taoiseach who happens to be Catholic but not a Catholic Taoiseach. A Taoiseach for all of the people, that's my job' (*Dáil Debates*, 12 June 2013). Perhaps he deserves credit for speaking in such terms but the bill he brought forward that summer was not designed to ease access to terminations even for women whose lives were at risk. It placed committees between them and their constitutional rights and denied them involvement in the decision-making process. It did not advance women's rights one iota. On the contrary, it reinforced the criminalisation of abortion in cases of fatal foetal abnormality, rape, incest, or when there is a risk to a woman's health or well-being (Protection of Life During Pregnancy Bill, 2013). On the same day, the Taoiseach did give an insight into the level and nature of a well-organised, woman-blind, anti-legislation lobby that he and other politicians were subjected to:

I'm now being branded by personnel around the country as a murderer, that I'm going to have on my soul the death of 20 million babies. I'm getting medals, scapulars, letters written in blood, telephone calls – and it's not confined to me. (*Dáil Debates*, 12 June 2013)

A year earlier, in summer 2012, *The Irish Times* had pointed to the Catholic hierarchy's 'aggressive political lobbying of the kind more usually found in the United States' as it attempted to prevent progress on any legislation that might arise from the 2010 ECHR judgement (2012a). Irish Catholic bishops contributions to public debate during 2013, in the months before limited legislation passed, were more nuanced than Cardinal Burke's, who declared: 'It is ... contrary to right reason to hold that an innocent and defenceless human life can be justifiably destroyed in order to save the life of the mother' (Murphy, 2013). Speaking soon after Ms Halappanavar's death, the Bishop of Cork and Ross, John Buckley, presented the same message but less directly, arguing that 'The Catholic Church has never taught that the life in the womb should be preferred to that of the mother', but emphasising the 'responsibility' to 'defend and promote the equal right to life of a pregnant mother and the innocent and defenceless child in her womb' if either was threatened (Buckley, 2012). Obstetricians giving evidence to an Oireachtas committee disclosed that they did intervene to save women's lives, perhaps as often as thirty times a year, but that they did so without the protection of Irish law and that there was a 'difficulty' when the risk was not 'immediate' (Coulter Smyth, 2013). Without the protection of legislation, how might a woman whose life was in danger fare if her doctor accepted Cardinal Burke's position?

Bishop Buckley also expressed a fear identifiable in other Catholic Church contributions to the debate. This was that the line against legislation must be held, at all costs, because even an apparently restrictive law might eventually be 'interpreted in an ever more permissive way' (Buckley, 2012). We know little of the private lobbying of politicians as the Oireachtas debated the Protection of Life During Pregnancy Bill 2013, but it was reported that the bishops sent them briefing notes and intimated that they might mount a legal challenge to the constitutionality of the new law (MacDonald, 2013).

Opposing the 2013 legislation on women's right to protection when their lives are at risk, the Catholic bishop of Limerick, Brendan Leahy, suggested that there were 'shades here of George Orwell's *Animal Farm* where all are equal but some more equal than others', the implication being that the balance of rights was being tipped in women's favour (Leahy, 2013). If the state fully accepted the Catholic Church's position, Ireland would for all time turn its back on those standards for the protection of women's lives and health that have been set out in UN and European conventions. Embryos and foetuses would continue to have rights equal to a woman's and pregnant women would, as Sir Nigel Rodley expressed it, be treated as vessels 'and nothing more'. The term 'Orwellian' might be better applied to that dystopian regime in which an all-male religious group consistently focuses on maintaining its control over women's bodies and threatens those who move to recognise pregnant women's human rights with excommunication. To break fully into the twenty-first century and protect those rights requires a courage which, to their shame, Irish politicians have failed to display. Until there is a genuine separation of Church and Irish state, women will remain condemned to second-class citizenship instead of sharing with men an equal right to life, health and bodily integrity.

4

Speech for Abortion Papers Symposium,

JUNE 2013

ANTHEA McTEIRNAN

*'We are a very small country. We live by our ideas. We live
by our values and we try to be open-hearted and
generous-spirited; that's who we are.'*

ON MONDAY, 12 NOVEMBER 2012, Tánaiste and Minister
for Foreign Affairs, Eamon Gilmore, was entitled to bask in
the reflection of glory as he welcomed Ireland's accession to
the top table of global human rights. Ireland had been working the
room for more than six years to secure itself a three-year stint as a representative of western countries on the United Nations Human Rights
Council (UNHRC).

Qualifying in third place behind the US and Germany, Ireland nudged
Sweden and Greece out of the running thanks to a stellar lobbying effort
that included a trip to the Broadway staging of the Irish musical *Once*.

The ascension of Ireland to the top table means that 'the huge
majority of member states of the UN value Ireland's role in human
rights', said Gilmore. What a PR campaign it must have been.

In March 2012 in Geneva, the UNHRC issued its four-yearly report on Ireland's human rights record, as it does with every nation. The report saw Spanish, Danish, British, Norwegian and Slovenian recommendations on reproductive rights rejected hands down by the Irish government. I wonder if those countries remembered that when they cast their votes.

As part of the review, the UNHRC looked at what the Irish government had done to implement the ruling by the European Court of Human Rights (ECHR) in the A, B and C case.

In December 2010, the Grand Chamber of the ECHR had found that the Irish state had failed to implement a woman's existing rights to a lawful abortion where her life is at risk, including from suicide. The rights derive from a 1992 Supreme Court ruling on the X case, bolstered by a referendum, where the Irish people voted to support the same. The Irish people also said in the tri-partite referendum that women have the right to information about abortion and to travel to have an abortion in another country.

It was an open-hearted and generous-spirited response by the Irish people to a complex, human dilemma. That's who we were twenty years ago. That's who we are now. Eamon Gilmore was right. The Irish people are 'open-hearted and generous-spirited'.

At the UNHRC meeting in March 2012, the Irish government stated that the expert group convened to make recommendations about how to implement the European Court of Human Rights judgement in the cases of A, B and C would report in July 2012.

Eight months passed. Nothing happened.

November arrived and Ireland had a seat on the same council it had palmed-off in March. That must have been some canvassing. Canvassing that presumably steered clear of questions about what women living in Ireland could do if they found their life was compromised by a pregnancy.

Meanwhile terrible things continued to happen to women in Ireland. Tragic, terrible, unnecessary things continued to happen to the women that Ireland spews across the sea to seek solutions in a foreign land. Terrible things continued to happen to the women of Ireland who couldn't escape this state's totalitarian reproductive regime in time to be saved.

On 28 October 2012, sixteen days before Ireland bagged its seat next to the great and good nations of the human rights community, Savita Halappanavar, a thirty-one-year-old Indian citizen working as a dentist in Galway, died in University College Hospital Galway. She was seventeen weeks pregnant and was suffering a miscarriage. Savita Halappanavar asked for an abortion on a number of occasions but was told that, because Ireland was a 'Catholic country', she could not have one while the foetal heartbeat was still present, even though it was non-viable. The foetal remains were removed several days later on 24 October. Savita Halappanavar suffered septicaemia and organ failure.

When he appeared at the inquest into the death of Savita Halappanavar in Galway on 17 April 2013, the former master of the National Maternity Hospital, Dr Peter Boylan, said that had she been given a termination on the day she was admitted (21 October) or the day after, 'on the balance of probabilities', Savita would still be alive. The real problem, he said, was the inability of doctors to terminate her pregnancy at an earlier stage because of the legal impasse in which we all find ourselves. By the time Savita's condition worsened and termination became possible, it was too late to save her life.

That situation has not changed. We await the promised legislation from the government. Every second we wait, women in Ireland continue to bear unconscionable risk. Savita Halappanavar paid the ultimate price for our state's fundamentalist reproductive policing. It is one that no woman in Ireland must pay again.

Of course, since the conception of the Irish state, women have been denied fundamental human rights. The collateral damage of this war on women has been bolstered and given meaning by the teaching of the Catholic Church (a topic to be dissected later – or on another day altogether!).

And it has been acknowledged and proven that the state has often presided over practices that have denied women basic human rights. In the Magdalene laundries, where women were incarcerated for lifetimes without trial and without hope, in the brutal wards of Irish hospitals where women were carved apart by symphisiotomy, a practice justified as a way of guaranteeing their ability to fulfil their Catholic duties as wives and mothers by producing more children from their butchered genitals. And what about the human rights of the mothers forced by Church and state to hand over their babies to strangers, never to see them again? And the rights of poor women, desperate women, terminally ill women, women sobbing for the unviable foetus they must carry inside them for nine months if they stay? What about all our human rights? That is the fundamental question. The fundamental human rights question.

In 1993, forty-five years after the Universal Declaration of Human Rights was adopted, and eight years after the Convention on the Elimination of All Forms of Discrimination Against Women (CEDAW) entered into force, the UN World Conference on Human Rights in Vienna confirmed that women's rights *are* human rights.

That this statement was even necessary is striking – women's status as human beings entitled to rights should surely have never been in doubt? And yet this was a step forward in recognising the rightful claims of half of humanity. It was a step forward in identifying the neglect of women's rights as a human rights violation. It was a step forward to draw attention to the relationship between gender and human rights violations. Steps we must now take.

As women in Ireland, human rights instruments and organisations are our friends. Without the A, B, and C Judgement from the European Court of Human Rights in November 2010, we wouldn't even be this far. On Thursday (6 June 2013) the Council of Ministers, which monitors the implementation of ECHR requirements in member states, reported that it is satisfied with the Irish government's progress thus far.

We will have to go back to the human rights trough yet. Unfortunately some of us will lose everything – our human rights, even our lives – in the process. Progress is coming, but it is coming on the backs of the suffering of Irish women and the dispassionate logic of international law.

Thank goodness for the UN Human Rights Council, which protects the human rights of *some* women in *some* states. It has a good track record in doing so. Just not good enough. Just what Ireland brings to the top table of the United Nations in terms of protecting reproductive rights we have yet to see. We are not optimistic.

Hopefully the twenty permanent UN representatives who attended Ireland's jolly to see *Once* in New York and possibly voted for Ireland to join the top table of UN human rights will have listened to Glen Hansard's lyrics to the theme song from the musical they attended and their vote for Ireland was cast accordingly – with open-hearted, generous spirit.

> Take this sinking boat and point it home
> We've still got time
> Raise your hopeful voice, you have a choice
> You'll make it now
> ('Falling Slowly', *Once,* by Glen Hansard).

5

Reproductive Justice and the Irish Context: towards an egalitarian framing of abortion

LEAH CULHANE

CONTROL OVER REPRODUCTION has been a long-standing concern for Irish feminists. The rhetoric regarding reproductive control, however, has evolved over time, giving rise to a variety of frameworks for thinking about abortion. How should we, as advocates, respond to these changes and how should we conceptualise and articulate abortion? Is it a choice, a right or a healthcare service? Realistically, it is all three and at the same time, it is none. Rather, it is a reality and a lived experience for millions of women globally. Analysing how we think and talk about abortion is, however, an important endeavour and more than just an exercise in semantics. Different frameworks have specific legal, political and moral implications and offer distinct ways of understanding abortion. Primarily, these understandings affect how abortion is implemented as a service insofar as the definition of a 'problem' affects the construction of the solution, which is provided through policy (Bacchi, 1999). Furthermore, they provide different representations of women seeking abortion and the world they inhabit.

It is therefore important to examine our own discourses and attempt to develop a framework that complements broader feminist and egalitarian aims. This chapter starts such an analysis by critically examining the three most dominant framings of abortion from a social justice perspective. Existing frameworks in the field have already mapped the dimensions of inequality, specifically drawing attention to resources, respect and power.[29] These three aspects offer a good starting point for re-thinking abortion discourse and strategies. Resources were a central concern for early feminists who asserted that abortion should not only be safe and legal but also free, in order to ensure equal access for all women. Respect and recognition are also salient issues that must be addressed. Abortion stigma in Ireland continues to deny those who have sought an abortion the respect that they are entitled to. A framework must therefore be developed that serves to contest, rather than sediment, negative representations of women who seek abortions. Finally, feminist advocates must attempt to work within a framework that highlights inequalities of power. Providing legal access to abortion is not enough to ensure a change in social relations with men or the state and thus abortion must be situated within a more transformative agenda. When critically viewed from this perspective, some of the most dominant framings of abortion seem to be somewhat lacking and a greater focus on social justice, and specifically on the three diverging dimensions of resources, respect and power, may be beneficial going forward.

CHOICE

Respect

Abortion advocates have long espoused the view that abortion is a woman's choice. With regards to respect, the choice paradigm has been both heralded and criticised by feminists. Despite the insistence on the need for legal abortion without explanation, the notion that it is a 'necessary evil' is still very much alive among pro-choice movements. It is not infrequently heard among advocates that it is a woman's control of her body that they are defending as opposed to abortion. Although it may be true that an unwanted pregnancy is not desirable, pro-choice discourses can add to the representation of abortion as negative. In order to dispel the myth of 'convenience' or 'selfish' abortions, feminist scholars have highlighted the difficulty of the decision for many women (Himmelweit, 1988; Fletcher, 1995), the cultural or material constraints of choice (Himmelweit, 1988; Petchesky, 1984) or the failure in contraceptive technology that leads to the tragedy of abortion as a 'last resort' (Rich, 1976). Although this line of thinking focuses on the conditions under which the abortion decision is made as opposed to the woman making the decision, it does imply that there is always something questionable about abortion even if it is justified. Thus, a large issue with the choice framework is that it merely tolerates abortion as opposed to accepting it. The choice paradigm is of course politically attractive insofar as it does *not* require the acceptance of abortion, just the acceptance that it is a woman's choice. However, this is equally problematic, as it does not offer legitimacy to the abortion decision.

Resources

In Ireland and many other countries, radical, socialist and liberal feminists have united around the pro-choice paradigm and asserted that the decision to have an abortion is a private issue and one that should not be subject to governance by morally imbued state policy. Whether abortion is a moral issue or not, such a claim states that it is the woman who must take on that decision and that it should not be interfered with by state or man. Although widely articulated, the choice paradigm is problematic insofar as it espouses an argument to be free from state intervention. In asserting one's individual autonomy with regard to the state, a demand for individual personal freedom and privacy can distort the issue of state responsibility by emphasising the need to decriminalise abortion without putting an onus on the government to fund or provide abortion services. The institutionalisation of 'choice' in the US context embodies this criticism by failing to provide women with material access in many cases (West, 2009; MacKinnon, 1984; Petchesky, 1984). Three years after the Supreme Court ruling of *Roe v. Wade* (which legalised abortion under a privacy rationale), the Hyde amendment was passed by US Congress, banning federal funding of abortion except for the most extreme cases (Boonstra, 2007).[30] Although this effectively inhibited access to abortion for working-class women, it was deemed legitimate by a choice logic in *Harris v. McRae* where the Supreme Court ruled that it did not violate the equal protection clause of the Constitution as 'although government may not place obstacles in the path of a woman's exercise of her freedom of choice, it need not remove those not of its own creation, and indigence falls within the latter category' (Boonstra, 2007).

According to the court, there is therefore no obligation on the state to enable a woman to avail of her various private choices, nor are structural inequalities maintained and reproduced by the state and law. Construed in this way, the choice rationale can be associated with a distinct ideology that implies individual responsibility. This notion is not specific to the US; it is at the heart of neoliberal ideology, which has become increasingly influential in Ireland and on a global scale since the 1970s. With a decreasing onus on the state to provide for its citizens, the individual is made responsible for their own successes and failures, masking the economic and political factors that shape markets and the choices available within them. Framing abortion as a 'choice' may therefore have significant legitimation costs where privacy and 'privatisation' express a withdrawal of state funding and intervention. Thus, 'choice' in the neoliberal sense of the word is an extremely conservative template, framing abortion as a consumer service as opposed to a public social good. In the US, this has facilitated a hierarchy of reproductive access based on resources (Smith, 2005; Solinger, 2001) and the opportunity to participate in a market-dominated provision of services (Petchesky, 1984) as opposed to equal and material access for all who require it.

Power

From a power perspective, the discourse of choice fails to challenge the hegemonic social relations of reproduction that define reproduction and childcare as a woman's responsibility (Petchesky, 1984). In claiming that abortion is a woman's personal choice, responsibility for a pregnancy, contraception, childcare and abortion all remain firmly rooted in existing unequal gender relations. Furthermore, by framing abortion as a private choice, we may run the risk of framing having children as one. If having children is construed as an option, chosen by women in full knowledge of the responsibilities associated with such a choice, the claim for state or fraternal assistance falls thin (West, 2009). 'Choice' therefore has serious implications for women who need financial support for parenting, does little to demand a change in women's relationship with the state, family and men and further reinforces the public/private divide. As reproductive justice activist Marlene Gerber Fried stated so accurately:

The women's movement fought to bring women's reproductive lives out of the private sphere, arguing that our personal choices were political. How ironic that the pro-choice movement now argues that abortion is private and personal, not political. (Fried, 1990, p. 6)

The notion of 'choice' when applied to birth control more generally also raises questions regarding power and control when reproduction is enabled for certain groups of women but not for others. The 'freedom to choose' is problematised when it is exercised in a position of oppression: can an option to which there is no viable alternatives truly count as a 'free' choice? For a woman who does not have the resources to raise a child, for example, abortion does not appear a 'choice' in the normal sense of the word. Similarly, in the absence of state supports for the disabled, women's choices about raising a disabled child are severely restricted.

A choice rationale therefore conceals the racial and economic structures that constrain women's choices including the prerogative for certain women to bear children. Yuval-Davis (1997) points out that although they are not always immediately obvious or seen internationally to the same extent, policies of reproductive discouragement or encouragement towards specific sections of the population are features of most countries and are part of a eugenicist discourse regarding the nation and purity. In particular, the forced or coercive sterilisation of poor women and women of colour during the 1970s in the US led many activists to question the idea of choice, when the right of specific groups of women to bear and care for their children was an ongoing struggle not solely for resources but for power and legitimacy. For such women, the *choice* not to have children does not describe their particular position or experience. It is not solely poverty or ethnicity that brings discouragement. Depending on the context, women engage with complex social and culturally specific meanings regarding motherhood, meanings which they are transformed and judged by. Motherhood is a moral status depending on one's position. In Ireland, a woman's marital status has traditionally determined legitimacy, with the Magdelene laundries offering a grave example of how motherhood under undesirable conditions has been condemned.

RIGHTS

Respect

The language of rights is a powerful one and extremely beneficial to abortion advocates. Feminist activists have articulated the principled foundations of the right to abortion through various existing rights claims including the right to equality, bodily integrity, dignity and individual liberty and furthermore have highlighted the indivisibility of these rights. The claim that abortion is a woman's right is particularly useful when considering issues of respect and recognition in that it asserts a demand for justice and presents abortion as an entitlement, as opposed to a need or a want. Claiming a right is not considered irrational, selfish or needy; it is an empowering language insofar as it allows recognition of a benefit owed to all. Thus, rights claims offer women a certain amount of legitimacy with regard to the abortion decision in comparison to other frameworks.

Resources

Discursively speaking, rights are a much stronger rhetoric than choice with regard to resources. Whereas choice can be interpreted as a consumer-orientated language that benefits those with money, rights insist on universality (Solinger, 2001). Indeed it is hard to imagine campaigning for the freedom to choose food or shelter; inherent in the language of rights is that they are applicable to all. There is a problem with rights, however, in that they have been traditionally confined to political and civil liberties, which tend to be 'negative' liberties as opposed to an insistence on positive state commitments to citizen well-being. The right to abortion can easily be interpreted as the right not to be prevented by the law from having an abortion, while the right to avail of publicly provided access to abortion seems to be tied to a larger and more controversial struggle for positive social rights. Rhetorically, claiming abortion as a right is strongest precisely when it does not constitute a claim for resources, which is problematic when it comes to ensuring equal access.

Power

With regard to power relations, individual rights claims are somewhat limited. Feminist critical legal theorists have been quick to point out how individual rights are often isolated from a broader social context of structural inequality. Thus, the legal right to abortion in the absence of equality in other areas may seem hollow. MacKinnon (1989), for example, argues that an individual legal right to abortion has separated control over reproduction from control over sexuality by presuming that the intercourse prior to conception was co-equally determined. It is presumed that women have full control over sex, over their choice of partner and over the use of contraception, thus ignoring the conditions under which mass numbers of women get pregnant against their will. For these reasons the complex issue of abortion and reproductive politics more generally cannot be reduced solely to a right. They suggest that using legally based and individual tools such as rights could hinder progress towards a full restructuring of power relations and a more transformative feminist programme. We must therefore be aware of what can and cannot be achieved through rights and place abortion rights within a wider frame of social justice.

THE MEDICAL PARADIGM

Respect

Increasingly abortion has come to be construed as a healthcare issue, a framing that is distinct from the other two paradigms. Discursively, the 'medicalisation of abortion' can be thought of as the perception of abortion in medical terms, using medical rhetoric to explain and describe it. Safe and legal abortion can and has been very easily advocated as a public health concern due to the annual deaths and bodily harm of thousands of women at the hands of unsafe and illegal backstreet abortionists.[31] It is also easy to see why medical discourse is appealing to feminist advocates. Medical rhetoric has significant legitimacy in that it conjures up notions of neutrality as opposed to political radicalism or social resistance. Furthermore, the body of work focusing on the sociology of medicine has examined how medicine functions (intentionally or unintentionally) to ensure compliance with social norms; specifically, by normalising behaviour once deemed deviant (Conrad, 1992). The construction of abortion as a health care issue also has the potential to legitimise the procedure and to normalise abortion by treating it like any other standard medical service.

Substantiating the claim that abortion is a medical issue, however, requires drawing on established medical rhetoric and norms. What is deemed 'medically necessary' with regard to abortion is subject to dominant healthcare ideology and shapes the way abortion on demand can be conceptualised. Mental health has therefore entered the arguments of feminist advocates who stress the emotional and psychological burden placed on women who are legally compelled to carry a pregnancy to term when it has been the result of incest or rape. Similar arguments have been made regarding women who are carrying a foetus with serious abnormalities or women who could not support a child due to a shortage of resources or due to personal problems. Although these burdens are undoubtedly a reality, their recognition has certain implications for the legitimation of abortion and the construction of women seeking them. Medical models of abortion have tended to focus on situations where extreme hardship is implied (Lee, 2003). Whether justified in the context of physical health, death or mental illness, women seeking a termination are generally represented as unstable victims needing help and guidance as opposed to 'possible shapers of their own destinies' (Cisler, 1970, p. 276).

Mental health arguments have been particularly strong in Ireland when seeking justifications for abortion due to the X case ruling.[32] The case was brought to the Supreme Court, which interpreted Ireland's law as permitting abortion when there was a real and substantial risk to the life of the woman, *including* the risk of suicide (ibid.).[33] Consequently, in order to obtain an abortion in Ireland, a woman who does not face a clear physical threat to her life must declare that she is suicidal. The debate running up to the Protection of Life During Pregnancy Bill which legislated for X was marked by attempts to legitimise the protection of mental health as grounds for abortion as opposed to drawing on notions of reproductive freedom, justice and equality. This is of course an understandable tactic considering that the Irish Constitution and the X case have set the discursive parameters within which Irish feminists must work. The assertion of mental instability in order to gain reproductive freedom is, however, at odds with the recognition of women as moral individuals acting as agents of self-determination. Indeed it is an assault on women's dignity and a denial of respect to have to make such a declaration.[34] Scholars who have commented on the medical model have therefore outlined its stigmatising potential. Indeed there is a significant oppression in the characterisation of people as ill, frail, incapable or helpless when they are not (Silvers, 1999).[35] Thus, while a medical rationale may be politically compelling as it highlights the serious need for terminations and thus attempts to deconstruct the notion of 'frivolous abortions', it significantly negates the respect and recognition that should be afforded to women seeking to gain reproductive control.

Resources

The consideration of abortion purely in medical terms can also remove some responsibility from the state as the enablers of abortion, masking the socio-political nature of the procedure. Thus, it may be construed as any other procedure provided or not according to the facilities of a heterogeneous medical system. In Canada for example, there has actually been a nationwide decrease in the number of hospitals that provide abortion services since abortion has been decriminalised and has gained status as a medical service. In 1977, 20.1 per cent of hospitals provided abortion, in 2003 it was 17.8 per cent and in 2006 the number stood at 15.9 per cent (Sethna et al., 2013). On Prince Edward Island, there is no hospital that provides the service. Thus, a lack of political commitment to providing abortion as a very specific health service leaves it vulnerable to opposition by individual healthcare providers.

Power

Institutionally, the medicalisation of abortion has been used to denote the complete removal of abortion from criminal legal law so that it becomes a 'health service', regulated and provided at the discretion of health providers. Although this can enable a relatively liberal abortion regimen, as is the case in Britain, it raises questions regarding power and who is in control of the decision. Drawing on Foucaultian concepts of power, Sheldon (1997) questions the medical model in Britain from this perspective, evaluating what forms of power continue to operate after legal boundaries have been reduced. Criticising the 1967 Abortion Act, she argues that abortion has been removed from the political agenda and the question of *who* controls access to abortion services has now been hidden. Considering that abortion was defined as a medical issue in Britain, judgement was afforded to the professionals in that area. It is therefore two doctors who decipher whether a woman's case is acceptable and appropriate as opposed to the woman herself. Thus, the physician takes the role of authority, deciding whether each individual case is legitimate. Other scholars have used a Foucaultian framework to look at the micro-institutionalisation of power through the direct interaction of women and their doctors, arguing that doctor–patient relations are highly political and can function as sites of oppression or liberation (Morgan, 1998). The requirement of a woman to consult a doctor before an abortion, or as is the case in some countries, attend mandatory counselling, allows a medical authority to impart an opinion or a worldview on the woman and influence her decision. Of course feminist scholars have long attempted to problematise the mediating role that medical experts are afforded with regard to women and their bodies. Women's healthcare has always been a political drama and a struggle not for the provision services but for women's agency, autonomy and control (Morgan, 1998). In Ireland, this has been particularly salient due to the role of the Church in the provision of healthcare services. This should be taken into account when considering medical frameworks for abortion. Just because abortion is deemed an apolitical health service by law or state does not necessarily make it so.

TOWARDS A REPRODUCTIVE JUSTICE APPROACH

In response to some of the issues outlined, scholars and activists have begun to conceptualise abortion in a broader social inequality framework (Price, 2010; Fried, 1990; Solinger, 2010; Luna, 2010). One result has been the emergence of the reproductive justice movement, which flourished in the United States in the early 1990s. Fundamental to this line of thinking is the notion that women's reproductive decisions are hindered by power inequities relating not only to their gender but also to their ethnicity, ability, class, sexuality and immigration status. In placing inequality at the heart of the paradigm, reproductive justice activists have thus attempted to connect reproductive rights and reproductive health with broader issues of social justice and therefore simultaneously offer a criticism of neoliberal capitalism, sexism, white supremacy, colonialism and heteronormativity (Price, 2010). The problem is therefore defined not as inaccessible abortion per se but as the subordination of women and their lack of control over their own lives. The solution, reproductive justice, is:

the complete physical, mental, spiritual, political, economic, and social well-being of women and girls, and will be achieved when women and girls have the economic, social and political power and resources to make healthy decisions about our bodies, sexuality and reproduction for ourselves, our families and our communities in all areas of our lives. (Asian Communities for Reproductive Justice, 2005, p. 1)

With reproductive justice as the aim, abortion becomes a means to a far greater egalitarian end, where women have real power over their lives. In order for reproductive justice to be achieved, however, quite a lot more than safe, legal and free abortion would need to be secured.

A central criticism of all three paradigms is that they offer an individualist, often reductionist, view of abortion without viewing it within a wider context. Of course the existence of safe, legal and free abortion should be a positive feature of any society and is a prerequisite for gender equality. However, legal or not, abortion is not in itself sufficient for women's liberation and in the absence of equality it can be a last resort for women who are powerless in other spheres of their lives. It does not enable women to control their reproduction insofar as women do not control the conditions under which they get pregnant, nor the conditions under which they would raise a child. When reproductive responsibilities remain unequal, contraception remains inadequate and inaccessible, and coercive sex simply remains, women have limited power to control the occurrence of unwanted pregnancy. Nor does abortion socialise the responsibility for childcare or address the conditions that sanctify motherhood for some but damn it for others. In terms of power relations, abortion *does* however enable women to gain some power over their own lives. As Petchesky (1984, p. 385) argues, it allows a woman 'to move from one point in her life to the next [...] to navigate some of the more oppressive patriarchal and institutional forces that are beyond her control'. If we accept that abortion itself cannot solve inequality, but only empowers women to overcome some of the negative outcomes of it, abortion must be placed within a wider framework where various structural inequalities would need to be addressed. Unless one is committed to tackling the conditions that result in unwanted abortions as well as unwanted pregnancies it is hard to argue for a framing of abortion as a fully empowering decision. Advocates of reproductive justice therefore assert the need for a wide range of realistic reproductive options for *all* through active state commitment to both gender equality and general social equality. They assert the need for a change in relationship between women and men and women and the state.

Of course if we accept that abortion cannot solve gender inequality, we must also reject the view that equality can 'solve' abortion. Germaine Greer (1999), for example, argues that a credible feminist movement needs to be 'pro-woman', as opposed to 'pro-abortion', by providing real alternatives. This however is misguided. A reproductive justice movement needs to be 'pro-woman' by refusing to offer excuses for abortion. There is no doubt that a wider variety of reproductive options should be available to all; however, they should be advocated as part of a women-focused agenda of reproductive justice which offers equal legitimacy to both and refuses to shy away from abortion as a dirty word. In terms of the three dimensions mentioned, reproductive justice is quite reflective of egalitarian thinking and offers a more robust context for dealing with inequalities of power, respect and resources. In terms of resources, it highlights the need to advocate for state-funded support for parents as well as state-funded abortions and contraceptives. In terms of respect and recognition, it implies the necessity of addressing the division between acceptable and unacceptable motherhood, in addition to acceptable and unacceptable abortions. In terms of power, it is informed by the need to tackle gender injustice more broadly. This involves addressing the assumption that reproduction, contraception and childcare are solely women's responsibilities. Furthermore, inequalities in economic, racial and sexual relations are integral to such a project. Reproductive justice acknowledges that if women are to have some level of control over their lives social justice must be achieved through certain state supports and commitments with regard to both reproduction and societal welfare more generally. It therefore connects abortion to broader issues of inequality while simultaneously examining how inequality affects access to abortion itself.

CONCLUSION: WHAT CAN A REPRODUCTIVE JUSTICE APPROACH OFFER THE IRISH ABORTION STRUGGLE?

Much of the writing on reproductive justice comes from a context where abortion has been decriminalised but remains inaccessible or unsatisfactory. Some of the arguments made here may therefore appear irrelevant to Irish feminists who must continue (most rightly) to struggle for the most basic of access to abortion. Ireland is, however, at a key point in the debate and there are lessons to be learned from other contexts where certain frameworks have been institutionalised. As feminist scholars have demonstrated, the frame which is perhaps the most representative of a movement's aims is not necessarily the one that will be the most successful in eliciting change as the political acceptance of equality claims partially depends on their ability to resonate with prevailing social norms in a specific institutional context (Ferree, 2003). The tension proposed here is not, however, between 'resonance and radicalism' (ibid). Rather, it is an attempt to show how a reproductive justice framework might strengthen and make explicit some of the social justice aspects that are already articulated within the movement. Without couching abortion within a broader social justice agenda we run the risk of losing what is being demanded in the struggle for abortion and what it represents more broadly. In the purely legal battle for abortion, rights claims are of course indispensable and should not be discarded as a tool to advance the struggle for reproductive justice more broadly. Furthermore, the medical aspect of abortion cannot be ignored and feminists must strive to have abortion implemented, normalised and funded as a health service. A reproductive justice perspective however, acknowledges the limits of these frameworks when viewed in isolation from issues of inequality and gender injustice. In a reproductive justice framework, women remain central to the decision, the state remains a central actor in supporting and enabling the decision, and medical intervention is seen as technically necessary for implementing the decision. If one thing is most notable from other contexts however, it is that power, resources and respect must remain at the centre of reproductive and abortion struggles. These three issues could be useful for shaping an Irish reproductive justice agenda and could contribute to developing a more well-rounded and transformative abortion discourse in the future.

6

Towards a Reproductive Justice Model in Ireland

LESLIE SHERLOCK

To HEAR ABOUT the high-profile cases where women have been denied access to abortion in Ireland, it could seem on the surface that these circumstances were extraordinary. Their status as high profile could lead us to imagine there was something unique about these women, and perhaps this sentiment is magnified when the names – particularly of those who have passed – become household names, or when we reify their faces, their court cases or their stories as part of our activist battles. It can seem comforting, and can feel like self-protection, when we 'hope' that the unthinkable would never happen to us. Putting stories to names, and names to faces, and faces to placards feels simultaneously humanising and othering. We refuse to forget their stories, because we know they represent countless more stories which will never be told. We refuse to let these women's circumstances slip away from public discourse, and their humanity helps to strengthen the dialogues, to fuel our movements.

But there is another side to this well-intentioned and actually necessary humanity that the Irish public and activist communities are increasingly displaying, and we need to be careful. With every story, we are given a chance to relate to the heroine, and also to separate ourselves. Theirs will never be exactly our story, precisely our circumstances; something about each and every narrative will be similar, and something will be different from our own lived realities. Sometimes, we might even attempt to convince that part of us which feels in such close proximity to some of the circumstances within these women's stories that 'it could never happen to us' *because* of these very differences.

It is for these reasons that I will argue the need to strengthen our abortion rights movements by becoming more intersectional, more aware of and reflective upon our diversity, and especially more pensive about privilege. Of course we *know*, intellectually and academically, about the varied nature of each of our lives. We know we need to be constantly aware of aspects such as class, ethnicity, age, immigrant status, marital status, mental health, dis/ability and gender, as well as access to and engagement with state and non-governmental organisation (NGO) services. As feminists, we know that privilege and oppression are two sides of the same coin, and that our varied identities and circumstances combine to position us diversely within state and social systems. We endeavour to check our privilege, and to be good activists by highlighting and acknowledging the compounding power mechanisms in place within the countless other cases where abortion has been restricted, denied or refused. We are aware, or at the least we are beginning to become aware. Using this awareness as a starting point, it is time to take our activism and our work a step further.

In the wake of the disappointing Protection of Life During Pregnancy Act 2013, our movements need to regroup while managing to maintain the momentum that exploded following Savita Halappanavar's tragic death in late 2012. In reimagining an activist landscape moving forward, and strategising new approaches to advocacy and services, it will be prudent for us to examine those precise aspects which have made the cases so diverse, the many life circumstances which impacted upon, and likely compounded, these women's lack of sexual and reproductive health and rights. It is easy to see our similarities. It is easy to simply say we are fighting for abortion rights for women in Ireland, but I am increasingly unconvinced that this is an inclusive statement.

Our identities outside of our status as 'women' matter. In fact, from a gender inclusion perspective, even the term 'women' must be problematised. Indeed, it is not our gender identities that are being restricted from reproductive rights, it is our reproductive *bodies* which are being denied reproductive rights. It can easily feel that taking extra care with our language will muddle our messages or create confusing discourse. It can be easy to fear that making a statement about who is included when we say 'women' might lessen our credibility after we have fought so hard and gained so little in the political battlefield. But the reality is that a status as 'woman' is always already unstable and contended (Wittig, 2000). In a context of rigid gender norms, the reified and socially imagined caricature of 'woman' in Ireland is an image very different from the heroines of our movement. Indeed, the socially imagined ideal of 'woman' is different for each and every one of us.

THE NEED FOR INTERSECTIONALITY

The midwife's words spoken to Savita Halappanavar in her final days, as the reason given for denying her the life-saving abortion she requested, echoed around the world: 'This is a Catholic country' (RTÉ 2013). How might this dialogue have been different if Savita had been perceived as Irish and Catholic herself? What other intersectional elements have been and will continue to be at play in the many instances of struggle in accessing essential and life-saving reproductive services in Ireland? Most importantly, how can we make visible and address directly these intersectional elements which affect our circumstances and our access to reproductive choices?

Savita Halappanavar's immigrant status mattered in the days leading up to her death. Her physique,[36] religion and her educational, occupational and socioeconomic status mattered, too – especially in the coverage following her death. Ms X's young age mattered, as did her mental health status as a result of having been raped. Ms A's socioeconomic status and mental health status mattered, and particularly mattered when combined with the fact she was unmarried and had multiple children, most of whom were in care and one of whom had a disability. Ms B's health status mattered, her socioeconomic status mattered, and so did her social circles and her privilege. Ms C's health status mattered, her immigrant status mattered and so did her lack of access to services. Ms D's age and the diagnosis she received of fatal foetal abnormality mattered. For the women in this list who are Irish, this also mattered. So did the intersection of other health status, monetary situations, support networks and structures as well as logistical awareness of and access to information and services.

We know each of these 'official cases' represents hundreds or thousands of more nameless people whose cases will never be common knowledge or the topic of public discourse. The intersection of our identities and personal histories has profound impact on our experiences in navigating the circuitous and hidden path that leads some people to access much-needed abortion services abroad, and many others to deal with or surrender to tragic circumstances when that path cannot – for a variety of reasons – be taken. Most of these stories will remain unnoticed and untold, kept secret through the powerful functions of shame and stigma that have characterised sexuality in Irish society for far too long.

As we regroup, it is important that we reflect on the less-talked-about dynamics fundamentally present where functions of reproductive health are inaccessible to people throughout Ireland. It is vital that we honour the complexities of the stories we know, while maintaining awareness that the dynamics of those untold stories are unquestionably more diverse. We must contemplate the intersectional elements of experience and identity that shape 'lack-of-reproductive-choice' for all of us, and identify a model for ensuring that intersectionality of our movement is embedded in all of our work. I would like to propose a model of reproductive justice for Ireland as a template for critical integration of intersectionality in our activism and in our services moving forward.

REPRODUCTIVE JUSTICE AND INTERSECTIONALITY

In the 1980s in the United States, the movements to obtain access to reproductive rights were led primarily by white middle-class women, while the more disenfranchised communities of colour, immigrants and impoverished women most affected by restrictions on reproductive rights were not yet organised to advocate on their own behalves (Silliman et al., 2004). The models and movements organised by and for white middle-class 'normative' women were not doing justice to the complex realities affecting those who existed outside of that norm. The multiple oppressions which compounded lack of access to services and information had not begun to be unpacked, examined or acknowledged as corroborating factors in individual reproductive landscapes (Smith, 2005). Once the more disenfranchised communities started to break through the cultural taboos that are so often barriers to doing reproductive choice work, these groups got organised. When the dialogues opened up about sexual health and reproductive issues, there was a widespread sense that the term 'pro-choice', which had been used by activist groups up until that time, was simply not adequate (ibid.). Some started to use 'reproductive rights', while others teased out what a notion of 'reproductive justice' might look like (Silliman et al., 2004).

Reproductive justice deliberately names and recognises the intersectional ways in which aspects of positionality and identity such as race, religion, gender, class, economic status, marital status, sexuality and nationality are connected to the control, regulation and stigmatisation of bodies in a reproductive context (Cook et al., 2003). As with the distinction made between social policy and social justice, the term 'justice' is expressly chosen for its active, engaged and productive nature (Lynch, 1999). Reproductive justice acknowledges that lack of access to abortion is just one of the *many* factors acting to disenfranchise the reproductive choices of more marginalised communities. Reproductive justice explicitly links abortion access, reproductive rights and healthcare, and sees reproductive and sexual health problems as not isolated from other areas of inequalities. Groups and organisations which have gotten on board with reproductive justice work are committed to addressing, as ongoing and integral, the intersectional ways in which power, privilege and oppressions function related to reproductive rights and sexual health.

Central aims of the movement include to situate access to reproductive functions in a culturally and contextually specific milieu, fight against population control and make visible the links between the right to have children and the right not to. It seeks to organise within race and ethnic lines in order to engage with other movements. It acknowledges the multiple ways that these oppressions function, and deliberately strives for services and campaigns which have been skilled in the areas of marginalised identities such as LGBT. For example, reproductive justice movements in the United States have recognised eugenics laws, immigration reform, refugee and asylum seeker conditions, sterilisation, targeted family planning and welfare restrictions as structural efforts for population control containing racist, homophobic, anti-immigrant, classist and cissexist[37] ideologies as core tenets (Cook et al., 2003).

Reproductive justice requires sexual health and reproductive service providers to be inclusive and culturally aware, to implement practices that are informed through collaborations with communities rather than stereotypes, norms and societal (mis)conceptions. A true use of the reproductive justice model makes a strong statement about intersectionality within sexuality and reproductive rights movements.

ENVISIONING REPRODUCTIVE JUSTICE IN IRELAND

Recognising the intersectional power dynamics at play when considering individuals' experiences with access to (or lack of) reproductive and sexual health services is vital to a sustainable movement which can bring disparate groups on board and accomplish access in a comprehensive and just manner. In Ireland, we can begin by examining who staffs, operates and avails of mainstream sexual health and reproductive services, as well as who sets the agendas and how those agendas are informed. Once we scratch the surface, it is not difficult to see racial, ethnic, cultural and societal norms at play. Alliances between mainstream movements and efforts aimed towards those experiencing multiple oppressions are newer concepts in Ireland. Indeed, the emergence into abortion rights activism is recent, or still under consideration, for many groups representing marginalised experiences. Such alliances are only recently beginning to form and to receive wider cultural acceptance.

The age of sexual consent in Ireland is seventeen,[38] and the age of medical consent is sixteen.[39] This is in some cases enforced by general practitioners (hereafter GPs) acting as gatekeepers to contraception for young people (Sherlock, 2008; IFPA, 2011; Sherlock, 2012). This situation is compounded by lack of proper implementation of a sex-uality education curriculum in Irish schools (Maycock et al., 2007), including a fear and varied interpretation of what religious ethos looks like in practice (Sherlock, 2012). Young people are disproportionately marginalised within a reproductive health landscape, mostly due to *interpretation* of ethos and the law, rather than articulated restrictions brought on by these policies in the first place (IFPA, 2011).

Reproductive justice positions young people at the forefront. When we speak about access to abortion for 'women', we rarely envisage younger women and girls for whom access to any reproductive health service, including contraception, is already incredibly restricted. When efforts are implemented to reduce instances of teenage pregnancy in specific and targeted locales, it is possible that an undercurrent of population control ideologies underpin these initiatives. Compounding the situation for young people is an extreme lack of access to free, non-judgemental, accessible and non-moralising sexual health clinic services in Ireland. Countries like Sweden have expansive networks of accessible, youth-friendly sexual health clinics throughout the entire country, creating a different type of culture of responsibility and prioritising access to services for some of the most vulnerable individuals (Sherlock, 2012).

People with intellectual disabilities in Ireland have to break the law in order to have sex outside of the context of marriage.[40] This in and of itself is an inhumane violation of reproductive rights, and unquestioningly has practical as well as legal implications for people with intellectual disabilities trying to access reproductive services. In this instance, the law compounds and upholds existing societal stigma and exclusive norms concerning who sex and reproduction is for, and who is not expected to have sexual and reproductive needs. Emergency contraception is now, since 2011, provided in chemists throughout Ireland, but research is beginning to find that chemists will refuse provision or use a consultation session to moralise over the behaviour of the person seeking emergency contraception (see www.realproductivehealth.com).

The appalling conditions for asylum seekers in Ireland living in 'direct provision' compound the reality that many of these individuals are simultaneously coping with traumatic pasts while living with an uncertain future under conditions which are sub-standard, lacking in privacy and contain limited health care options (Breen, 2008). Further barriers to services exist for undocumented immigrants, as well as anyone residing in Ireland who has restrictions on travel. The right to travel for abortion services is not a right for everyone in Ireland.[41] Irish Traveller communities have social as well as logistical scenarios which complicate access to services, particularly reproductive and sexual health needs (McGorrian, 2012). An increasing number of people are in limbo between having earnings too high to warrant issuance of a medical card, yet too low to be able to afford adequate health services. Further complications arise for those who do hold a medical card, in that when their GP refuses services, such as to prescribe emergency contraception, under the grounds of conscientious objection, sometimes there is not an easy option for a second opinion or to see another GP (see also www.realproductivehealth.com). Lack of reproductive 'choice' in Ireland has many different connotations and manifestations.

Those in same-sex relationships are disallowed from adopting children as a couple, and it is often the case that the non-biological parent of a child does not have custody or parental rights.[42] The children's rights in this and many other scenarios are also complicated, with policies not reflecting the diverse realities of modern family constellations. Sexual orientation is often presumed by health workers, and even when practitioners are aware of sexual diversity assumptions can be made about what it means to have a specific sexual identity (for example, assumptions that a lesbian woman will never have sex with a man, or will never have sex with a woman who has had or is having sex with men).

Lack of legal gender recognition in Ireland has been a fundamental piece to a policy scenario whereby transgender (hereafter trans*[43]) experiences are completely ignored and off the radar when it comes to sexual health and reproductive rights.[44] Trans* exclusion from policy translates to lack of awareness and exclusion in financing of efforts to include diverse experiences of gender. Practically, this includes recognition that not all individuals who can become pregnant identify as 'women', and that the trans* community has unique reproductive needs such as requirements to freeze sperm or ova prior to medically transitioning. Ignorance of these scenarios contains presumptions about who reproduction is for, and who it is not for. The 'women-centric' language used in most sexual health and reproductive rights discourse ignores the fact that many trans-masculine[45] people also have wombs and can be reproductive. Furthermore, despite being often de-sexualised or fetishised by media and wider society, trans* people have all of the sexual health concerns that cisgender people do.[46] Medical professionals are often uninformed about the medical diversities of trans* and intersex bodies, which leaves these already-marginalised groups to advocate for themselves in attempting to achieve inclusive health care.

Lack of cultural awareness in sexual health care and reproductive rights advocacy permeates throughout Irish society, with many nationalities and cultural backgrounds unaccounted for, leaving some already quite oppressed groups in even more oppressive and vulnerable scenarios when attempting to access competent services. Language barriers can further complicate culturally inappropriate interventions, affecting non-native English speakers as well as deaf communities, to name only a few. Physical accessibility barriers often compound other restrictions to services and inclusive movements. Any time a service or a political action is located in an inaccessible building or without good access to transport, we are excluding some of those who need to be included most.

As discussed previously, age is another factor that compounds lack of access to services, with individuals under eighteen experiencing particular vulnerabilities where access to reproductive and sexual health services and information is concerned. Limited financial resources are a particularly restrictive force for many in austerity Ireland, especially when considering that Ireland's abortion needs are outsourced to other countries. It is a very different scenario for those who have the financial resources to be able to book a flight or a ferry to the UK for a termination than it is for individuals who cannot afford to do so. Those lacking in the ability to travel, for financial, immigration or other reasons, are literally stuck with Ireland's insufficient abortion legislation and all that it implies.

CONCLUSION

For people who require a specialised service, where specialised services exist, it is often the case that alternative services are not available and second opinions are not possible. This is the reality for LGBT people, those who have experienced FGM[47] and those who have language or physical accessibility limitations. The same is true of activism; when individual stories are iconised, or when a handful of spokespeople are relied upon to speak for 'people like them', our view of reproductive realities becomes limited. These scenarios leave our movements uninformed about the diverse experiences we all have, and the complex ways in which norms and privileges create exclusions in our lived realities. Issues like bodily autonomy, and efforts to achieve these rights, characterise the struggles of many groups in our society. It is time to put these intersectional realities at the forefront of our reproductive justice work.

The intersectional facets of our lives combine in interesting ways, meaning each person's experience of reproductive health in Ireland is nuanced and unique. All of the complex scenarios within reproductive landscapes combine with many other factors I have undoubtedly failed to mention. My own positionality and privileges as a white, English-speaking, Western, middle-class, bisexual/queer, able-bodied, educated cisgender woman researching and doing activism in this field influences my vantage point. My experiences shape what I can see, and what I fail to see. If we are to one day accomplish greater access to abortion as well as reproductive and sexual health services in Ireland, without having considered and included the complex realities that further restrict reproductive justice, we will not have accomplished anything besides further exclusions. As rights are gained for a normative 'majority', we further marginalise those who are already oppressed by the conventional visions we all conjure up when imagining *who* we mean when we fight for reproductive rights.

Oppression and exclusions are not isolated incidents, not solely the experiences of 'the other'. They affect every single one of us and our complex realities. A reproductive justice movement sees these complex-ities as central, rather than add-ons. It takes intersectionality as the starting point. Importantly, it also builds in a function for working towards and celebrating countless smaller achievements on the road towards a 'holy grail' of widespread access to abortion. Most of the lived realities affected by lack of access to abortion services in Ireland, and the difficulties and tragedies resulting from this lack, will never be told. A reproductive justice model makes visible all of the smaller barriers that contribute to lack of reproductive choice, and in doing so actually gives our activist movements more power and more 'choices'. Reproductive justice is the intersectional movement that Ireland is ready for, and the time is now.

7

The Eighth Amendment: planting a legal timebomb

STEPHANIE LORD

I N OCTOBER 1983 article 40.3.3 of the Irish Constitution was signed in to law declaring that: 'The State acknowledges the right to life of the unborn and, with due regard to the equal right to life of the mother, guarantees in its laws to respect, and, as far as practicable, by its laws to defend and vindicate that right' (article 40.3.3, Bunreacht na hÉireann). It is a law that has had the effect of very clearly subordinating pregnant women's lives to the lives of the foetus they carry, rendering abortion entirely illegal save for a situation in which an abortion is medically necessary in order to save the life, as opposed to the health, of the pregnant woman. Whether a pregnant woman has been a victim of rape or incest, or her foetus has a fatal abnormality with little or no chance of survival outside of the womb, or even if the pregnancy poses long-term risks to her physical or mental health short of being life-threatening, or if she simply does not want to be pregnant, is irrelevant to the Irish legal and medical systems. The law maintains that death must be a very real prospect for a pregnant woman before a legal abortion may be countenanced (United Nations, 2013). The artificial distinction created between a risk to health and a risk to life has left it so the hands of doctors are tied when it comes to assessing risk and providing necessary medical care, leaving many women who are simply told to travel to access abortion services overseas. Despite the enactment of the Protection of Life During Pregnancy Act 2013, there is still a lack of clarity as to the point at which a risk to health will constitute a risk to life.

Women who do not have access to the funds to travel may be forced to continue their pregnancies against their wishes. Further to this, women who are in precarious immigration positions, such as the asylum-seeking processes, or with disabilities, or in abusive situations, or in care, may find it difficult to leave Ireland in order to travel to access health care in another jurisdiction. Despite this, constitutional provision on abortion has not had the effect it was designed to have. Many women in Ireland still have abortions by either travelling overseas to procure abortions in private health clinics or ordering abortifacient medications online to induce their miscarriages at home (Brown, 2013). The Irish abortion law and its effects are draconian, and have led to a range of cases taken in both domestic and European courts which have drawn attention to the issues, and resulted in criticism of the law from international human rights bodies including the UN Human Rights Committee, the UN Committee on the Elimination of Discrimination against Women and the Council of Europe Human Rights Commissioner.

For the groups that favour restricting women's access to abortion and disregarding their rights, it is not about protecting children or families, it is a view very clearly based on how they view women's position in society, ultimately underpinned by conservative religious teaching that for women, there must be consequences for having sex. Many of the groups which campaigned in favour of the Eighth Amendment in 1983 still exist today. Quite a number of politicians who debated it in the Dáil (Irish parliament) chamber that year are still in office, or still politically active. The wheels of reproductive justice in Ireland have turned so slowly and the law has moved on so little, it is impossible not to see how many of the arguments from 1983 are still being fought today. Peter Sutherland, while acting as attorney general to the Irish government, termed the proposed constitutional provision which eventually became the Eighth Amendment banning abortion in Ireland a 'legal timebomb' (Riegal, 2012). He was right.

Article 40.3.3 of Bunreacht na hÉireann does not mention the word abortion, and yet it is because of its existence that 158,252 women from Ireland have travelled overseas to have abortions during the last thirty years (IFPA, 2013a). It is the reason that thousands more have risked jail terms by procuring abortifacient medication on the internet in order to induce abortions here in Ireland. It is the reason Savita Halappanavar died in a hospital bed in Galway in 2012.[48] While the Eighth Amendment to the constitution remains a part of the legal framework, there will always be a risk to women when serious complications resulting from pregnancy arise.

CONTRACEPTION AND ABORTION

Abortion is illegal in Ireland in almost all circumstances and had up until very recently been criminalised under sections 58 and 59 of the Offences Against the Persons Act 1861, introduced while Ireland was under British rule. These offences were not to be taken lightly and a woman convicted of unlawfully administering to herself 'any poison or other noxious thing' or of unlawfully using 'any instrument' with the intent to procure a miscarriage would be subject to life in penal servitude on conviction.[49] Up until 1979, contraception was illegal and the importing and sale of contraceptives was an offence punishable by a fine of up to £50 and six months in prison.[50] Spending most of your adult life pregnant was not an unusual prospect for Irish women and the sheer volume of time spent being pregnant meant that the rates of women working outside the home in Ireland were very low. The Protection of Life During Pregnancy Act 2013 has amended the potential punishment of life in penal servitude under these laws, to a potential jail sentence of fourteen years.

The law in Britain moved on from the 1861 Act, with MP David Steele introducing a private member's bill which led to the enactment of the Abortion Act 1967 decriminalising abortion in that jurisdiction in a range of circumstances. Sections 58 and 59 of the Offences Against the Persons Act remained on the Irish statute books. Steele's intention with the Abortion Act was to reduce the amount of disease and death associated with illegal abortion, and although there were divisions and heated debate there was a free vote in Westminster (BPAS, 2007). There was recognition at the time that the illegality of abortion in Britain was not preventing women from actually having abortions but it was increasing their risk of death or infection from the abortions. It is a recognition that has never been acknowledged by the Irish legislature.

While the sixties saw a period of social change throughout Europe, after 1967 fears began to take hold in Catholic organisations that legislative developments overseas would result in a call for legalisation of abortion in Ireland. In 1973, the US Supreme Court, while re-iterating that privacy was a fundamental right, held that this right extended to a woman's right to abortion in *Roe v. Wade* (*Roe v. Wade*, 410 US 113 (1973)). 1973 also saw Ireland join the European Economic Community, which was seen as a threat to the state's restriction on abortion. As a condition of membership, Ireland was required to allow Community law to take precedence over Irish law leaving a risk, according to the religious right, that Ireland would be required to introduce a liberal abortion regime similar to other European states. Furthermore, freedom of movement between member states of the EEC was protected, allowing women to travel from Ireland to Britain and other countries to procure abortions resulting in this being perceived as a normal option for women, (O'Reilly, 1992).

Pressure to legalise contraception built steadily over the seventies and in 1971, a group of women from the Irish Women's Liberation Movement took part in the 'contraception train' journey from Belfast to Dublin, arriving in Connolly train station waving contraceptive packets at mortified customs officials (Workers Solidarity, 2008). Despite the fact that contraception was illegal, Irish women took matters into their own hands with many women being prescribed the contraceptive pill as a 'menstrual regulator' by sympathetic doctors.[51] Much like the women turning to Women on Web in Ireland today to receive abortion medication in the post, many received their contraceptives through the post.

A turning point for the law on contraception was the McGee case. Mrs McGee was a mother of four children including twins, all born within twenty-three months of each other. She became ill during her pregnancies and suffered a stroke during one. She was advised by medical professionals against becoming pregnant again and attempted to import spermicidal jelly in the post which was confiscated by customs officials. Mrs McGee challenged the constitutionality of this confiscation. This resulted in the Irish Supreme Court ruling in the case of *McGee v.*

Attorney General in 1974, that in reference to the 'imprescriptible rights, antecedent and superior to all positive law' of the family (Article 41), conferred upon spouses a broad right to privacy in marital affairs (*McGee v. Attorney General* [1974] I.R. 284). This right to privacy included the right of marital couples to contraception.

THE RELIGIOUS RIGHT

The anti-choice/religious conservative movements had also galvanised support after Pope John Paul II visited Ireland in 1979. A quarter of the population, 1.25 million people, turned out to see him in the Phoenix Park and it was a visible demonstration of the influence that the Catholic Church still had in Ireland (O'Reilly, 1992). There was also a view that the European Union, seen by conservative elements as the monster who had foisted equal pay upon Ireland, would force Ireland to adopt a liberal 'abortion on request' regime.

The privacy decision in *Roe v. Wade*, which legalised abortion in the US, had shocked conservative Ireland – it was after all an extension of a 1965 US privacy ruling on the right to contraception. It was feared by those in conservative circles that at some point, a case would arise and the Supreme Court would decide that the right to marital privacy in marital affairs not only included a right to contraception as in McGee – but a right to abortion as well. As far as the conservative elements of Ireland were concerned, what was needed was a provision in the constitution that was designed to ban abortion outright, and not leave it open to the Supreme Court to ever interpret a right to abortion within the constitutional right to privacy. It was this fear that drove them to begin an intensified campaign to change the law with ramifications for thousands of women in Ireland that we are still living with today.

THE PRO-LIFE AMENDMENT CAMPAIGN

The first call for a constitutional amendment appeared in a leaflet produced by a fundamentalist Catholic lay group, the Irish Family League, headed by John O'Reilly and specifically targeting the McGee ruling. It stated that the matter of contraception was far too important to be left to the Supreme Court or the Oireachtas, and that the Constitution should define 'a citizen as a citizen from the moment of conception and a prohibition on artificial contraception be inserted under clause 41'. John O'Reilly would go on to be one of the leading voices of the Pro-Life Amendment Campaign (PLAC).

However, the seventies gave rise to a massive transformation in the lives of women in Ireland. Due to the (albeit limited) availability of contraception, the previous situation where married women would have large families and spend years of their lives being pregnant was finally changing. 1980 even saw the establishment of a Women's Right to Choose group in Ireland (see Threlfall, 1996). However, in 1981, a conference was held in Mount Carmel hospital that brought together a range of right-wing organisations under the PLAC umbrella, including the Society for the Protection of Unborn Children, the Catholic Secondary School Parents' Association, the Guild of Catholic Pharmacists, the Catholic Doctors Guild, National Association for the Ovulation Method, the Catholic Young Men's Society, the Responsible Society and a number of members of the Knights of Columbanus. The Knights of Columbanus are still active today. A Catholic lay organisation, they had a central role in the fight for article 40.3.3. Emily O'Reilly in her book, *Masterminds of the Right*, describes them as a 'patriarchal, secretive catholic fundamentalist network of influential men who seek to exert power and influence through the infiltration of hostile groups and organisations, anonymous lobbying and the targeting of individuals hostile to their orthodoxy', with their fundamental aim being the 'creation and maintenance of a catholic state for a catholic people', (O'Reilly, 1992, p. 25).

The Pro-Life Amendment Campaign took advantage of the influence held by their Knights of Columbanus members and only three days after their launch in early 1981, they visited government buildings to lobby the then Fianna Fáil taoiseach, Charles Haughey, for a referendum on abortion, as well as the leader of the opposition Fine Gael TD, Garrett FitzGerald. Both meetings were a success, and the PLAC members left with commitments from both party leaders for a referendum on abortion if they entered government after the forthcoming general election. Frank Cluskey TD, leader of the Labour Party, also committed his party to a referendum stating that his party was 'unequivocally opposed to abortion'.[52]

PLAC were well organised and there was an implied threat that failure to commit to a referendum that would introduce a constitutional ban on abortion and protection for the 'unborn' would result in a campaign being mounted against them, drastically reducing their chances of being re-elected. Given the range of influential bodies and organisations that PLAC members had control of, combined with the traditional conservatism of those male-dominated political parties and genuine fear that women would somehow be granted access to abortion, it is unsurprising that they were quick to agree to hold a referendum.

Indeed, the fears of counter-canvassing were not unfounded, and two left-wing TDs, Deputy Jim Kemmy (Democratic Socialist Party) and the current president of Ireland, Deputy Michael D. Higgins (Labour) saw visible campaigns against them from local media, clergy and members of the Labour Party in their own constituencies. Both of these members also saw massive declines in their first-preference votes between February and November 1982. It is a well-tested and well-honed tactic that anti-choice lobby groups are still renowned for using today (Farry, 2013).

THE EIGHTH AMENDMENT

There were five general elections during the 1980s in Ireland, with three of those taking place in an eighteen-month period between 1981 and 1982. May 1981 saw the return of Fine Gael leader, Garrett FitzGerald, as taoiseach. Haughey and Fianna Fáil had appeared to be more popular but the general election, due for spring, was postponed due to the Stardust tragedy. Fine Gael proposed tax-cutting plans that appealed to the electorate over Fianna Fáil's proposal to increase public spending. Furthermore, the Anti-H-Block Movement abstentionist candidates undermined the credibility of Fianna Fáil members, emphasising their republican credentials. However, the budgetary plans – which included a plan to put VAT on children's shoes – of the Fine Gael–Labour government were defeated in 1982, leading to a general election in February of that year, which in turn led to a restoration of a Fianna Fáil government led by Haughey. It was Haughey's government that drafted an initial wording for a constitutional amendment to ban abortion, in the Eighth Amendment to the Constitution Bill, but before the referendum could go ahead, the government collapsed, leading to another general election in November 1982. But the relentless lobbying and campaigning by the right-wing religious conservatives of PLAC had paid off – commitments to hold a referendum on abortion still remained central planks of all the main political parties' policies (O'Reilly, 1992, p.73).

The Fianna Fáil amendment was as follows: 'The state acknowledges the right to life of the unborn and, with due regard to the equal right to life of the mother, guarantees in its laws to respect, and, as far as practicable by its laws, to defend and vindicate that right.' It was a formula of words drafted by the Pro-Life Amendment Campaign. When the formula of words was introduced, it was generally opposed by those considered to be on 'the left' in Ireland, although many of these were at pains to say they were not in favour of legalising abortion. The Catholic Church supported the amendment but many of the Protestant churches spoke out against it (National Archives, ref no. 2012/90/881).

Of course, it is now a matter of public record that while Garret FitzGerald did initially support the wording of the proposed amendment, state papers show that the legal advice received by the government had warned the taoiseach that the wording was ambiguous and might have the effect of preventing the safeguarding of the life of a pregnant woman as was the case already. The implications of this amendment became clear in 1992 when the fears of Garret FitzGerald and Attorney General, Peter Sutherland, became realised when the Supreme Court held in the X case that a woman did have a right to an abortion where there was a real and substantial risk to her life that could only be averted by provision of an abortion.

An alternative wording had been proposed by Michael Noonan, who was minister for justice at the time, that stipulated: 'Nothing in the Constitution shall be involved to invalidate or to deprive of force or effect a provision of a law on the grounds that it prohibits abortion.' Dáil debates ensued on which formula of words to go with. The vote in the Dáil on the wording led to government parties being split on the preferred choice of wording but in the end it was the Fianna Fáil wording that won out. Fianna Fáil, Fine Gael, the Catholic Church and the Pro-Life Amendment Campaign strongly supported the amendment and the Labour Party, the Workers' Party, Sinn Féin, the Anti-Amendment Campaign, Senator Mary Robinson and the taoiseach himself campaigned against it. However, it passed with 66 per cent of the electorate supporting it, but it was defeated in five of the Dublin constituencies and the numbers on the day demonstrate that the winning margin was much smaller in urban constituencies than rural areas.

PROTECTING PUBLIC MORALITY

The contributions in the Dáil on the Eighth Amendment Bill are fascinating insights into how issues of 'public morality' in general were viewed in Ireland in 1983. What is also remarkable is that the tone and some of the language that was used then is not dissimilar to more current debates on abortion in the state parliament. In the 1983 debates there are accusations from Fianna Fáil's Dr Sean McCarthy that Garret FitzGerald had been influenced by the 'pro-abortionists in Young Fine Gael' because of his campaign against the Fianna Fáil wording.[53] Deputy Oliver J. Flanagan's contribution also makes for interesting reading, where he speaks of the obligation of parliamentarians to uphold 'public morals'. The transcripts of his contribution show he verges on the point of obsession with public morality, and quotes *Humanae Vitae* at length and then proceeds to castigate a number of individuals including Bernadette McAliskey, the Right to Choose Group, Jim Kemmy and the Democratic Socialist Party among others.[54] Those who are familiar with Oliver J. Flanagan may also be aware that he was known for his views and his leanings towards uber-Catholic pronouncements in the Dáil, not to mention anti-Semitic outbursts. In one Dáil debate during 1983, Deputy Flanagan pronounced that:

> ... we must bear full responsibility in the area of legislating for public morality. We must be concerned about the quality of Irish life that we wish to pass on to those who will come after us. It has been said that we cannot legislate for virtue but that we can legislate for non virtue by way of creating conditions and trends whereby the struggle to be virtuous is rendered very difficult ... Abortion is nothing less than murder, but it is a practice that is growing steadily in various parts of the world. We in Ireland have an opportunity to display to the rest of the world our total concern for the protection of the unborn ...

The reasons of the Minister for Justice, Michael Noonan, for opposing the original wording in the same debate seemed chillingly prophetic in the context of what was to happen in the course of the X case in 1992:

Briefly, those defects are twofold: first, that the expression the 'unborn' is very ambiguous; second, that the reference to the equal rights of the mother is insufficient to guarantee that operations necessary to save the life of the mother but resulting in the death of the foetus may continue.

On the first point, it is scarcely necessary to say that objection is not being raised simply on the basis that there is a certain degree of ambiguity. Some ambiguity is probably inescapable – language is not a precise instrument. The criticism in this case is the extent of the ambiguity, a criticism which is strengthened by the fact that it was obviously accepted in order to avoid argument.

On the second point, I would like the record to show very clearly what is being said by way of criticism – and what is not being said. It is not being said that the wording would be held to make the operations in question unlawful. Nobody could say with certainty what interpretation a court might put on the words. What is being said is that, on the ordinary meanings of words, that should be the interpretation and that therefore there must be a definite risk.[55]

The Workers' Party proposed amendments, but as there were not sufficient numbers in the vote, the house was not divided, and all these were lost. Even though they opposed the amendment overall, they proposed to make the amendment a lesser harm or clearer in its meaning and these proposed changes to the original wording highlighted the nuances of the discussion at the time. In November 1982, two days before a vote of no confidence in the Dáil, the Fianna Fáil government announced the wording despite having been warned by their own attorney general, Patrick Connolly, that a 'pro-life' amendment 'might well have the effect of threatening the right of the mother' to have a life-saving operation.

The State Papers for 1982 also show that he foresaw some of the problems that could be thrown up by a difficult case, like the 1992 X case that was to follow, and noted that 'whatever my personal views be' a 'rape victim could not be exempted from any constitutional prohibition nor, in the current climate of what is sought to achieve, could the amendment exempt abortion where the mental health of a woman was at serious risk' (Humphreys, 2012).

He was the second attorney-general to have argued that it would create serious legal problems in the future if enacted. The Fianna Fáil government also had advice from the previous attorney general, Peter Sutherland, who argued that the amendment would create serious legal ambiguities. State Papers show that senior officials in the department of the taoiseach told Mr Haughey that 'this view may well be shared by many legal experts' (Humphreys, 2012). However, the advice was dismissed and records of the time also demonstrated how Mr Sutherland's advice was withheld from Mr Connolly in an effort to speed up the process. Pressure from PLAC was mounting behind the scenes.

Current Taoiseach, Enda Kenny, also made a number of representations between 1981 and 1982 on behalf of constituents to expedite the processing of the referendum. Many of the forces behind the 1983 referendum still have a hand in shaping the laws governing reproductive rights in Ireland today.

THE X CASE

The X case in 1992 shocked the nation. The parents of a fourteen-year-old girl pregnant as a result of rape, who became known as 'X', contacted the Gardaí in order to find out if DNA evidence from the foetus could be used in a prosecution. The Gardaí were unclear if this was permitted and sought advice from the DPP. The DPP in turn contacted the attorney general, Harry Whelehan, who issued an injunction to prevent the girl from travelling to access an abortion outside of the state. Although she had already left Ireland, the threat of legal action hanging over them brought her home. The matter ended up in the courts, and X, who was suicidal as a result of the pregnancy, stated quite clearly to a consultant psychologist that she would take her own life if forced to continue with it. The Supreme Court found within the wording of the Eighth Amendment that a woman had a right to an abortion where there was a real and substantial risk to her life, including the risk of suicide (*Attorney General v. X*, [1992] IESC 1). It was obvious that the intention of PLAC, to ban abortions in all circumstances, regardless of the consequences, had failed.

THE ANTI-AMENDMENT CAMPAIGN

A broad range of civil society groups against the amendment, comprised of organisations including the Well Woman Centre, the Irish Family Planning Association, the Irish Council for Civil Liberties, the Council for the Status of Women, and the Women's Right to Choose Group, launched a co-ordinated Anti-Amendment Campaign (AAC) in June 1982. The group also had a number of left-wing activists, non-Catholic clergy, journalists and academics involved, and other groups such as Doctors Against the Amendment and Lawyers Against the Amendment campaigned vigorously in conjunction with the AAC on the basis of numerous well-thought-out and reasoned arguments against the proposed wording, including the central opinion that a woman's right to life would be subordinated by the right to life of the 'unborn', and fears that forms of contraception such as the IUD might be made illegal as they prevented implantation in the womb. Strategic decisions were made within the AAC to not silence openly pro-choice demands, but rather to 'mute' them in order to appeal to a broader audience (McAvoy, 2008). They further argued that a more worthwhile endeavour for PLAC would have been the pursuit of improvement to the quality of life for families and children – an argument still being put forward by pro-choice groups in 2014 in reference to ongoing campaigns to roll back the very restrictive and narrow right to abortion that women have.

Regardless of the arguments put forward by the AAC they had a very clear understanding of what was going on with PLAC and the political structures of the time:

> ... this Constitutional amendment campaign represents a reactionary and anti-democratic movement to counter the progressive liberali-sation of opinion within Irish society. Nor is the title 'pro-life' for this amendment an honest one. The campaign is anti-abortion only, and to be consistently pro-life it would have to call for the ending of legal discrimination against children born outside of marriage and oppose capital punishment. Furthermore, the blatant disregard for the welfare of women (whose rights are always deemed secondary to that of the fertilised ovum, embryo or foetus) inherent in the attitudes of its leading supporters raises the question of what it means to be genuinely pro-life. (Women's Right to Choose Campaign, WRCC, 1982 Statement quoted in McAvoy, 2008)

CONCLUSION

In 1997 Garrett FitzGerald expressed regret for his hand in the 1983 referendum, referring to it as a debacle (Sheehan and Hand, 2012). What became clear as the years went on and more women sought access to abortion through the Irish courts was that the political leadership of 1983 had proceeded with a referendum for which there had been no real popular demand. It arose from pressure by the Pro-Life Amendment Campaign to do so. Transcripts of the Dáil debates during the course of 1983 demonstrate clearly that those who were involved in moving the referendum forward had very little understanding of abortion or the issues surrounding it. There is very little discussion concerning the reasons why a woman in Ireland might want to have an abortion. The realisation that nobody really knew what 'the unborn' was, or what the implications of attempting to define it would be, was not new to the deputies in Dáil Éireann debating the matter in 2012 and 2013 – two different attorney generals said so quite clearly in 1982. The level of ignorance in the debates is palpable but, sadly, similar to what is still seen today in that same institution. The recurring theme seems to be a notion that any liberalisation of abortion law will lead to masses of women having abortions – the underpinning idea is that sex for women should have consequences, i.e. pregnancy and childbirth.

Deputy Alan Shatter told the Dáil on 17 February 1983: 'I have no doubt that if [the amendment] in its present form becomes part of our Constitution it will essentially secure a constitutional judgement in the not too distant future requiring the House to enact legislation to permit women to have abortions.' That is exactly what happened in the Supreme Court's decision on the X case in 1992. The then minister for health, Labour's Barry Desmond, summarised the flaws in the amendment and what would likely happen if it was passed:

> It will lead inevitably to confusion and uncertainty … Far from providing the protection and certainty which is sought by many of those who have advocated its adoption it will have a contrary effect … a doctor faced with the dilemma of saving the life of the mother, knowing that to do so will terminate the life of 'the unborn', will be compelled by the wording to conclude that he can do nothing.

It was exactly this that led to the withholding of an abortion from Savita Halappanavar in a Galway hospital in November 2012.

Since 1983, there have been three further referenda held in order to clarify the meaning of the Eighth Amendment to the constitution. The Eighth Amendment had the effect of restricting access to information on abortion, and led to women having to seek recourse in the courts in order to ensure their right to travel to access abortion overseas. Even today, now that abortion has been legislated for where there is a real and substantial risk to the life of a woman, including a threat of suicide, women with risks to their health will still travel. It still has an impact on the maternity care that women will receive, with screening for genetic defects generally not being made available – the underlying fear in Catholic-run maternity hospitals is that if women are given such information they might have an abortion. In 1983, Deputy Michael D. Higgins stated: 'The government has decided to go to the people to ensure that, in the rare cases where a woman is prone to suicide, she will go to England.' The legislative hurdles that a woman must jump through when she is suicidal, in order to access abortion here, mean that women who are suicidal will travel rather than put themselves before panels of psychiatrists, risking involuntary detention under the Mental Health Act 2011. Overall, as far as the law concerning abortion is concerned, and the political structures that have protected, enabled and bolstered it, remarkably little has changed.

8

Abortion and the Law in Ireland

IVANA BACIK

I RISH LAW ON ABORTION is highly restrictive – criminal prohibition dates back to 1861. In 1983, the law became even more restrictive when the Constitution was amended to give 'the unborn' equal right to life with 'the mother' (the Eighth Amendment). A pregnancy may only be terminated legally under this provision in order to save the life of the pregnant woman. There is no right to abortion in any other circumstance; even where a woman or girl has been raped or abused, or her health is at risk.

Despite this highly repressive law, more than 150,000 women and girls from Ireland have had abortions over the last forty years. Most recent figures show that approximately 4,000 women travel to Britain each year to terminate their pregnancies. Yet these women's stories are never told publicly at home. The cultural taboo on speaking out about abortion and crisis pregnancy has been strengthened by the intimidatory tactics of anti-choice campaigners. Abortion represents their last line of defence since contraception and divorce were finally legalised in the 1990s. These conservative lobbyists have brought disproportionate influence to bear on fearful politicians over many years.

But the tide is now turning. In 2013, after a long and hard-fought campaign, legislation was passed which specifies when abortion may be carried out legally to save women's lives (the Protection of Life During Pregnancy Act 2013). Although abortion remains a criminal offence where carried out for any reason other than to save a woman's life, this legislation marks significant progress. It represents the first time that abortion in any form has ever been legislated for in Ireland. Public opinion has also significantly moved on in recent years – until the mid-1990s, it was illegal even to provide Irish women with information on how to obtain abortion in Britain, but now opinion polls show that most people favour legalising abortion on grounds beyond those of risk to the woman's life. This article seeks to chart the development of Irish law on abortion in recent decades, and to assess the prospects for future progressive change.

THE LEGAL CONTEXT

Until the enactment of the Protection of Life During Pregnancy Act 2013, abortion was a criminal offence in Ireland under sections 58 and 59 of the Offences Against the Person Act 1861. Section 58 made it an offence for a pregnant woman unlawfully to 'attempt to procure a miscarriage', i.e. to undergo an abortion, while section 59 criminalised anyone who assisted a woman in having an abortion. The maximum penalty was life imprisonment.

For many years after 1861, prosecutions were taken against persons performing backstreet abortions in both England and Ireland. However, the legal position in England was altered after the 1939 case of *R v. Bourne* ([1939] 1 KB 687). Dr Bourne was prosecuted under the act for performing an abortion on a young girl who had been gang-raped by a group of soldiers. The trial judge directed the jury that the doctor would have a defence if he or she carried out an abortion to preserve the life of the pregnant woman; and the doctor would also have a duty to carry out an abortion if the effect of the continuation of the pregnancy would be to make the woman or girl a 'physical or mental wreck'. This judgement led to an increase in the availability of backstreet abortion in England, as doctors were able to rely upon the *Bourne* defence. As a result, women began to travel from Ireland to England for abortions, and the numbers of Irish prosecutions for abortion and infanticide fell considerably. They rose again during the years of the Second World War, when restrictions were placed on travel to England from Ireland. The last prosecution for a backstreet abortion in Ireland was in the infamous Nurse Cadden case in 1956. The nurse, reputed to have performed many abortions, was the last woman sentenced to death in Ireland following the death of one of her patients. This sentence was later commuted, and she died in prison in 1959 (Kavanagh, 2005).

In Britain, largely as a result of pressure from the medical profession concerned at the many deaths of women undergoing abortion in poor sanitary conditions, the Westminster parliament passed the Abortion Act 1967 which provides legal access to abortion. Once the act was passed, the numbers of women travelling to England from Ireland for terminations began to increase significantly, peaking at 6,673 women in 2001. The numbers travelling have fallen since, reducing to 3,982 in 2012.[56]

These figures demonstrate the extent of the need for legal abortion in Ireland. At present, for many Irish women this is addressed through the availability of travel to Britain. But the needs of the most vulnerable women, who find it hard to travel because of youth, poverty or legal status as asylum seekers, are not being met. These are women who face a 'double crisis'. On top of their crisis pregnancy, they also face the added crisis involved in the practical, financial and emotional difficulties in making the journey to England. (For anonymised accounts of these experiences see IFPA, 2000.)

In recognition of the need for legal abortion, in 1979 a group of feminist activists established the first Women's Right to Choose group in Ireland, demanding the legalisation of both contraception and abortion. In March 1981 this group held a public meeting at Liberty Hall, Dublin. Linda Connolly has described the effect of this development:

> The counter right made itself visible and increasingly mobilised in 1981 by diverting the abortion debate into the legal/constitutional arena – an area which required extensive resources and expertise. Tactically, it aimed to block the women's movement from providing its services by actively campaigning for a constitutional referendum on the 'right to life of the unborn' ... (Connolly, 1997, p. 561)

THE 1983 EIGHTH AMENDMENT

The impetus for this campaign for a referendum derived from the dramatic changes in abortion law that had occurred in other countries, not just in England and Europe but also in the US. In 1973 the US Supreme Court had held in *Roe v. Wade*, building on earlier case law on rights to privacy and contraception, that women had the right to abortion under the US Constitution (*Roe v. Wade* (1973) 410 U.S. 113). This decision acted as a catalyst for conservative forces in Ireland to lobby for a constitutional referendum to reinforce the legislative prohibition on abortion, so as to prevent the Irish courts from taking a similar approach. The same year that *Roe* was decided, the Irish Supreme Court had held in *McGee v. Attorney General* that a right to marital privacy was implicit in the Constitution, thereby enabling a married couple to import contraceptives for their own use (*McGee v. AG* (1974) IR 284).

The decision in *Roe*, and the legal reasoning of those who saw *McGee* as offering a back door to the legalisation of abortion, had 'a clearly visible effect on the development of Irish law and policy on abortion, in giving an impetus to the Pro-Life Amendment Campaign (PLAC) which resulted in the passing of the Eighth Amendment to the Irish Constitution in September 1983' (Kingston et al., 1997, p. 260). The bitter and angry referendum campaign has been described as a 'second partitioning of Ireland' (Hesketh, 1990). Many commentators have identified the outcome of the referendum as a pivotal setback in the history of the Irish women's movement (see Smyth, 1992; McAvoy, 2008; Schweppe, 2008).

The Eighth Amendment became article 40.3.3 of the Constitution, which recognises the 'right to life of the unborn' and expressly sets that right up in potential conflict with the 'equal' right to life of the pregnant woman.[57] Inevitably, that conflict did arise, only nine years after the passing of the referendum, after a great deal of litigation had taken place which was to extend the effect of the provision well beyond that publicly envisaged by its advocates.

THE 'INFORMATION' CASES

Very shortly after the passage of the referendum, the Society for the Protection of Unborn Children (SPUC), established in 1980, began to use the new provision as the basis for a series of cases taken against those providing women with information on abortion facilities in Britain. SPUC first issued proceedings against two non-directive pregnancy counselling agencies, Open Door Counselling and the Well Woman Centre. Both offered pregnant women information on all the options open to them, including the contact details of clinics offering abortion in Britain. SPUC argued that the provision of this information amounted to a breach of the constitutional right to life of the unborn. This argument required a breathtaking leap of logic in order to succeed, based on the assumption that women would not choose to terminate their pregnancies if they were not provided with information. Yet it succeeded – Judge Hamilton ruled against the counselling agencies in the December 1986 *Open Door* case, stating that their right to freedom of expression could not be invoked to interfere with the 'fundamental right' to life of the unborn (*Attorney General (SPUC) v. Open Door Counselling Ltd* (1987) ILRM 477). This High Court decision, subsequently upheld by the Supreme Court, established that the provision of information on abortion was unlawful under the Constitution.

The agencies however appealed to the European Court of Human Rights, which in the October 1992 *Open Door (No. 2)* case ruled that the Irish government's ban on abortion information was in breach of the freedom of expression guarantee in article 10 of the European Convention on Human Rights, since it (the ban) was 'overbroad and disproportionate' (*Open Door No. 2* (1993) 15 EHRR 244).

In the meantime, the judgements in the *Open Door* case had a dramatic effect on the availability of information. Other counselling agencies, in fear of being closed down, stopped providing information on abortion. An underground helpline run by the Women's Information Network (WIN) was established, and linked up with the London-based Irish Women's Abortion Support Group (IWASG) to provide women with information and practical help. Other underground groups in Ireland also provided information through informal networks (see for example Conroy, 1996). However, the only organisations that continued to provide abortion information openly in Ireland were students' unions.

Shortly after initiating the *Open Door* litigation, SPUC began legal action against the officers of a number of students' unions, which were providing information on abortion in their handbooks. The student officers, of whom this author was one, were from the national Union of Students in Ireland (USI), University College Dublin and Trinity College Dublin. Once again, SPUC succeeded in obtaining court orders against the students from the High Court and Supreme Court, prohibiting them from distributing this information. They even sought to jail the four officers from Trinity College, who had already distributed their student handbooks prior to the High Court case. Mary Robinson, then a senior counsel, defended the students, and succeeded in persuading the court to refer the case to the European Court of Justice. In its 1991 judgement in the case, known as *Grogan*, that court defined abortion as a 'service' under EC law – and prohibition of the provision of information in one member state on a service lawfully available in another member state would normally be in breach of EC law. However, ultimately the court concluded that because there was no commercial connection between the students' unions and the British clinics, the information ban could not be regarded as a restriction under EC law – so the students' case was returned to the Irish High Court, where in August 1992 Judge Morris granted a permanent injunction restraining the students from providing information on abortion. This was finally lifted by the Supreme Court in March 1997, by which time many more legal and social developments had occurred.

In the context of EC law, two further significant developments took place following the decision in *Grogan*. First, in November 1991, the Irish government negotiated a protocol on abortion, to be adopted as part of the Treaty on European Union (the Maastricht Treaty).[58] This was to become highly controversial in the aftermath of the X case.

THE X CASE

The two rights outlined in the Eighth Amendment were finally brought into direct conflict in February 1992, with the X case. X was a fourteen-year-old girl who had been raped and became pregnant as a result. She wished to terminate the pregnancy and her parents took her to England for that purpose. They notified the police that they were leaving the country for this purpose because they wished to use DNA samples from the foetus in any subsequent rape prosecution. The attorney general then sought a High Court injunction to stop the girl from travelling out of Ireland for the abortion; this was granted by Judge Costello. The nightmare scenario predicted by those who had campaigned against the 1983 amendment had come to pass; a pregnant child had effectively been imprisoned in her own country.

X and her parents were already in England when notified of the injunction, but they cancelled their appointment at the clinic and returned to Dublin. Political uproar ensued. There was popular outrage at the notion that a child rape victim might be forced to proceed with an unwanted pregnancy. In the face of mounting public pressure, an appeal was heard within a matter of weeks, and the Supreme Court reversed Judge Costello's decision, allowing the girl to travel. The court found that because the girl was suicidal, the continuation of the pregnancy would have threatened her right to life. Thus, the two rights were in direct conflict. In such situations, the court ruled, the right to life of the girl prevailed. Chief Justice Finlay stated that:

> ... if it can be established as a matter of probability that there is a real and substantial risk to the life, as distinct from the health, of the mother, which can only be avoided by the termination of her pregnancy, such termination is permissible. (*Attorney General v. X* (1992) IR 1)

In a separate judgement, Mr Justice McCarthy commented on the lack of legal clarity about the Eighth Amendment:

> In the context of the eight years that have passed since the Amendment was adopted ... the failure by the legislature to enact the appropriate legislation is no longer just unfortunate, it is inexcusable. What are pregnant women to do? What are the parents of a pregnant girl under age to do? What are the medical profession to do? They have no guidelines save what may be gleaned from the judgements in this case. (1992, p. 90)

The judgement meant that X could legally have an abortion in Ireland (in fact she travelled again to England). However, it also meant that where a woman was not facing a threat to her life, then not only would it be illegal for her to have an abortion in Ireland, but she could be prevented from travelling abroad for abortion. Further, because of the Maastricht Treaty Protocol, a pregnant woman prevented from travelling could not rely upon the EC law guarantee of freedom of movement.

When it was realised that the Maastricht Treaty might have this effect, pro-choice groups launched a campaign against its adoption. Faced with the potential defeat of the Maastricht referendum, the government was forced to take action. First, in May 1992, they got the EC to adopt a 'Solemn Declaration' stating that the operation of the protocol would not affect freedom to travel or to obtain information. The actual legal effect of this declaration apparently contradicting the words of the protocol has never been tested. But its adoption reassured people that girls like X would not be prevented from travelling, and it helped to ensure that the Maastricht referendum was passed in June 1992.

The government also put three amendments to article 40.3.3 before the people in November 1992. The aim of the first (the twelfth amendment) was to rule out suicide as a threat to the life of a pregnant woman, thereby overruling the X case. The second amendment guaranteed the freedom to travel abroad, and the third allowed the provision of information on services lawfully available in other states.

The twelfth amendment was opposed by pro-choice groups who wished, at a minimum, to maintain the lawfulness of abortion in X case circumstances. Bizarrely, it was also opposed by some anti-abortion groups who, while seeking to overturn the decision in X, did not think that the proposed wording went far enough, in that it still allowed for abortion where necessary to save the life of the pregnant woman. They denied that abortion was ever necessary to save a woman's life.

It was hardly surprising in that context that the twelfth amendment was rejected by the people. However, in a clear victory for the pro-choice movement, the travel and information referendums were both passed (Kennelly and Ward, 1993, pp. 115–34). Following these amendments, the Regulation of Information (Services Outside the State for Termination of Pregnancies) Act 1995 was introduced, providing for the conditions under which information on abortion may be provided. The first comprehensive study of women and crisis pregnancy in Ireland, conducted subsequently, found however that information on both contraception and abortion was still difficult to obtain for many women and girls (Mahon et al., 1998).

THE 1997 C CASE

In November 1997, the High Court was asked again to deal with the issue of crisis pregnancy, in the C case, involving a pregnant thirteen-year-old rape victim. She was in the care of the health board, which obtained permission from the District Court to take her to England for an abortion. However, the girl's parents, having previously supported her decision, changed their minds, and appealed to the High Court. There, Judge Geoghegan held that the continuation of her pregnancy would pose a 'real and substantial risk' to her life, on the basis of psychiatric evidence that she was suicidal (*A & B v. Eastern Health Board and C* (1998) ILRM 464). Thus the abortion would have been lawful in Ireland, and so the health board was entitled to take her to England.

Following the C case, a number of further developments took place. First, the expert Constitution Review Group recommended in 1996 that legislation should be introduced to clarify the application of the X case test (Constitutional Review Group, 1996, pp. 227–9). Following consultation, a comprehensive Green Paper was then published by the government in 1999, which presented a total of seven options, ranging from an absolute constitutional ban on abortion (which they rejected as unsafe) to legislation allowing for abortion on request (Interdepartmental Working Group, 1999). This report was referred to the All-Party Oireachtas Committee on the Constitution (APOCC), which itself engaged in a further consultation process, holding oral hearings during 2000, and finally reporting to the Cabinet Sub-Committee on Abortion in November 2000 (All-Party Committee on the Constitution, 2000).

Among the recommendations agreed upon by APOCC was the need to invest resources in a programme to tackle the incidence of crisis pregnancy. As a result, the Crisis Pregnancy Agency was established in 2002. It was subsumed into the Department of Health in 2010, but for a time ran high-profile contraceptive and sex education programmes; it continues to provide funding to crisis pregnancy counselling agencies, including those providing non-directive counselling. It is noteworthy that the numbers of women travelling from Ireland for abortions have declined since its establishment.[59]

The members of APOCC could not, however, agree on a single recommendation for legal change, instead presenting three alternatives, including the option of seeking again to amend the Constitution to rule out suicide risk as a ground for legal abortion. The anti-abortion movement lobbied successfully for this option; so on 6 March 2002, the government again put an amendment to the people to reverse the decision in the X case.

A range of different feminist and civil liberties groups, along with the Labour Party, united against the referendum, under the 'Alliance for a No Vote' (ANV) banner; it was ultimately defeated. Unfortunately, while this was important symbolically, defeat did not mark any step forward for pro-choice campaigners. It simply stopped the clock turning backwards.

THE EUROPEAN COURT OF HUMAN RIGHTS – THE D AND ABC CASES

Following the defeat of the 2002 referendum, abortion slipped off the political agenda altogether for some years, although the courts continued to deal with the human impact of the Eighth Amendment. In 2007, a seventeen-year-old woman in the care of the state and with an anencephalic pregnancy sought permission from the HSE to allow her to travel to obtain an abortion. The High Court ruled that she had a right to travel (*D v. District Judge Brennan, HSE and Ireland*, High Court, 9 May 2007).

A similar issue then arose in a case before the European Court of Human Rights taken against Ireland by another applicant, also D, whose pregnancy had resulted in the diagnosis of a fatal foetal abnormality. She was forced to go to England to terminate the pregnancy, and argued that this breached her rights under the European Con-vention. In its decision, however, the court found the application inadmissible because the applicant 'did not comply with the requirement to exhaust domestic remedies as regards the availability of abortion in Ireland in the case of fatal foetal abnormality' (*D v. Ireland*, Application No. 26499/02, ECHR, at para.103).

The court accepted the rather hypocritical argument made by the Irish government, that:

> there was 'at least a tenable' argument which would seriously be considered by the domestic courts to the effect that a foetus was not an 'unborn' for the purposes of Article 40.3.3 or that, even if it was an 'unborn', its right to life was not actually engaged as it had no prospect of life outside the womb. In the absence of a domestic

decision, it was impossible to foresee that Article 40.3.3 clearly excluded an abortion in the applicant's situation in Ireland. (para 69)

In accepting this argument, the court made reference to the APOCC Report of November 2000. The court noted that the Committee during its deliberations had met the masters of the three major Dublin maternity hospitals, and that: 'All three [Masters] spoke in favour of permitting in Ireland termination of pregnancy in cases of foetal abnormality ... where the foetus would not survive to term or live outside the womb ...' (para 40).

Thus, the court concluded in the D case that there was 'a feasible argument to be made that the constitutionally enshrined balance between the right to life of the mother and of the foetus could have shifted in favour of the mother when the "unborn" suffered from an abnormality incompatible with life'. If she had initiated legal action before the Irish courts, the court stated that D's case would have been 'an arguable one with sufficient chances of success' to mean that a domestic legal remedy was therefore in principle available to her, and she should have pursued her case through the Irish courts before applying to the ECHR (at paragraphs 90–92 of the judgement).

Accordingly her application was deemed inadmissible. However, the judgement clearly envisages that terminations of pregnancy in cases of fatal foetal abnormality would be declared lawful in any relevant case taken before the Irish courts, even under the terms of the Eighth Amendment.

In December 2010, the European Court of Human Rights gave its crucially important judgement in *ABC v. Ireland* (Application No. 25579/05, ECHR, 16 December 2010). This arose from a case taken by three women, all of whom had been obliged to travel to England to terminate their pregnancies, and who argued that in failing to provide them with access to legal abortion within the jurisdiction, Ireland had breached their human rights under the Convention.

The court ruled against the applications of A and B, but C won her case. In her case, the continuance of her pregnancy had posed a risk to her life due to her medical condition. The Court held that Ireland's failure to implement the existing constitutional right to a lawful abortion when a woman's life is at risk had violated the European Convention, because:

... the authorities failed to comply with their positive obligation to secure to [C] effective respect for her private life by reason of the absence of any implementing legislative or regulatory regime providing an accessible and effective procedure by which [C] could have established whether she qualified for a lawful abortion in Ireland in accordance with Article 40.3.3 of the Constitution. (para 367)

A new government (Fine Gael/Labour) was elected in February 2011, just months after the European Court decision. It committed to establishing an expert group to review the judgement and its implications. This group reported to government in November 2012, setting out the framework for legislation to clarify the criteria under which abortions may be carried out in order to save a woman's life (Department of Health and Children, 2012). In advance of the expert group's findings, a private member's bill on abortion was introduced in the Dáil in April 2012 (Medical Treatment (Termination of Pregnancy in Case of Risk to Life of Pregnant Woman) Bill 2012). Although supported by pro-choice campaigners, the bill was defeated by the government on the basis that it would pre-empt the expert group report.

Tragically, just before the publication of the report, in October 2012 a young woman named Savita Halappanavar died while undergoing a miscarriage at Galway University Hospital. Her death generated immense public anger and outrage, because she and her husband had requested a potentially life-saving termination of pregnancy – but this was refused. The lack of legal clarity as to when doctors could intervene to carry out a life-saving abortion had clearly contributed to the failures in her medical treatment.[60]

In the aftermath of this case, and following the publication of the expert group report, the government announced an intention to legislate at last to provide for the X case test, in accordance with the requirement of the European Court of Human Rights to provide an 'accessible and effective procedure' for women to vindicate their constitutional right to life.

Extensive hearings on the proposed legislation were held by the Oireachtas Health Committee in January 2013. The overwhelming majority of doctors and psychiatrists who testified agreed that legislation was essential to give women access to life-saving abortions. Doctors emphasised that the lack of legislation posed serious difficulties for them in cases where the continuance of a pregnancy posed a potential threat to a woman's life (Joint Oireachtas Committee on Health and Children, January 2013).

The general scheme of the bill was published by the government in April 2013. In May 2013 a further series of hearings on the scheme was held by the Oireachtas Health Committee (Joint Oireachtas Committee on Health and Children, May 2013). The Bill itself was introduced in June 2013; it was debated and passed through both Houses of the Oireachtas, and by August it became the Protection of Life During Pregnancy Act 2013.

PROTECTION OF LIFE DURING PREGNANCY ACT 2013

The passage of the act through the Oireachtas was marked by passionate and often heated debate in both Dáil and Seanad, and by the expulsion of some members of the larger government party, Fine Gael, for refusing to support it. Despite the immense controversy around its introduction, the act is very conservative. It is limited to clarifying when abortion may be carried out legally in accordance with article 40.3.3 and the X case test, where necessary to save a woman's life. It provides that an abortion is lawful in a range of listed general and maternity hospitals, where two doctors have certified that it is necessary to avert a 'real and substantial risk of loss of the woman's life from a physical illness'; or where three doctors, including one psychiatrist, have certified that it is necessary to save a woman who would otherwise be at real and substantial risk of losing her life by suicide.

There is provision for one doctor to carry out an abortion in a physical emergency, and for a review procedure where women have been denied abortion on grounds of risk to life. The act repeals the 1861 criminal offences, replacing them in section 22 with the new offence of 'destruction of unborn human life', which carries a maximum penalty of fourteen years.

Some commentators suggested during the hearings that the act was so restrictive in its terms that it did not meet the European Court test of providing an 'accessible and effective procedure' for pregnant women to access life-saving abortions. The act only came into effect on 1 January 2014 and its impact in practice remains to be evaluated.

But despite these doubts, and the conservatism of its provisions, the passage of the act is nonetheless highly significant. It represents the first positive development in abortion rights since the 1979 establishment of the women's right to choose group. Over the thirty-five years since then, the pro-choice movement has had to respond to a series of proactive referendum campaigns by the anti-choice lobby; and to successive court cases involving individual women or young girls denied access to abortion. Never before has a proactive legal step succeeded on the pro-choice side; the Irish legislature has never before had to confront the reality of crisis pregnancy. For far too long, the courts have had to deal with the fallout from the Eighth Amendment.

Indeed, for many Oireachtas members, the hearings in January and May 2013 illustrated for the first time the consequences for women and doctors of the harshly restrictive regime under article 40.3.3. In particular, many expressed the view that the article should be interpreted as allowing legal abortion where the baby has no prospect of being born alive. The government legal advice was to the contrary, despite the European Court judgement in the earlier D case, and the act does not cover such cases. But the brave and articulate women who spoke publicly of their experience of fatal foetal abnormality during the public debates on the act received strong public support; and in November 2013 they lodged a complaint with the UN Human Rights Committee arguing that abortion for this reason should be carried out legally in Ireland – as the Irish government arguments in the D case appeared implicitly to accept.[61] Public opinion, measured in polls taken around the passage of the act, show strong public support not only for allowing legal abortion in cases of fatal foetal abnormality, but also in cases of rape or incest; or risk to the health of the pregnant woman.[62]

However, such legislative change will not be possible without the repeal of article 40.3.3. Its existence has not prevented one crisis pregnancy, nor stopped even one woman travelling to England to terminate her pregnancy. It simply serves to compound the crisis of a crisis pregnancy, and to create a culture of secrecy and silence around the termination of pregnancy. Its retention maintains the hypocrisy that there is no abortion in Ireland – a hypocrisy that is now recognised by many (see for example Fletcher, 2005; Rossiter, 2009; Schweppe (ed.), 2008). Now that the tide is finally turning in favour of progressive change to Irish abortion law, the pro-choice movement must focus on repeal of the Eighth Amendment.

9

Discourses on Foetal Rights and Women's Embodiment

URSULA BARRY

INTRODUCTION

ISCOURSES ON FOETAL RIGHTS are the language and imagery of global anti-abortion campaigns, and represent a strategy to insert themselves centrally into debates around human rights, thereby gaining legitimacy for the very concept of foetal rights. A key aim is to consolidate those rights within legislative frameworks. In practice, under this ideology, the rights of the foetus are deemed as equivalent to the rights of a pregnant woman. It is an ideology that is pervasive in Ireland since foetal rights became part of the Irish Constitution in 1983, and has created a situation in which this country plays a leading part in the contestation of women's reproductive rights internationally.

The strength of foetal rights discourses in Ireland is the consequence of power exercised by the medical and legal professions, together with authority seized by both Catholic religious institutions and the state, to monitor and control women's bodies. It is a specific form of anti-abortion discourse and its use of brutal imagery and violent language has been targeted at young people in particular. Its influence has been evident in recent debates on abortion both inside the Dáil (parliament) and outside, within the legal and medical professions, and in the pronouncements of members of the hierarchy of the Catholic Church. One Catholic bishop (of Kilmore) stated that the new highly restrictive legislation that was finally brought into statute law in July 2013 (Protection of Life During Pregnancy Act 2013) was putting Ireland on 'the first step on the road to a culture of death' and conjured up the possibility of excommunicating politicians who voted for this legislation (*Irish Times*, 2012). Some months later Archbishop Martin provoked controversy within the Catholic hierarchy itself by arguing that legislators who supported abortion were excommunicating themselves (Irish Central, 2013).

Under the latest act abortion is to be provided only in cases in which there is 'a substantive threat to a woman's life, not her health' and designated hospitals are identified. The cumbersome assessment process involved is hugely controversial, particularly in cases of threatened suicide, and a penalty of up to fourteen years imprisonment is set down for a woman procuring an abortion, or anyone helping a woman to access abortion, in anything other than the prescribed circumstances. Just one year after this legislation was enacted the UN Human Rights Council (UNHRC) criticised its 'highly restrictive' nature and its failure to provide women with access to abortion in circumstances in which pregnancy is a result of rape, when a woman is carrying a foetus with fatal abnormalities and to explicitly recognise the priority of women's health in pregnancy. Its chairman, Nigel Rodley, stated that Irish abortion legislation treated women who were raped as 'a vessel and nothing more'. The Committee concluded that in giving power to doctors, obstetricians and psychiatrists to prevent vulnerable women from terminating their pregnancies generates *an excessive degree of scrutiny by medical professionals* and is in breach of human rights law and principles. The law leaves women, as some clinicians have stated, 'at the mercy of a local, moral and political lottery' (*Irish Times*, 2014; *Guardian*, 2014).

Just one month after the UNHRC's heavy criticism, the first appalling case under the new act ended up in the Irish courts, as they made decisions over a woman's body and her life. This most recent case involved a migrant woman who was effectively legally forced to give birth by caesarean section. It is reported that the woman looked for an abortion when she discovered she was pregnant at eight weeks but was refused, despite stating that her pregnancy was a result of rape and that she was suicidal. After a series of delays she went on hunger strike to protest the decision. Local health authorities obtained a court order firstly, to rehydrate the woman, and secondly, to deliver the baby prematurely, at around twenty-six weeks. It is reported that the woman had no choice but to eventually 'consent' (*Irish Times*, 2014).

This is the context of reproductive injustice in Ireland: bodily integrity has been displaced by the public physical dissecting of women's bodies; choice has been displaced by calculating risks between a pregnant woman's health and her life; privacy has been displaced by secrecy; compassion has been displaced by the threat of long-term imprisonment; reality has been displaced by denial. Women in Ireland are subjected to a culture of surveillance, and even of self-surveillance, driven often by imposed guilt and shame – and the focus of that surveillance has been highlighted by many writers on women's sexuality and reproductive activity (Barry, 1992; Inglis, 1998; Morrissey, 2004; Smyth, 2005, 2012; Conlon, 2009; Ferriter, 2012; Conroy, 2012). One unique voice, Irish author, Lia Mills, speaking of her personal experience of abortion debates in Ireland, concluded:

> Abortion is a highly charged, difficult subject. It sparks so much passion, fury and hatred that many women are afraid to speak out privately, let alone in public. I was afraid to write this. But, on balance, I think I'm more afraid of living in a country where I'm afraid to say what I believe and why. (Mills, 2013)

CONCEPTUALISING THE FOETUS

While Ireland is one of a few countries on the front line of the anti-abortion movement, the debate on foetal rights has developed globally, particularly in the conceptual analysis of foetal imagery. Barbara Duden speaks of a growing hegemonic anti-abortion discourse based on 'specific foetal iconography'... in which women are seen as an eco system, 'delicate and dangerous', which the foetus inhabits and consequently this eco-system must be subject to strict management and regulation (Duden, 1993, p. 28). Barbara Katz Rothman in her famous statement says that:

> The foetus in utero has become a metaphor for 'man' in space floating free attached only by the umbilical cord to the spaceship.

But where is the mother in that metaphor? She has become empty space. (Katz Rothman, 2000 p. 114)

In *Foetal Images: the power of visual culture in the politics of reproduction,* written in 1987, Rosalind Petchesky documents how:

> Beginning with the 1984 presidential campaign, the neo-conservative Reagan administration and the Christian Right accelerated their use of television and video imagery to capture political discourse and to establish their power. American television and video viewers were bombarded with the newest 'prolife' propaganda piece, *The Silent Scream,* marking a dramatic shift in the contest over abortion imagery. With formidable cunning, it translated the still and by-now stale images of fetus as 'baby' into real-time video giving those images an immediate interface with the electronic media; transforming anti-abortion rhetoric from a mainly religious/mystical to a medical/ technological mode; and bringing the foetal image 'to life'. On major network television the foetus rose to instant stardom, as *The Silent Scream* and its impresario, Dr. Bernard Nathanson, was aired at least five different times in one month. (Petchesky, 1987, p. 264)

Lisa Smyth, referring to the Swedish photographer Lennart Nilsson's infamous foetal photography published in *Life* magazine in 1986, argues that it represented a new departure, presenting:

> an autonomous foetal embodiment narrativised in 'moving picture' form within which woman is reduced to the maternal function – motherhood – separating womb from self. (Smyth, 2005, p. 28)

These writers make the compelling argument that a central role in the development of the ideology of 'foetal rights' is the development of foetal imagery. Rothman argues that the 'colonisation of the womb by patriarchy has led to its identification as a "dominated space" which is to say a space transformed and mediated by technology', a concept which she bases on the classic work of Lefebvre in *The Production of Space* (1991). Lefebvre had argued that one of the main principles and effects of the ideology of technology is its apparent attaining of 'neutrality'. Conlon and Carvalho in their 1994 paper, 'Spaces of

Motherhood', also apply Lefebvre's argument to the way in which the technology of ultrasound has been developed, and the way it is used in pregnancy.

> Technology as a neutral event produces the segmentation of space and blinds the relationship between space and its contents. Consider the use, and images, of ultrasound screening in pregnancy wherein the body of the mother is considered completely isolated from that of the baby. (Conlon and Carvalho, 1994)

It is worth posing the question of whether the widespread use and normalising of foetal imaging, made possible by scanning technology, has in practice fed into the ideology of foetal rights?

Taken together, the combined impact of the development of imagery is closely linked to the strength of foetal rights ideology. In practice, the systematic disembodiment of women is a counterpoint to the granting of legal rights to the foetus. The Eighth Amendment to the Irish Constitution establishes in our legal framework that a 'mother' has an equal right to life to that of the 'unborn' she carries. With largely unacknowledged consequences for women's autonomy and citizenship, questions thrown up by ascribing effectively 'citizenship rights' to the foetus are constantly recurring within the Irish legal and political system (Barry, 1992).

LANGUAGE AND IDEOLOGY OF FOETAL RIGHTS AND THEIR IMPLICATIONS

Historically, under both English common law and US law, the foetus has not been recognised as a person with full rights. Instead, legal rights have centred on the mother, with the foetus treated as an integral, rather than separate, part of her. Legal experts, in Ireland and elsewhere, have often argued the need to clarify the legal status of the foetus. US law has, in certain instances, granted the foetus limited rights, facilitated by those new developments in medical technology that have made it increasingly possible to directly view, monitor, diagnose and treat the foetus as a *patient*. In an important sense, technology has been used to bolster the case for regarding the foetus as independent of the mother.

The US Center for Reproductive Rights identifies what it analyses as:

> an emerging trend to extend a right to life before birth, and in
> particular from conception [which] poses a significant threat to
> women's human rights, in theory and in practice … [In their view,
> these efforts are often] rooted in ideological and religious motivations
> and are part of a deliberate attempt to deny women the full range of
> reproductive health services that are essential to safeguarding women's
> fundamental rights to life, health, dignity, equality, and autonomy,
> among others. (Center for Reproductive Rights 2014,
> www.reproductiverights.org/)

The Center documents a wide range of constitutional and legislative
changes across different countries that attempt to grant a right to life
before birth, recognising a prenatal legal personhood, which aims to
outlaw any procedure that terminates a pregnancy and sometimes make
certain forms of contraception and in-vitro fertilisation illegal. Legal
frameworks protecting life before birth include:

- explicit recognition of a constitutional right to life before birth, as
  in the national constitutions of Guatemala and Chile;

- constitutional protections that confer equal protection for the life
  of both the pregnant woman and the 'unborn', as in Ireland and
  the Philippines;

- legislation establishing that the right to life is subject to prenatal
  protection, as in Poland;

- a new constitution adopted in the Dominican Republic in 2010,
  which recognises a right to life from conception;

- sixteen Mexican states, which since 2008 have amended their
  constitutions to protect the right to life from either fertilisation
  or conception;

- The Protection of Life During Pregnancy Act 2013 in Ireland, which
  enshrined, for the first time, a definition of the foetus in law as 'a
  potential human being from the point of implantation in the womb'.

The ideology of foetal rights has been debated over decades through
the courts and legal systems of different countries, including the US,

Canada, El Salvador, Mexico as well as Ireland. Analysing selected case law reveals that the contested arena of foetal rights is as much about the regulation and control of the bodies of pregnant women, as about the specific issue of access to abortion.

The term foetal rights came into wide usage following the landmark 1973 abortion case in the US, *Roe v. Wade* (US Supreme Court, 1973). In that case, the Supreme Court ruled that a woman has a constitutionally guaranteed, unqualified right to abortion in the first trimester of her pregnancy. She also has a right to terminate a pregnancy in the second trimester, although the state may limit that right to situations in which the procedure poses a health risk to the mother that is greater than the risk of carrying the foetus to term. In making its decision, the court ruled that a foetus is *not a person* under the terms of the Fourteenth Amendment to the US Constitution. However, the court also maintained that the state has an interest in protecting the life of a foetus *after viability*, that is, after the point at which the foetus is deemed capable of living outside the womb (usually referred to as twenty-four weeks). As a result, individual states were permitted to outlaw abortion in the third trimester of pregnancy, except when the procedure is necessary to preserve the life of the mother (Tran, 2006).

Fifteen years later, in 1988, the Canadian Supreme Court effectively abolished its abortion law in *R. v. Morgentaler.*

> The Supreme Court determined that restrictive abortion provisions violated women's rights as set out in the 1982 Canadian Charter of Rights and Freedoms [2]. The court ruled that the Criminal Code violated women's rights because 'forcing a woman, by threat of criminal sanction, to carry a foetus to term unless she meets certain criteria unrelated to her own priorities and aspirations, is a profound interference with a woman's body and thus a violation of security of the person'. (Tran, 2006)

Following a hotly contested case, (Winnipeg Child and Family Services (Northwest Area) v. G. (D.F.), in relation to a pregnant women with serious drug addiction issues a landmark judgement was again delivered in October 1997 by the Supreme Court of Canada which ruled by a 7 to 2 majority that nobody has the right to interfere with a woman's pregnancy against her will, even if her behaviour threatens the foetus. Justice Beverley McLachlin (currently the longest serving Supreme Court Judge in Canada) wrote the decision for the majority.

She stated that 'the only law recognized is that of the born person. Any right or interest the foetus may have remains inchoate and incomplete until the birth of the child.' She concluded that any attempt to forcibly treat a pregnant woman would violate:

> the most sacred sphere of personal liberty – the right of every person to live and move in freedom ... A pregnant woman and her unborn child are one ... To make orders protecting foetuses would radically impinge on the fundamental liberties of the mother – both as to lifestyle choices and as to where she chooses to live.

McLachlin expressed concern that if the state were found to have a right to interfere with a pregnancy then women who smoke cigarettes or who exercise strenuously might be the next to be taken into custody. This could cause the problem to be driven underground: pregnant women might refuse counselling and medical help out of fear of being confined; some might even resort to having an abortion in order to continue their addiction. Justice McLachlin concluded, 'in the end, orders made to protect a foetus's health could ultimately result in its destruction.'

FOETAL PROTECTION POLICIES

Foetal protection policies are policies that bar women of reproductive age from specific jobs out of a supposed fear that those jobs may cause harm to any embryos or foetuses the women might be carrying. These policies came into widespread use by many companies in America during the 1970s and 1980s, until a landmark case was referred in 1991 to the US Supreme Court. In the case *UAW v. Johnson Controls* the court judged foetal protection policies to be a form of sexual discrimination that violates the US Civil Rights Act 1964:

> This Supreme Court ruling that declared foetal protection policies to be a violation of Civil Rights laws came too late for five women from West Virginia who were forced by their employer to choose between undergoing a sterilization procedure to avoid health risks associated with their higher paying jobs, remaining fertile but moving to lower paying jobs, or quitting their jobs. (Bettinger-Lopez and Sturm, 2007)

The women worked at an American Cyanamid factory in Willow Island, a poor region where decent-paying jobs were scarce. They were all among the first women to work in these factories which, until 1974, had employed only men. In 1978 the company stated that no women would be allowed to work in its lead pigments department, claiming that hazardous chemicals might harm women's reproductive systems. Fertile women under age fifty would have to be sterilised or take jobs in other areas of the company, all of which paid less. Men, whose reproductive systems might also be damaged by lead, were not subject to restrictions. The seven women then employed in the lead pigments department found themselves facing an agonising choice: whether to reduce or sacrifice their income or undergo a surgical procedure that would render them unable to bear children. Five chose sterilisation and the American Civil Liberties Union sued for damages on their behalf. In its final ruling, the US Supreme Court held that foetal protection policies unfairly discriminate against women because they do not demand that men make a similar choice regarding the preservation of their reproductive health in a potentially hazardous workplace.

Companies using foetal protection policies argue that they are necessary to protect their employees. Critics of foetal protection policies maintain that they effectively exclude all women aged fifteen to fifty from well-paying jobs unless the women can prove they have been sterilised. They also contend that such policies raise privacy questions because they often require women to provide proof that they cannot have children in order to take specific jobs. No company has created similar policies for men.

FORCED CAESAREAN SECTIONS

Another series of cases in the US were the result of pregnant women refusing to undergo caesarean sections. The 1980s saw an increasing number of cases in which hospitals and doctors sought court orders to force women to give birth by caesarean section. Women who choose not to undergo a caesarean section despite the advice of their obstetrician do so for many reasons, for example: concern about the risk of surgery; experience of former caesarean section/s; possible consequences of repeated sections; lack of information and/or understanding of its implications; religious, cultural, or moral beliefs. This situation has generated specific legal questions. Should a woman be forced to undergo a caesarean section or other surgery in the interest of the health of the foetus? To what extent is a woman obliged to follow the advice of her doctor regarding assessment of the best medical care of her foetus? Again technology is implicated. Because of improvements in foetal monitoring and surgical techniques, obstetricians increasingly recommend that women give birth by caesarean section, a surgical technique that involves removing the foetus through an incision in the woman's abdomen.

The American Medical Association (AMA) in its submission to the court stated that it opposed the use of criminal prosecutions against mothers. Imposing criminal sanctions, it said, does not prevent damage to foetal health and may violate privacy laws between doctors and women, making doctors and hospitals agents of prosecution. The American Civil Liberties Union (ACLU) supported the AMA in their submission, arguing that 'prosecutions of drug-addicted women for harm to their children will greatly damage women's health, their relationship to the health services community, and their ability to control their own body' (Cook and Dickens, 2003).

IRELAND – FOETAL RIGHTS IN PRACTICE

Being on the frontline of global foetal rights campaigns has meant that woman after woman has found herself forced into Irish and European courts to have her rights and bodily integrity judged against Irish laws. Women's health is set against the health of the foetus she is carrying. The enormous controversy that erupted in Ireland in 2012 following the tragic death of Savita Halappanavar is referenced across this book. Despite the fact that Savita was diagnosed as having a miscarriage and the foetus was deemed non-viable, repeated requests for an abortion were refused on the basis that the foetal heart was still beating. In this situation, the implications of the foetal rights amendment to our Constitution became blindingly clear. Medical staff continued to weigh up whether the threat to Savita's life was severe enough. What followed were days of simple cruelty and torture as Savita was made to go through appalling suffering and distress in one of our main so-called *public* hospitals, before she finally miscarried. This is the balancing act that women's lives in Ireland are forced to undergo. In the words of Coliver:

health has become a politically powerful category, in which we have
seen women's health utilised by forces ... [such] as the 'anti-choice'
religious right, ... to promote and obscure their own agendas.
(Coliver, 1995, p. 2)

There are other Irish stories out there that confound ethical, moral or
political sense, but which at the same time illustrate the power of foetal
rights ideology in practice.

Michelle Harte, terminally ill with cancer, was forced to travel to
Britain for an abortion and successfully sued the state for violation of
her human rights. The hospital had advised her to terminate the pregnancy, the obstetrician was willing to perform the termination but the
hospital ethics committee in the large Irish public hospital decided
against authorising an abortion on the basis that her life was 'not under
immediate threat'. Huge delays occurred in this process, the cancer
worsened and Michelle had to be helped onto the plane when she eventually travelled to Britain for an abortion. Her lawyers sued under the
A, B, C case of the European Convention on Human Rights (ECHR).
The Irish Health Services Executive (HSE) paid substantial compensation to settle her claim out-of-court in July 2011. Michelle died in
November of that same year (*Irish Times*, November 2012). What is
evident from this case is the way in which Catholic ideological constructs
have been, as Jacqueline Morrissey argues,

> filtered and interpreted by the Irish medical profession, embedded
> in medical practice, and ultimately embodied and implemented by
> the institutions of the Irish State. (Morrissey, 2004, p. 14)

Ireland had already been found to be in breach of the ECHR primarily
because of a lack of clarity of the circumstances in which a pregnancy
could be terminated in Ireland (*A, B, C v. Ireland* 2012). The under-
the-radar settlement in the case of Michelle Harte demonstrates just
how aware the Irish state is of the dangerously contradictory position
it is in.

One other example illustrates the implications of foetal rights
discourses in practice. The perpetration of this ideology culminated in
the discussion of a very particular form of brutality on an Irish national
television broadcast on 12 June 2013. During *Prime Time*, Sarah

McGuinness from the organisation Termination for Medical Reasons (TFMR) argued that she should have had the choice to access termination of her pregnancy in Ireland following the diagnosis of the foetus she was carrying as non-viable. Her decision to travel for a termination and in her words 'leave our daughter in a morgue in the hospital in Liverpool' was partly based on the terrible prospect of putting herself through a daily process in her workplace and community of people regularly asking 'when is the baby due?' Confronted with the inhumanity imposed on this woman, brave enough to present her experience on national television, Dr Berry Kiely, medical advisor to the Pro-Life Amendment Campaign, claimed that to allow for such a termination would lead to 'people in a situation like this who would argue for post-birth abortion'. In her view, the situation could be resolved instead by providing hospice care to a pregnant woman to ensure that her non-viable foetus would be brought to full-term: 'Every mother in her situation should be offered … a perinatal hospice which would provide infinitely more support than what we are able to provide'. It is worth pausing and closing your eyes for just a moment to try and imagine what a perinatal hospice would be like. In her reply, Sarah McGuinness made the compelling argument:

> But why make a woman break her heart even further for another three months. Let me go to work and people asking me 'Is your, is your nursery all ready? How are you keeping?' What about women's mental health? You would have to lock yourself away. I would've in my case for another three months. (RTÉ, *Prime Time*, 3 May 2013)

Yet another twist in the sometimes surreal abortion debate in Ireland, is highlighted in the Case of *D v. Ireland* under the ECHR when the Irish state argued for the first time that 'she should have applied in the Irish courts first, because she had a reasonable chances of establishing that the Constitution did not apply to a foetus with a lethal anomaly' (ECHR, 2012; Hewson, 2007). This again raised a crucial issue of reproductive justice – the right of a pregnant woman to access a 'medical termination' in circumstances of fatal foetal abnormalities. Ms D had been refused an abortion in Ireland and was forced to travel to Northern Ireland. This refusal was made even though her remaining foetus (she was originally carrying twin foetuses) was diagnosed as carrying a fatal foetal abnormality and would not survive outside the womb. She tells of her shock:

> I assumed there would be a system in our hospitals where there would be a sympathetic arrangement [instead she was left to 'go home and sort it out' herself]. I found on our own island (Northern Ireland) there was a place where compassion and sympathy and tolerance prevailed. If there can be that sort of tolerance on our island just across the border I don't see why we don't have that here. (Deirdre Conroy, RTÉ *News at One*, recorded in *Irish Times*, 2 May 2013)

Effectively, the state argued in *D v. Ireland* that the foetal rights amendment to the Irish Constitution did not protect the life of a foetus in circumstances where its survival was diagnosed as terminal. Yet, in 2013, when the ministers for health and justice were defending the limitations of the new PLDPA, they argued that they were prevented by the Constitution from allowing for abortion in cases of fatal foetal abnormality and as a result no provision was made.

As one woman recounting a similar story on the website of the US Center for Reproductive Rights states:

> I realize that abortion is and will always be a highly contentious issue, but when your baby is not going to live, how can it be justified that a pregnant woman must sneak over to England like a criminal to do what she feels is the most humane thing? (Center for Reproductive Rights, 18 August 2013, www.reproductiverights.org/)

Opinion polls overwhelmingly show that nearly 80 per cent of Ireland's population supports legalisation of abortion in circumstances that go far beyond current legislation. The latest *Irish Times*/IPSOS MRBI poll revealed that 89 per cent support abortion in cases when a woman's life is at risk; 83 per cent in cases of fatal foetal abnormalities; 81 per cent in cases of sexual abuse and rape; 80 per cent when there is a risk to a woman's health (*Irish Times*, 13 June 2013). Irish politicians are a long way behind the rest of the population on this issue and completely out of line with international human rights standards. Ireland allows other countries offer support to women and couples faced with excruciating decisions. Human rights bodies from Europe and the UN have repeatedly called for action to humanise Irish abortion law in order to safeguard women's fundamental rights.

Lisa Smyth (2006) in *Abortion and Nation* analyses how the anti-abortion rhetoric that 'Ireland has no abortion' has been used in the construction of representations of the Irish nation – a nation uncontaminated by the practice of abortion. According to the latest data published by the UK Department of Health, almost 4,000 women from Ireland travelled to England or Wales for an abortion in 2013 and since 1995 they estimate that over 140,000 women who gave Irish addresses (likely to be an underestimation) have had abortions in Britain (UK Department of Health, 2013).

CONCLUSIONS

Ireland, its laws, regulations and courts are at the very opposite end of the spectrum to Canada. Canada has seen judgements in case law recording strong positions of bodily integrity and choice from the stand-point of women, and has also taken the highly significant step of situating abortion outside of its criminal law entirely – where it becomes a question of reproductive health and justice, exercised by a woman drawing on medical and personal advisors. Drawing on the power of conservative right-wing ideology, key countries, including traditional majority Catholic countries such as Ireland and El Salvador, have been identified as flagship countries for establishing and reaffirming foetal rights. Political parties central to drawing up legislation, and the courts central to interpreting legislation, are the main targets but the ideological warfare is even more widespread and pervasive.

The 'foetus' has been legally constituted in Ireland as the moral and ontological equivalent of a pregnant woman and it is now protected under statute law unless a woman is facing death by continuing her pregnancy. This constitutes a politicised ideological construction of gender and reproduction. It represents a hostile deconstruction of women's embodiment and bodily integrity, based primarily on the un-equal distribution of reproductive justice. The 1983 Irish Constitutional Eighth Amendment that defines the life of a pregnant woman – denoted as 'mother' – as equal to the life of the foetus she is carrying has been predictably exposed as denying women's right to bodily integrity and reproductive justice. Renewed, stronger calls have been made by women's organisations, human rights groups and many service providers, academics, doctors and activists to have that amendment finally deleted. As one recent dissertation on obstetric violence concludes, we have moved from a situation in which the *foetal patient* has now become the *foetal citizen*, with clear consequences for the dis-embodiment of pregnant women (Campbell, 2014). The power of foetal rights ideology and imagery means loss of life and undermining of autonomy for women as courts and medical authorities dissect women's bodies, making life-threatening and degrading decisions. Ireland is at the forefront of the battle for women's bodily integrity, her embodiment.

10

'On the Run': a story from the London-Irish abortion underground

ANN ROSSITER

FROM THE START, she wasn't like the others. Alright, so she was a bit like a few of the others who had made it to Heathrow (or Gatwick, or Luton, or Stansted), but balked at taking the final hurdle.

It was about eleven when she phoned. She sounded panic-stricken and blurted out in a little-girl voice, 'I'm here!' 'Right', I said. Somewhat annoyed, I thought, 'Oh my goodness, you're a city girl. Surely you can make the last few yards from the airport arrivals hall to the tube station on your own?' She and I had talked through the London travel end of things on the phone the night before and she was word perfect. She stood stiff and immobile at the Information Desk, looking as if she hadn't moved since we spoke. Taking in that she was in shock, I mouthed the usual inane pleasantries, 'Hello, I'm Ann. So you made it, then. Do you fancy a cup of tea or coffee, something to eat, before we head off?'

What struck me was how incongruous she looked: a Barbie doll of a young woman made up to the nines. She was a platinum blonde sporting a Charlie's Angels hairdo (you know, the one Farrah Fawcett had made all the rage once upon a time in the 80s) and tight black

Lycra top and pants. She looked like a woman well able to find her way around.

But not this time round, it seemed …

At the clinic that afternoon she made it through the pre-op medical routines. Her blood tests done and dusted, and her fee paid, she got herself signed and certified to say that she was qualified for an abortion under the British 1967 Abortion Act. The only glitch was when she appeared grim and strained coming out of a much longer than usual counselling session. I wondered what had been going on in there, but all I could bring myself to say was, 'Are we done?' I burbled a few comments about us going home and putting the dinner on, and continued with whatever nervous chitchat one engages in to disguise troubled situations.

The night was interrupted by a seemingly endless series of telephone calls on our landline – those were the days before mobile phones. We, the host family, sat in the kitchen thinking it unwise to take to our beds, only to be woken again by very loud and very fraught exchanges with her husband/partner/boyfriend who clearly didn't want the pregnancy terminated. She sounded adamant about her decision to go ahead. At six in the morning, after a few hours' sleep, I was awakened as a head appeared around my bedroom door, asking, 'Where do you keep the hairdryer?' It was hard to know what to make of such a request in the early hours. I was knackered, suffering from a version of 'the morning after the night before' syndrome. But I dragged myself up and furnished her with the required item.

She was already washed, dressed and kitted out with enough war paint for a night on the town. I looked askance at her face, saying rather peevishly, 'Chances are you'll have to wipe all that off before you go under the anaesthetic.' Immediately, I felt bad, but she seemed unperturbed and replied, 'It's what I face the world with; it's my armour, you know.'

As a kind of afterthought, she added, 'Sorry about all the fuss and bother last night. That was my brother on the phone. He can be such an arse when he's drunk.'

This is a true story, albeit with modifications to protect the identity of the woman concerned. It is an unusual story of an abortion seeker; in fact, it is one of the few cases of incest I have knowingly experienced as a member of the London-based Irish Women's Abortion Support

Group (IWASG) for twenty years, and as a 'freelancer' supporting women before and after the existence of the group (see Rossiter, 2009 and Irish Women's Abortion Support Group, 1998). It goes without saying that the majority of women who came to IWASG for help did not do so in such mind-blowing circumstances. However, I have chosen this particular story because it illustrates only too well what can happen when women find themselves with an unwanted and, in this case, crisis-laden pregnancy, in either of the two Irish states.

In 1980, the formation of IWASG in London was a logical step in the formalisation of an already existing tradition of Irish women (and some men) supporting relatives, friends and friends-of-friends seeking the termination of an unwanted pregnancy 'across the water'. In the days before the internet, mobile phones, cheap flights and credit cards, IWASG members provided information, accommodation in their homes, financial support, and acted as go-betweens for abortion seekers and the clinics. These services were particularly important in the years 1986–1992 when a ban was imposed on providing information on, and referral to, British abortion clinics. Last, but not least, IWASG offered help and support in a non-judgemental manner, as well as always being on tap with a sympathetic ear.

The group was a non-hierarchical feminist collective with members that included those defining themselves as either LGBT or straight, Catholic or Protestant, agnostic or atheist. They were from both working-class and middle-class backgrounds, from both north and south of the Irish border, or were British-born second- and third-generation Irish. In other words, they were a 'mish-mash' of female London Irish life united by a fundamental belief in 'a woman's right to choose'. The work was on an entirely voluntary basis with funds for abortion seekers raised through a whole range of activities from staging cultural events, such as céilís, sponsored walks, swims and 'slims' (weight loss), and working as barmaids at outdoor music venues like the annual Glastonbury Festival. Apart from fundraising for abortion seekers, considerable sums were also raised to support the legal battles being waged on three Irish students' unions, the Dublin Well Woman Centre and Open Door Counselling by the Society for the Protection of the Unborn Child (SPUC).

As the new century approached and the Celtic Tiger was in full blast our services were less and less in demand, with abortion seekers having access to easy – or at least, easier – credit, cheap air fares thanks to Ryanair and EasyJet, as well as widespread use of the internet. As a result, IWASG disbanded. However, it did not reckon with the island-wide collapse of the economy and women with unwanted pregnancies desperately needing financial help. The baton has now passed to the Abortion Support Network (ASN) which very ably provides not only finance, but the whole gamut of services once offered by IWASG.

11

Civic Feminism and Voluntary Abortion Care:

A story of ESCORT's contribution to reproductive justice[63]

RUTH FLETCHER

INTRODUCTION

FEMINIST ACTIVISM IN IRELAND, the UK and elsewhere has occupied difficult terrain as concerned individuals and groups respond to urgent contemporary needs. Acting against historical wrongs and in the hope of a better future, feminism has used a diverse and mixed range of strategies (Dhaliwal and Yuval-Davis, 2014; Rowbotham, Segal and Wainwright, 2013; Connolly and O'Toole, 2005; Grewal and Kaplan, 1994). Advocacy and campaigns for law reform have sought to recognise experiences of harm and affirm survivors' knowledge. In directly providing paid and unpaid services to women in hostels and clinics, feminists have often stepped in to address gaps in public and private provision (Southall Black Sisters, 1990). As they mediate access to professional services on behalf of the women they support, feminists have developed expertise in bringing about organisational change. In all these ways, feminist activism has developed an important social presence, a presence that is engaged increasingly seriously, even as feminism questions the effects of that engagement (Kantola and Squire, 2012; Barry, 2008).

Here I want to build on this important work on the diversity of feminisms as social actors and think more about the contributions of smaller feminist groups as kinds of 'civic feminism'. Rather than approach feminism as a social movement that mobilises for change through campaigning and consciousness-raising of various kinds (Hoggart, 2010; Connolly, 2003), I want to concentrate on small-scale, relatively short-lived, practice-focused groups who organise so as to have a beneficial impact on women's lives. Often such groups participate in broader coalitions and movements, so I don't mean to draw a clear boundary around them, but instead to focus on the significance of their practice. In other words, these civic feminisms acknowledge the presence of state and market, but are not directly focused on changing or engaging with the relations of either.[64] Secondly, their feminism is defined less by a set of principles which mark them out as feminist (or a particular kind of feminist), and more by a set of practices which generate feminist community in response to specific problems. These civic feminisms make a difference by acting so as to enhance women's sense of belonging in spaces where they have been made feel 'out of place'. Civic feminism does this by identifying its members' experiences and commitments as resources, resources which are mobilised towards accommodating women's requests. In thinking about how civic feminism comes into being I want to consider the way that experiences, commitments and connections operate as the glue that holds such feminisms together.

Access to abortion care has generated extensive feminist engagement in order to support women in resisting both pro-natalist and anti-natalist assumptions about their 'proper' reproductive roles (Petchesky and Judd, 1998; Fried, 1990). Although feminist legal and political struggles for better access have probably received most attention (Connolly, 2003, pp. 53–77; Sheldon, 1997), the direct and indirect provision of abortion care has also been a site of feminist activity in lots of different ways. Feminists have organised within and without health care in order to enhance women's access to abortion (Gomperts, 2002). Here I am concerned with the kind of pro-choice activism that focuses on caring for abortion-seeking women through a range of practical activities including: providing information and facilitating discussion on the phone, by email or in person; meeting and accompanying women to the clinic; and providing room and board (see further Abortion

Support Network, 2013; Kimport et al., 2012; Rossiter, 2009). Through this provision of support, activists respond to a public care deficit and provide interesting insights into what abortion care might be.

In the context of activism on reproductive rights, some feminists are increasingly framing themselves as advocates for reproductive justice (McAvoy, 2008; Silliman et al. 2004). Although there are interesting debates about the significance of this language (Bristow, 2013; Furedi, 2013; O'Brien, 2013; Fried et al. 2013), I want to leave that aside for the purposes of this chapter. I'm using reproductive justice here for two reasons. First, reproductive justice signifies a commitment to working across the diversity of reproductive needs and desires, to linking sexual and economic justice, and to solidarity across locations. Second, however reproductive justice goes on to be used and developed, this framework has been brought into being by the activism, commitment and critique of Women of Color in the United States (Silliman et al., 2004). In drawing on research I have been doing with abortion support groups and care organisations to focus on ESCORT's contribution, reproductive justice seems an appropriate framework for analysing how civic feminisms generate knowledge.

ESCORT was a Liverpool-based support group that supported Irish abortion-seeking women in accessing abortion care between 1988 and 2004. ESCORT has never, as far as I know, explicitly talked about its activities within the language of reproductive justice. But I consider their activism as a contribution to civic feminism's struggle for reproductive justice because they worked to destigmatise abortion-seeking by providing socio-economic support. As they sought to diminish the obstacles experienced by travelling abortion seekers, they had to be sensitive to women who were accessing abortion for very different reasons and acting on different needs and desires. They acted to provide women with the means to implement their sexual and reproductive choices, sometimes in difficult and constrained circumstances. And they reached out to women from other jurisdictions who they would likely never meet again.

I tell a story about ESCORT's feminist activism drawing on two pseudo-anonymised interviews with past co-ordinators of the organisation. In answering questions about who ESCORT's members were and who they supported, I show how they contributed to imagining and enacting reproductive justice in two key ways. They constituted a civic feminism by mobilising their experiences and commitments as volunteers and students in order to affirm and support abortion-seeking women. Secondly, their mobilisation was responsive to and sought to connect with the experience and commitments of the women they supported. To ESCORT's co-ordinators, abortion-seeking women were resilient and creative in addressing their own needs and in tackling discrimination. Although clearly not a representative account of ESCORT's members, abortion activists or abortion-seeking women, this story of ESCORT's contribution to reproductive justice helps us think about the different possible features of 'just abortion care' as we struggle to bring it into being.

WHO WERE ESCORT?

ESCORT's members shared some of the characteristics of other feminist support groups in that they were committed volunteers. They also tended to be students, or to have become members when they were students. This was partly because students have historically played a role in these kinds of civic support groups in the UK and elsewhere (Brewis, 2014). But it was also because ESCORT came into existence at a time when Irish students' unions were playing a key role in fighting restrictions against abortion (Bacik, 2004, pp. 114–15; Fletcher, 2000). One of the ways that ESCORT was different from, the London-based Irish Women's Abortion Support Group (Rossiter, 2009), was because cultural belonging in the form of some identification with Irishness was not an important aspect of membership. ESCORT was also distinct from the more contemporary Abortion Support Network, which began operating in October 2009, because they didn't have social media and because they didn't provide funds towards the cost of fee-based abortion, but provided 'in-kind' forms of support. Rather ESCORT generated a civic feminism by mobilising their affiliations and commitments as volunteers and (past) students to carve out a safe space for abortion seekers.

Volunteers

There has been some tendency to explain and represent voluntarism as an activity of the middle classes, who had the time and resources, particularly in a Victorian age, to engage in philanthropy. But the diversity of voluntarisms has become more obvious through a range of histories and sociologies (Hilton and McKay, 2011) that emphasise the 'adaptability, renewal, complexity and variety' (Clements, 2012) of the voluntary sector. Being unpaid volunteers was a defining and important feature of ESCORT's membership. For some, the unpaid volunteer role also meant that they were 'not professionals'. This distancing of feminist voluntarism from professionalism echoes Wainwright's earlier comments on the ways in which the women's movement made politics personal, and not simply a matter for professionals (1980). As a feminist 'fragment', ESCORT's voluntarism was key to their efforts to affect everyday life and provide an alternative so that women did not have to rely on professionals if they did not wish to.

> We tried to make it clear to the volunteers that we weren't counsellors, and we weren't pretending to be counsellors. We weren't qualified to be counsellors. We weren't there to try and [provide] any professional things. (Ciara, 2004)

'Not being a professional' was important in terms of boundary maintenance and integrity. They were there to help as volunteers, and they worked against misunderstandings of their role. But they also thought that their unpaid participation was important to the women they served.

> I think that what's good is that it [when the women found out that ESCORT were unpaid volunteers] broke down barriers, because I was no longer in their eyes a kind of professional person who perhaps they had experience of in Ireland. Suddenly I became just another person who cared about the same things they did, and so they relaxed much more. Perhaps they knew then there weren't going to be any forms they had to fill in or procedures to go through. (Liz, 2004)

For Liz, the non-professional, voluntary nature of the organisation helped put women at ease. As 'ordinary people,' ESCORT members were more likely to be perceived to be on the same level as the women users, and less likely to be seen as official gate-keepers to services. Interestingly, Liz was also keenly aware that awareness of ESCORT's voluntary role had the potential to produce a 'guilty' response.

They often assumed that this was a paid job, and when they realised that it was just something that people did altruistically ... they were so, so grateful. But to the point where you felt that was just another thing to feel guilty about. So you had to insist that you wouldn't be doing it if you didn't want to and that no, you didn't need any money. (Liz, 2004)

Sometimes awareness of ESCORT's voluntarism actually made women feel worse, or at least a bit bad, about being the triggers for altruism. Here we can hear the gratitude to the volunteer carer for her altruistic support, but also a sense of discomfort about being cared for by volunteers in this way (see, on a related note, Uí Chonnactaigh, 2014). As they seek to assure themselves that their supporters are not out-of-pocket, perhaps abortion-seeking women are saying that they don't want to be the objects of heroic altruism.

Students

ESCORT had strong associations with university students by virtue of their historical emergence at John Moore's University in Liverpool. As a group of university students they were motivated to do something practical on women's issues. The connection with students was also live at the time out of solidarity with students and students' unions in Ireland, who had been taken all the way to the Irish Supreme Court and the European Court of Justice over their provision of information about abortion clinics in other countries (Rossiter, 2009, p. 12; Fletcher, 2000).

In the early days we probably had about sixteen [members] because we had such a strong student base. (Liz, 2004)

Their status as university students gave them access to certain resources and ways of organising, which were very important for the group.

Every year we made ... we were probably like the annoying aunts, or something ... we knocked on the door of the women's officer and just wouldn't leave them alone. (Liz, 2004)

National Union of Students funding was our first major confirmation that we were here for the long haul, because we weren't just relying on fifty quid here and there, we got £1,000 per year from the NUS which was an incredible amount of money, it was very generous. (Liz, 2004)

But changes in the governance of students' unions in the UK in the 1990s eventually made it more difficult for ESCORT to draw down financial and organisational support from local and national students' unions.

As the politics of students' unions changed in the 1990s, their willingness to be seen to support marginal political causes also waned. The Student Union [National Union of Students] stopped supporting ESCORT on the grounds that their work fell outside the remit of the SU in the sense that ESCORT's work was not exclusively targeted at helping students, but at helping Irish women who travelled for abortion. (Liz, 2004)

Changes in members' status as students and 'younger people' also had an impact.

As we graduated as students, we got jobs and we had families and we bought houses and we took on full-time jobs, and it became more and more difficult. (Liz, 2004)

Ciara expressed some of the changes as time went by a little differently. She associated a change in ESCORT's activities more with ageing and energy levels, which overlapped with, but was distinct from, 'not being a student any more'.

In the early days, we were more political and more prone to devote time to raising awareness, and we still do do that, but we just haven't had the energy or the time recently to get as involved as we would like … you know, we're older. (Ciara, 2004)

Although ESCORT's resources as students contributed in substantive ways to their organising in support of abortion-seeking women, their student-related experience also reflected the transience or impermanence of this form of abortion care.

WHO DID ESCORT SUPPORT?

The women that ESCORT supported don't represent Irish abortion-seeking women in the sense of providing a representative sample of their experiences. We know that most of the 5,000 women who travel every year didn't and don't use support services (Mahon, Conlon and Dillon, 1998). And clearly any picture of abortion-seeking women that does emerge here is also one that is mediated by the memories and reflections of the interviewees. But ESCORT's understanding of the women they met is an important source of knowledge about the under-represented experience of abortion-seeking. It has often been remarked that public abortion debates (Enright, 2014; Quesney, 2012; Smyth, 2005; Oaks, 2002; Fletcher, 1995) are conducted with little or no reference to the thoughts and experiences of the women at the very heart of these debates. Campaigns to destigmatise abortion experiences like the IFPA's video,[65] blogs of anonymous abortion stories,[66] media contributions by groups like TFMR[67] and individual interventions like Janet Ní Shuilleabháin's tweeted story[68] are all important developments in registering the voices of women and couples themselves. Listening to volunteers who themselves listened to abortion-seeking women is another important way of learning more about abortion-seeking experiences. As ESCORT's co-ordinators talked about the women that they supported, they revealed a civic feminism. This feminism responds to women's requests by working with the women themselves in order to address need and have an impact on their lives.

ABORTION-SEEKERS IN NEED

ESCORT's servicing of a care deficit was such an obvious theme of my conversations with Liz and Ciara that I almost neglected to foreground it when I came to write this. ESCORT came into being because women who needed abortion care were not being accommodated by the health-care system of their home state. Those women were prepared to travel to address the problem they had with continuing that pregnancy at that time. Therefore the women that ESCORT encountered were ordinary women trying to do their best with the hand that life had dealt them. They weren't acting on political views as such. They were getting on with sorting out a problem.

For lots of women I think they cut themselves off from how judgemental people are being because they're there for a reason, they want to get it over with and get home. (Liz, 2004)

A lot of women will say to me, 'I would have judged and I would have been dead against abortion until this happened to me, and now I'll never judge anybody else.' (Ciara, 2004)

Although ESCORT saw abortion-seekers as being engaged in ordinary problem-solving, it was clear that ESCORT regularly met women who were seeking out abortion in particularly difficult circumstances. References to such circumstances remind us that a failure to provide abortion care can become cruel treatment of women, treatment that exacerbates rather than relieves suffering.

If there was a particularly troubled set of circumstances, like a case of rape or a very, very young girl, I would only ever put them with very experienced volunteers. (Liz, 2004)

Some suffer from domestic violence … I've even had one who was date raped, with a date drug, didn't even know she'd had sex, then found out she was pregnant. (Ciara, 2004)

I've had a lot of sixteen-, seventeen-, eighteen-year-olds, refugees who have gone through torture or trauma or whatever in their own countries, and then find themselves in Ireland and have to go through the trauma of coming over here. (Ciara, 2004)

Feminist volunteers were stepping into the breach again when women who needed care and support were being ignored. Sometimes ESCORT's members thought that the domestic failure to provide abortion care was disadvantaging the already deprived.

I mean it doesn't shock me anymore, but the level of deprivation amongst some Irish women. I mean … illiteracy is a big thing. (Ciara, 2004)

ESCORT themselves aimed to prioritise the most needy as receivers of support given their limited resources. But such prioritisation was difficult to manage given the informal networking nature of their activities.

As the organisations that were linked with ESCORT spread, I felt the very important conditions to women using the service were also diluted ... And the only reason for me for those limits was to make sure that we always helped the most needy, when you have to prioritise ... (Liz, 2004)

Diversity among abortion-seekers and change in their circumstances over time were also observed features of ESCORT's constituency.

They really were so different, as in there was ... I didn't get a strong sense of them being mostly from a particular set of circumstances, or social class, or anything like that. I say recently meaning perhaps the last four years, that the organisation has probably helped as many asylum seekers as it has Irish women, so that is a definite shift. (Liz, 2004)

You get absolutely every kind of woman ... You've got everything from the forty-five-year-old who's already had five kids and can't take another one, to the thirteen-year-old. (Ciara, 2004)

But I think the much younger women were the ones who were like just so frightened, but mainly because they hadn't ever left their hometown. Some of them in the early days were really fearful about being found out. But I would say that's changed the last seven years or so, there was a lot more confidence. (Liz, 2004)

VICTIMS OF DISCRIMINATION

Having to travel for abortion care sometimes exposed women to local British discrimination, as well as to their home state's refusal to care for them. Liz and Ciara's comments raised the familiar theme of ethnic discrimination working with gender discrimination to construct racialised women, Irish abortion-seeking women in this instance, as particularly victimised (see further Yuval Davis, 2014; Rossiter, 2009; Luibheid, 2006; Fletcher, 2005; Connolly, 1997; Southall Black Sisters, 1990).

We always said that we were not only supporting Irish women in a practical way, but we were advocates when needed. And that did happen more times than it should have, where Irish women felt that they had been treated badly. (Liz, 2004)

You can sometimes tell by the look on the receptionists' faces, that they think, 'Oh, god, it's just another thick Irish woman who hasn't got a clue'. That kind of attitude which isn't explicitly said but is intrinsically felt, so there's some of that, I'm sure. And as I say, just because they see one after the other, it's a production line of women. (Ciara, 2004)

Organisations where people have been around for too long, and they've got total compassion fatigue, they stereotype enormously and I have to say that the stereotyping of women from other countries is phenomenal, it's really disturbing. (Liz, 2004)

Both Liz and Ciara were very clear in our discussions about calling people out over discriminatory treatment when it was necessary. But part of what's interesting is the way in which they both independently flag up social conditions that have contributed to this situation. Not only do you have a situation to which the Irish state has contributed by failing to care for abortion-seeking women. You also have 'compassion fatigue' and 'production lines' of clients, which make clinic workers less likely to see clients as individuals with personal stories and more likely to see abortion-seekers as trouble-makers who are making their lives difficult. Having said that, it's clear that there are many more stories of good, respectful care from clinic workers than otherwise. But it is still important to acknowledge how racialised stereotyping contributes to the experience of abortion-seekers and their supporters, at home and abroad (Fletcher, 2005).

RESILIENT AGENTS

Because Liz and Ciara had both been ESCORT co-ordinators for years, they were acutely aware of the lengths to which abortion-seekers would go in order to get access to care abroad. Lots of arrangements had to be made in order to make the abortion journey as smooth as possible. These arrangements involved organising travel at short notice and getting childcare cover, as well as fundraising and making the necessary, sometimes multiple, appointments. ESCORT existed in order to minimise the exhausting effects of such arrangements when women were already under pressure and probably not feeling their best. But as ESCORT worked with the women to get abortion access, they observed a great deal of creativity, energy and organisation. Sometimes being good at organising things was a way of getting back control over a situation.

> You know what it's like, when you have a crisis and you've got … you have to put some practical things in place to try to get out of that crisis. There was a lot of focus organising the trip over. (Liz, 2004)

Part of ESCORT's care work was about being there if needed, but another part was about recognising that women were getting on with resolving this problem in their lives right now. They didn't necessarily need much help beyond affirmation that they were on the right track.

> You can usually tell by talking with them whether they'll be able to find their own way. And if they've got the money, then you might say, 'Get a taxi to such and such a place when you get to the airport.' (Ciara, 2004)

As Liz talks about the resilience and strength of the abortion-seeking women she met, her sense of their moral agency and creative strategising becomes explicit.

> They had such resilience and strength. They were on a kind of mission to see through the two days that they were here. I experienced a lot of exceptionally well-organised and resourceful women. (Liz, 2004)

In this view, abortion-seeking women were needy and discriminated against, but they were also resilient and strong. They could be all these things at the same time. ESCORT's experience shows that making women travel for abortion does not stop them accessing abortion, but it does stigmatise their moral choices and deplete their energy.

CONCLUSION

In listening to ESCORT's past co-ordinators talk about their activist support for Irish abortion-seekers, I learned about different dimensions of feminist interventions into abortion care. Researchers and advocates of abortion care have long acknowledged the important role that abortion plays in meeting women's health care needs and in recognising women as moral experts of their own lives (Silliman et al., 2004; Fletcher, 1998; Sheldon, 1997; Gerber Fried, 1990; Petchesky, 1990). ESCORT came into being because a group of feminist volunteers acted on this recognition of abortion as a necessary health care service and a means of women's reproductive control. Over a sixteen-year period they deployed the resources they had at their disposal to make abortion-seeking strangers feel more at home in implementing their decisions and accessing abortion care. In doing so, they showed how to constitute feminism through the mobilisation of civic experiences and commitments – as students and volunteers – towards having a direct impact on women's lives. Their feminism was also civic in its engagement with the women they supported. ESCORT wasn't 'rescuing' abortion-seeking women and it wasn't helping them 'because they were women'. Rather ESCORT responded to the women's initiating call and worked with women's ideas and solutions to make their abortion-seeking experience easier. Through this activist provision of abortion support, ESCORT showed how civic feminisms connect users and activists in a creative, needs-addressing exchange.

12

Speaking Up! Speaking Out! Abortion in Ireland,

exploring women's voices and contemporary abortion rights activism

ANNE QUESNEY

BORTION REMAINS one of the most contentious and stigmatised issues of our times. Even in the twenty-first century, when millions of women across the world have abortions every year, legally or illegally, and many more have, at the very least, faced the dilemma of an unplanned pregnancy and considered it, abortion remains taboo. When it is discussed, it is mostly couched in the bitter feud between those who support it and those who oppose it. For the many women who need to access it, whatever their circumstances, it is a reality. In practice, however, abortion is part of a complex debate which goes beyond the classic binary opposition between the rights of the woman and those of the foetus. It is a debate that is deeply embedded in societal constructions of family, motherhood and gender norms, infused with politics, religion and misogyny. Ultimately, the debate is about who controls the means of reproduction (Petchesky, 1990). This heady mixture impacts directly on individual women's lives, who, beyond the pro- and anti-choice rhetoric of rights and wrongs, beyond even the legal status[69] of the procedure itself, go on to make the decision to end unintended, unwanted or impossible pregnancies. And it is not an easy decision to make – even if women are certain about terminating the actual pregnancy. There are a range of factors that make it a challenging, sometimes even gruelling, experience, not least because of the derogatory discourse it is shrouded in and especially for those who are unsupported, alone, in financial difficulties or living in a country where abortion is highly restricted. Ireland has one of the most restrictive legislations in the world, in spite of the recently enacted Protection of Life During Pregnancy Act. Yet, the near-ban is not stopping women from having abortions. Instead, every year, thousands undertake the journey to England or elsewhere to access legal abortions, in a climate of secrecy and stigma (Randall, 1986; Kumar et al., 2009) that excludes their experiences and silences their voices (Fletcher, 1995; Human Rights Watch, 2010).

This article examines the contemporary abortion debate in Ireland, highlighting the role of the state and the Church in the construction of women as 'mothers' and 'homemakers' and their impact on the production of the abortion narrative. It is grounded in feminist theory, methodology and practice, in that it is written by a woman, with and for women, and seeks, beyond the pursuit of knowledge per se, to bring about social change to empower women (Daly, 2000). I am hoping that it will help contribute to feminist epistemology about the social structures that hinder women's reproductive autonomy and, by giving women a voice, challenge the abortion stigma and 'normalise' the issue in public discourse. Research interviews were conducted with pro-choice activists and women who had had an abortion. Some of the women interviewed shared their stories anonymously; their names have been changed.

A BRIEF RETROSPECTIVE OF ABORTION IN IRELAND

For Irish women the struggle for reproductive autonomy remains a salient issue, one that has been dominated over decades by political inertia and imbued with traditional Catholic dogma (Randall, 1986; Barry, 1988; Murphy Lawless, 1993; Hadley, 1996; Rossiter, 2009). The Irish legal framework is, ironically, still based on the British 1861 Offences Against the Persons Act, which allows abortion only to save the life of a pregnant woman but makes it a punishable offence, including a life sentence, in every other case, as per article 58; and the Protection of Life During Pregnancy Act 2013 only allows abortions to be carried out in cases where there is a serious threat to the life of the mother.

The first Constitution of the Irish Free State, in 1922, granted women the vote, making Ireland one of the first countries to do so. It also enshrined the family as 'a moral institution, possessing inalienable and imprescriptible rights' in article 41 (Murphy Lawless, 1993) and confined women's economic, social and political roles within the limited parameters of the home in article 41.2.[70] Women's fortunes were further undermined by the prominent role of the Catholic Church in Irish politics. Catholicism's construction of women as inferior to men (Rossiter, 2009) legitimises and commends normative gender roles and women's subordination to men, including in all matters sexual, and as such the Irish Catholic Church acted as a moral arbiter whose conservatism has profoundly impacted on the country's institutions and attitudes, not least vis-à-vis sex. The portrayal of the 'ideal' woman as chaste, pure, obedient and respectable also provided strong justific-ations to impose political restrictions against her. From the outset, the Irish Free State legislated industriously about sex, introducing a number of repressive measures against divorce and contraception and reflecting the Church's puritan social doctrine in the legal framework (Peillon, 1982; Hayes and Urquhart, 2001).

It was not until the 1970s that a growing Irish feminist movement brought to the fore the scale of the discriminatory practices women had endured and began to challenge hegemonic discourses and inequities more openly. Then, in 1973, the *McGee v. Attorney General* case led to a Supreme Court ruling which granted married couples the right to acquire and use modern contraceptives.[71] In many other Western countries, meanwhile, the late 1960s and 1970s coincided with a wave of liberalisation of abortion laws – Great Britain (1967), the United States (1973), France (1975) and Italy (1978). Significantly, since it had become legal in Great Britain, an increasing number of Irish women began travelling there to procure abortions, thus making the issue more visible and sending inevitable shock waves through the more conservative layers of society.[72] The perceived threat of a change in the law mobilised the right wing, avidly supported ideologically and financially by the Catholic Church (Smyth, 2002). They formed a broad alliance under the umbrella of the Pro-Life Amendment Campaign (PLAC) and successfully campaigned to enshrine the 'rights of the unborn' in the Constitution, by way of referendum.[73] The Eighth Amendment, 1983, grants the foetus – 'the unborn child' – rights which conflict directly with those of the pregnant woman – 'the mother' – making Ireland the first and only country to have voted a ban on abortion into its Constitution[74] (Hadley, 1996).

A decade later the X case and the C case erupted, revealing the intrinsic brutality of Ireland's anti-abortion stance, which treats women with contempt and silences them to keep the country 'abortion free'. It wasn't until 2011, when the European Court of Human Rights (ECHR) delivered its ruling on the *A, B, C* case that the debate was properly reignited.[75] The ECHR held that Ireland had violated the human rights of one of the plaintiffs, C, on grounds of the lack of clear abortion guidelines. An expert group was set up and, almost instantaneously, anti-choice groups went into a frenzy. In July 2012, Youth Defence unveiled their campaign posters, representing a sad-looking woman with the caption: 'Abortion tears her life apart – there is always a better solution'. These appeared on buses and billboards. They were closely followed by the Pro-life Amendment Campaign's – 'Did you know that 79% of women want Fine Gael to keep its pro-life commitments?' – featuring a woman holding a baby.

Two prominent issues emerged from these campaigns. First, a clear indication that the anti-choice lobby was suddenly escalating its abortion-related activities after a period of focusing on other issues. As with PLAC in 1981, the perception was that Ireland's 'pro-life' position was under threat (Randall, 1986), which as Smyth (2002) observed is symptomatic of their resistance to a 'more modernising, and in many ways a more radical and human rights oriented culture. And one in which women [are] very determined to be free'. The second observation relates to a perceptible rhetorical shift in anti-choice discourse, away from the foetus and onto the woman. Foetal imagery has long played a prominent role in anti-abortion campaigns and continues to permeate the cultural landscape (Petchesky, 1990); the foetus has become a potent symbol of helplessness in need of patriarchal protection – from essentially selfish women (Petchesky, 1990; Boyle, 1997). Anti-abortion groups have, however, become judicious and have recognised the need to appeal directly to women, who might otherwise feel alienated by their foetus-centred approach.

While it is not within the scope of this article to analyse them in depth, it must be noted that these tactics encroach directly on pro-choice discursive territory around reproductive autonomy and women's decision making, which are core to the movement. They also promulgate the myth that abortion is harmful, an idea which has gained considerable currency and has become a central feature of many recent abortion-related psychological studies aiming to demonstrate its negative impact on women's mental health. In 1992, the year of the X case, the Psychological Society of Ireland issued the following statement:

> Evidence from the most rigorous scientific studies available shows that legal termination of unwanted pregnancy does not have severe or lasting negative consequences for most women undergoing the procedure. (cited in Fine Davis, 2007, p. 32)

These findings clearly refute anti-choice claims and concur with more recent publications that 'abortion in itself does not lead to depression, unless other life issues remained unresolved before the pregnancy' (IFPA, 2000). However, in the public consciousness contradictory interpretations only lead to further dichotomisation of an already distorted debate, and at a time when it is precisely women's health and well-being that are being legislated on.

Many people, north and south of the border, perceived Youth Defence's poster campaign as disingenuous and misplaced. It led to a great deal of resentment as well as a vociferous response from women's groups. As a matter of fact, it has spurred a whole new generation of pro-choice activists to get involved in campaigning for abortion rights. Savita Halappanavar's tragic death, in November 2012, after being refused a life-saving abortion, caused further consternation and anger. It provoked a national and international outcry against what was increasingly perceived as political incompetence to recognise that Ireland had changed and that there was growing support for women's reproductive rights.

STRADDLING THE PUBLIC AND PRIVATE SPHERES

One of the reasons abortion remains polarised, is that it sits uncomfortably between the public and private spheres (Petchesky, 1990).

On the one hand, it is a very public matter, discussed or decided by parliamentarians, churchmen, medical professionals, the media and civil society, all predominantly male; and, on the other hand, abortion is a private, or rather personal, matter for women, a decision they make within the context of their own lives, not a political exercise of the right to do something (Fletcher, 1995). Abortion is a private concern for women and one which they should be entitled to decide as individuals, regardless of their circumstances, but it is also a healthcare need that should be provided to them by the state, like it is in many countries. For as long as reproductive health policy is restrictive in Ireland, it will bear evidence of the economic, social and legal gender-based inequalities. As one of the interviewees remarked:

It indicates that women are still an oppressed minority. (Gill, 2012)

In this section, I will consider the implications of restrictive legislation and pejorative public discourse on women choosing abortion, specifically evaluating the material and emotional barriers they face, including stigma and silence. Finally, I will contemplate how women's voices and agency might play a role in reconfiguring the terms of political discourse around abortion.

Obstacle Course

The women who travel to access an abortion face the same barriers today as they did three decades ago. The legal restrictions place an undue burden on women, especially those who are poor. Financial hardship is a very real obstacle for women having to raise between £400 and £2,000 or more (Abortion Support Network), depending on gestation, thus bringing to the fore the intersection between gender and class as well as ethnicity, as is the case for asylum-seeking or Traveller women. The Abortion Support Network (ASN) reports a trebling in the number of women who have contacted it in the three years since it was opened, many facing dire circumstances.

Of course women can travel to England but that is a very different proposition for women without means. Thousands travel every year and for every woman who is travelling there is probably another five that are not travelling because they cannot afford it. [...] A lot of the trauma for these women is not the abortion but how they will be able to afford it. Women with money are more likely to have some sort of support network, somebody they can talk to and if not they have the resources to buy someone they can talk to. [...] Whereas the women we hear from, just by the nature of their poverty, they're already disenfranchised in some way. They are already at a disadvantage to the majority of society. (Mara Clarke, 2012)

All the women I interviewed identified the costs of having to travel abroad as an immediate concern once they had made the decision to have an abortion; many had to borrow the money from friends, family or even 'loan sharks', leaving them in a vulnerable position. The cost of the actual procedure does not include additional 'direct' costs, such as flights and accommodation, or 'indirect' costs, such as loss of income or childcare; these are then further compounded by practical arrangements.

Money was a major problem and childcare also. It's all very difficult to organise on a practical level – if you live in England you can just go to the clinic and then straight home. I had to hang around and wait to fly back in the evening. You've already had all the expenses, taxis and stuff; you can barely afford to buy a sandwich. (Ruth, 2012)

Most women also expressed a sense of isolation and frustration that comes with having to travel.

The whole experience of organising the flight and the appointment was stressful ... I'd also like to say how traumatic it was waking up in the recovery room. There were five of us – sobbing our hearts out. There was sadness – probably just circumstances – but to be so far from home and not to be able to hold my kids ... that was really hard. (Carla, 2012)

Adverse economic circumstances and ensuing stress related to the practicalities of organising the procedure and journey are further exacerbated by an endemic lack of adequate and reliable information. The current situation leaves the door open to unregulated, or so-called 'rogue', agencies to provide inaccurate or misleading information and related services, such as counselling, in an effort to delay or dissuade women. Modern means of communication have of course changed how information can be accessed but offer no guarantee as to the content.

Prevalent Stigma

Abortion is a complex issue, most of all for the women who undergo it, and the way it affects each woman is contingent on a myriad of circumstances (Buttenweiser and Levine, 1990). The multiple barriers they encounter when they choose to end a pregnancy are magnified by the high degree of stigmatisation (Petchesky, 1990; Fletcher, 1995). There is little doubt that Ireland's constitutional construction of women as 'mothers' and 'homemakers' has impacted on attitudes to female sexuality and reproduction. As Boyle points out, 'we take for granted particular constructions of the individual and of their relationship to the social world' (Boyle, 1997, p. 6) and this is particularly pertinent in the case of abortion where social and cultural contexts still frame the category 'woman' and reproductive policy, resulting in inevitable stigma for those who seek abortions but also for those who provide and advocate for them. Several participants concurred with this activist's statement:

> ... stigma is a huge barrier to the individual woman because it cuts her off from the community that might be supportive to her because the assumption is that she has done something wrong and that she will be shamed and will not be supported ... But I think stigma has [also] been internalised by us as advocates and by clinicians and that is a huge barrier to building the connections that would support providers and women and mobilise neighbours. (Jane, 2012)

Link and Phelan theorise that stigma can be produced and reproduced through a cascade of consecutive social processes:

> In the first component, people distinguish and label human differences. In the second, dominant cultural beliefs link labelled persons to undesirable characteristics so as to accomplish stereotypes. In the third, labelled persons are placed in distinct categories so as to accomplish some degree of separation of 'us' from 'them'. In the fourth,

labelled persons experience status loss and discrimination that lead to unequal outcomes. (cited in Kumar, Hessini and Mitchell. 2009, p. 2)

This cycle can be applied to abortion in Ireland, and elsewhere. Kumar et al. (2009, p. 4) defined 'abortion stigma' as 'a negative attribute ascribed to women who seek to terminate a pregnancy that marks them, internally or externally, as inferior to ideals of womanhood' – and womanhood is usually associated with motherhood. The concept of motherhood has been theorised in terms of its construction of women's socially prescribed reproductive roles. However, at the level of public discourse, motherhood is routinely represented as part of the natural order (Chancer, 1990; Boyle, 1997). According to Kumar et al. the abortion experience transgresses at least three classic constructs of the 'feminine': 'female sexuality solely for procreation, the inevitability of motherhood and instinctual nurturance of the vulnerable' (2009, p. 4). It is therefore unsurprising that abortion is presented as deviant and that the focus on women as mothers restricts the ways in which women themselves feel about abortion (Boyle, 1997).[76] Having children is the ultimate expression of femaleness and a reassurance to a patriarchal society that women, who undertake most of the responsibility in child-rearing, will continue to conform to their 'natural' role (Neustatter, 1986).

'I feel guilty, especially when I see people with babies, I think that should be me. Having had the abortion is really making me want to have another child – maybe to make up for what I did. (Ruth, 2012)

Her statement is a further indication of the powerful social context which has constructed motherhood and the idea of 'maternal instinct' as an intrinsically natural state for women (Badinter, 1981; Boyle, 1997).

Yet, abortion is also described as an act of defiance by women who assert control over their own bodies and challenge long-held expectations about their gendered roles (Petchesky, 1990; Kumar, 2009), but even then, it does not transcend stigma. Most of the women I spoke to said they were clear about their decision to terminate the unwanted pregnancy, but found it difficult to escape the stigma, precisely because the power dynamics that underline abortion form part of an ideological struggle about the meaning of sexuality, motherhood and family.

Stifling Silence

Stigma can be located in different spaces and mechanisms, and impacts on vulnerable women the most (Kumar et al., 2009). This is particularly the case in countries like Ireland, where it is exacerbated by the illegal nature of the procedure and where a derogatory discourse leads to stereotyping, demeans women's healthcare needs or silences them (Boyle, 1997):

> The public and private silence surrounding abortion has such intricate personal and socio-cultural meanings that any single explanation will inevitably simplify and distort its complexities. People remain silent or reticent about abortion in different ways and for different reasons ... Various political or personal reasons may compel one to be silent, to 'choose' not to speak out. (Jing Boa, 2005, p. 31)

The reasons why women remain silent about their abortion experience are too many to explore here; however, silence reinforces their sense of secrecy and isolation. Not knowing who to tell, not knowing who else has had one, not knowing what people will think; with so many unknowns it often seems easier and safer to keep quiet. As one activist pointed out, 'what is a private experience in countries where abortion is legal, such as England, becomes a secret because of perceived disapproval'.

> It's good to hear other women's stories; it makes you feel less like a psychopath, you know ... I don't really want people to know about it because I know how society works, I know how judgemental people are but you can't judge someone until you are in their shoes. I have actually had conversations with people that are anti-abortion and who think you should be ashamed of yourself. (Ruth, 2012)

Silence acts as a powerful mechanism, which 'influence[s] the production of the political abortion rhetoric' (Fletcher, 1995). It enables politicians and the anti-choice movement to pretend abortion is not happening in

Ireland and ignore the humanity of the women behind the statistics. 'Silence is almost necessary in Irish society so it can keep a good opinion of itself' (IFPA, 2000).

CONCLUSION: PUTTING THE WOMEN BACK IN THE ABORTION DEBATE – FROM PASSIVE TO ACTIVE SUBJECT

This article shows the extent to which the heteronormative power structures in Ireland are oppressing women and constructing abortion as deviant, as the antithesis of the 'ideal mother and homemaker' represented in the Constitution. It also suggests that there is growing resistance and mobilisation from a new generation of feminist and pro-choice activists, against the institutionalised gender order and patriarchal ideology that is forcing thousands of women to travel in secrecy and shame. Women's silences are a central feature of the abortion debate in Ireland, but there is an increasing recognition that their stories and their voices can provide a more balanced and contextualised account of women's actual experiences, one which makes fewer assumptions about the nature of abortion and challenges the discourse which depicts abortion as wrong and regrettable (Boyle, 1997).

In *Ireland's Hidden Diaspora*, Rossiter (2009) bemoans the absence of abortion seekers' voices, asserting that 'we still wait to hear them speak out in their own name'. Speaking out in a hostile environment is an act of bravery not many women are prepared to undertake and nor should they be expected to. When Rossiter herself spoke out in the past, at best she was met with silence, at worst ostracised. There is no tradition of or expectation that Irish women who have had abortions will share their stories – because in actual fact they have been rendered invisible. Sandra McAvoy recently observed that even the composition of the 'expert group', for example, is a stark reminder that abortion policy is determined by the professional and medical elites and not by the women who need it. Several participants in this study expressed caution about women speaking out:

> Women's voices are very important, they do make it human and they do highlight the fact that it's our mothers, daughters, sisters, friends; but we as a movement, we who are working in abortion,

have a really big role to play in terms of telling these women's stories. (Mara Clarke, 2012)

In 2000, the IFPA published *The Irish Journey*, a collection of women's personal accounts that attempts to shed some light on the complexities of the abortion experience and tackle the taboo by giving women a voice. As Ruane explicates in her introduction, '[i]n all the talk and high rhetoric of the endless abortion debate, the story of Irish women is usually authored by someone else, with few women daring to speak for themselves, to become visible' (IFPA, 2000). Out of the six women I spoke to and who had had an abortion, two have spoken publicly about their experiences; the others have spoken to partners, friends, family or in activist circles, i.e. what was described and considered as a 'safe' environment.

Of late, more women have spoken publicly and, increasingly, there is a sense that women's voices have been sidelined long enough. Earlier this year, three women, all of whom had to terminate wanted pregnancies due to fatal foetal anomalies, spoke out and have since formed the organisation Termination for Medical Reasons (TFMR). As one respondent indicated:

> I think that has had a huge impact. These women are quite mainstream, not politically active. They are more like your woman next door talking about the law and how it's impacted on them. And that is really important. [...] And I think the more women from diverse backgrounds ... who have had abortions can speak out to help break down the stigma [...] will make it easier for public to understand women's circumstances. (Liz, 2012)

Not all women connect their personal abortion experience to the political debate about their reproductive rights, or choose to talk about it publicly for a range of very valid reasons (Fletcher, 1995). However, those who do can help expose the reality that abortion *does* exist in Ireland and that the women who figure every May in the British Department of Health statistics are indeed real.

> All the Irish accents in the waiting room will never cease to amaze me and it made me feel quite sad. So I decided to speak out, because it's easy to simplify the whole issue because no-one talks about it

and challenges the anti-abortionists when they talk about taking a life. (Rhonda, 2012)

Thus, in the face of Irish society's resilient 'pro-life' culture, women in their tens of thousands have, over the past decades, exercised the necessary agency to defy the legal restrictions imposed on their reproductive bodies – albeit silently. This project underscores that women's marginalised experiences of abortion 'attest to the[ir] capacity for autonomous action in the face of often overwhelming cultural sanctions and structural inequalities' (McNay, 2000, p. 10), and that their accounts combined with the work of pro-choice activists may have a significant impact on attitudinal shifts that could in turn contribute to the social transformation necessary to change Ireland's regressive reproductive policy framework. They might provide additional impetus to contest '[t]he existing terms of the political discourse ... which is fundamentally discriminatory in relation to women, and are able to do so because of women's historical, material and symbolic relation to the domestic' (Squires, 1999, p. 31).

Of course, any such project must give careful consideration to women's subjectivities and recognise differences among women as well as create a safe space where all women's accounts can be validated and respected and where women could become empowered protagonists rather than having their stories played back at them by someone else. Such initiatives have taken place in many locations over time, in the US, in the UK and in France, and could take place in Ireland also.

It's so important for women to hear these stories, to hear that it's OK, that I haven't done a terrible thing ... So few people in Ireland are willing to speak out ... We still don't know Miss X's name or Miss C's; we simply don't know who these women are. But if there was that kind of critical mass, the 'anti-choicers' can't pick on you as an individual ... and for women to see that it's not just me and those other Irish women, it's the English women, the French women, the Italian women and Spanish women, that it is a universal experience. (Choice Ireland, 2012)

I think [women's voices] will be vital in opening debate and in dispelling the stigma. (McAvoy, 2012)

This paper seeks to inform the discussion around the role women's stories can play in 'normalising' and de-stigmatising the derogatory abortion discourse. At the time of writing, Ireland's first public 'Speak Out' event has taken place. Thirty years after women were equated with foetuses under the Constitution, they are standing up and sharing their accounts to make a collective impact towards validating and improving every woman's experience of abortion.

13

Prison Sentence for Abortion is Cruel and Unusual Punishment*

PEADAR O'GRADY

ON THE NIGHT BEFORE the general scheme of the Protection of Life in Pregnancy Bill was published, two women, whose pregnancy involved a fatal foetal abnormality, appeared on *Prime Time* on RTÉ to describe their lonely and at times harrowing journey to the UK to have an abortion. The distress they experienced at first, with the appalling news of the impending inevitable loss of an expected baby, was cruelly compounded for them by the bewildering information that followed: they could not have an abortion in Ireland.

The day after they bravely told their story, 'Head 19' of the bill said that an abortion in their circumstances, if it were carried out here rather than elsewhere, would be punishable by up to fourteen years in prison 'due to the gravity of the crime'. It was a shock to many that some anonymous drafter of legislation thought that what these women had to go through was the equivalent of a 'grave crime'. I have not met anyone yet who believes that it is. In 1992 a majority voted that there should be no impediment to travel for an abortion; a decision incompatible with the idea that such travel would constitute a 'grave crime'.

At the Oireachtas hearings I put the question of who exactly supported the idea of imprisoning women or children for having an abortion but not one senator or TD present volunteered any support for a prison sentence. As someone recently asked: with sentences of eighteen months or two years being handed down in the courts for raping a child, could a child who is raped and takes abortion pills at home possibly end up spending longer in prison than her abuser?

So this criminalising of women and children is certainly offensive and absurd, but it is also dangerous. Savita Halappanavar's death was due to being repeatedly refused an abortion due to the 'chill factor' of the 1861 act's threat of a prison sentence. 'Legal clarity' was supposed to help remove the chill factor not reinforce it, as the threat of fourteen years in prison will certainly do. Also, in the case of medical abortions, women should obviously be able to properly consult with a doctor before they take medication but they should certainly be able to tell their doctor what medication they have taken in an emergency. There is very real concern that this information will continue to be withheld by women through fear because of the threat of imprisonment.

The only possible justification for criminalisation is that it would in some way reduce the number of abortions. However, the research does not support this. A study published in the medical journal, *The Lancet*, in 2012, reports that restrictive abortion laws are not associated with lower rates of abortion (Sedgh et al., 2008). The region with the highest rate, with thirty-two abortions per thousand women aged fifteen to forty-four, is Latin America, where 95 per cent of abortions are illegal. The region with the lowest, with twelve abortions per thousand, is Western Europe where abortion is available on broad grounds and almost all are safe and legal.

According to Reuters, a report presented at the world's largest conference on women's health called 'Women Deliver' describes how: 'In Bolivia, Brazil and Argentina, women who sought or had abortions were handcuffed to hospital beds and placed under police custody as they recovered while doctors and nurses were subjected to police raids and investigations.' Some 47,000 women died from unsafe abortions in 2008 according to the World Health Organisation and five million women were disabled. Unsafe abortion, by untrained staff in unsuitable facilities, happens where there is restricted access to legal abortion services and is one of the top three causes of maternal mortality in the world. One of the reasons that Ireland can boast such low levels of maternal mortality is because we have access to safe and legal abortion, mainly in the UK. Restriction of access to abortion in Ireland is on the basis of ability to travel, and that restriction nearly killed the child in the X case and, tragically, did kill Savita Halappanavar.

Protection of Life During Pregnancy Act 2013 can only help to ensure that women who are unable to travel for an abortion do not die. It is important to amend the legislation to remove unnecessary delays through multiple certification and other institutional restrictions but legislators should also include fatal foetal abnormalities and remove prison sentences entirely as this is truly 'cruel and unusual punishment'. Amnesty International's Colm O'Gorman called for the prison sentence to be revoked and went on to say that 'Until Ireland's laws allow for abortion in cases of rape and incest, risk to a woman's health or cases of fatal foetal abnormality, they will be out of line with international human rights standards.'

Law lecturer, Ruth Fletcher, in her evidence to the Oireachtas public hearings, supported the inclusion of fatal foetal abnormalities in the bill by excluding a foetus with this condition from the definition of 'unborn' as previously argued by counsel representing Ireland at the European Court of Human Rights in *Ireland v. D*. Fletcher argued very convincingly that the Irish state could '... vindicate unborn life by investing in pregnancy-related care and research into miscarriage. In choosing to punish women rather than to adopt more neutral or positive measures for the support of foetal life in pregnancy, the Legislature would be acting unfairly. Head 19 is unfair because it asks women, rather than the state, to bear the weight of the public duty to vindicate foetal life (Fletcher 2013).

Sadly, the Oireachtas failed to find the courage to show humanity and compassion by providing services for those who choose abortion in these circumstances and could only resort to threats of imprisonment.

* This piece first appeared in the *Irish Times* as "Oireachtas should amend Bill's criminalisation of women and doctors" on 18th June 2013.

14

Ireland's Abortion Ban: honour, shame and the possibility of a moral revolution

LISA SMYTH

NTHONY APPIAH (2010) argues that collective forms of identity are infused with moral norms, in ways which direct and give meaning to our actions. What he describes as 'honour codes', namely bundles of norms which define the moral character of a collectivity, are an important feature of social identities, since they motivate and authorise how we act, what we believe and how we mutually evaluate each other. The honour, or esteem, of both collectivities and their individual members depends, to a large extent, on conformity to the code, an important source of shared, as well as personal, pride.

Violations of honour codes tend to produce intense responses, not least in the form of shame, a deeply social emotion which supports and sustains the moral norms captured by such codes (Scheff, 2000; Solomon, 2007, p. 100). Appiah argues that the restoration of collective honour following a violation can depend on punishing, excluding or even executing an individual who has brought shame on the group. However, this is not to argue that honour codes are static or determining. While powerful as a means of generating social conformity, such codes do rely on intensive suppression of dissent and are vulnerable to pressure in various ways, which can ultimately result in what Appiah describes as moral revolutions (2010, p. 162).

What follows aims to explore Ireland's long history of struggles over access to legal abortions in the state through this lens, considering whether and to what extent the recent enactment of legislation allowing for pregnancies to be legally ended can be understood as a significant step towards a moral revolution. While the history and politics of these events is well documented (e.g. see Girvin, 1993; Hesketh, 1990; Hug, 1999; Mullally, 2005; O'Carroll, 1991; O'Reilly, 1992; Smyth, 1992; Smyth, 2005; Smyth, 2008), it is worth considering the emotional tensions this honour code has generated, and the ways in which it has eventually resulted in something of a reversal.

ESTABLISHING AN HONOUR CODE: THE 'PRO-LIFE' NATION AND THE BAN ON ABORTION

The constitutional prohibition on abortion, ratified in the Republic of Ireland in 1983, was legitimised by advocates as a vital support for the moral heart of the nation in the face of impending change. This view was popularised through the deployment of a moral panic concerning national survival (Smyth, 2005). A concerted effort was made from the late 1970s to define the nation in terms of a principal moral norm, described as 'pro-life', and taking the form of an almost absolute ban on abortion. This was intended to set the Irish nation apart from and above its significant others, who had, it was argued, lost sight of the value of human life as a consequence of the grip of modernity. Not only would the abortion ban allow Ireland to maintain its supposed moral character as it moved into a more open democratic national and international situation, but it would do so in what was claimed to be a highly democratic manner, by allowing the sovereign 'people' to vote directly on the status of 'pro-life' morality in the state. The paradox at the heart of this type of defensive traditionalist politics, depending as it does on modernist ideals of progress and democracy, while at the same time perceiving such values as damaging to traditional forms of human sociality, are well-known (e.g. Hall, 1988).

This legal change, which elevated the status of abortion regulation from criminal to constitutional law, only changeable by the people through a referendum, was the result of a deliberate effort to sustain the deeply gendered vision of Irishness shaping nationalism since the latter part of the nineteenth century (Ward, 1983). It was an important strategy in bolstering the position of an elite of the time, in the face of a changing social and political landscape (O'Carroll, 1991; O'Reilly, 1992). The international women's liberation and civil rights movements during this era were actively politicising the gender order, in ways that were generating some degree of change, as well as resistance. One important consequence was changes to abortion law elsewhere, not least in the United States (Ginsburg, 1989; Luker, 1984). The 1973 US Supreme Court decision in *Roe v. Wade* opened up limited access to legal abortion in that jurisdiction, on grounds of an individual right to privacy. This contributed to the anxieties of Ireland's conservative elite, concerned that events could take a similar turn for them. Indeed, the 1973 Irish Supreme Court decision in *McGee v. Attorney General* allowed for married couples to import contraceptives on the related ground of a right to family privacy (Gearty, 1992).

In Ireland around this time, a number of other important changes were also taking place. Women were travelling from Ireland to legally end their pregnancies in increasing numbers following the introduction of the 1967 British Abortion Act (Randall, 1986). Secondly, the Catholic Church lost its 'special position' in the institutions of the state following a referendum in 1972, which removed this designated status from the Republic's Constitution. Thirdly, the state joined the European Economic Community (EEC, now European Union) in 1973, and consequently had, among other things, become answerable to the rulings of the European Courts of Justice and Human Rights. The possibility loomed that gender norms, and the institutions upon which they depended, not least a patriarchal family structure, inheritance system and labour market, might be destabilised by these changes. Thus, anxiety concerning the future of the nation, constructed as 'traditional', familial and deeply gendered, yet finding itself increasingly open to international influence, was crucial in motivating efforts, however divisive, to establish a 'pro-life' honour code in the culture, through the Constitution. While the formalisation of this code had been secured through what was described at the time as a 'moral civil war' (Smyth, 2005, p. 67), depicted by one commentator as generating a 'second partitioning' of the country, parallel to the border dividing north from south (Hesketh, 1990), it nevertheless sought to encapsulate and represent a single, deeply gendered account of the nation's moral character.

Indeed, it proved relatively successful in doing this, as abortion became, and remained for some time, an unspeakable practice, shrouded in shame, an emotion which Solomon argues is so painful that people will go to great lengths to avoid it (2007, p. 96). Literary, biographical and social science reflections and commentary on the practice and experience of seeking an abortion abroad provide ample testament to the ways that the ban had acquired the status of an honour code. Abortion, for any reason, was regarded as a deeply shameful, secretive practice (e.g. see Fletcher, 1995; Independent.ie, 2011; Mahon et al., 1998; McCafferty, 2004; O'Brien, 1997; Rossiter, 2009). Public debate on the moral and political issues involved tended to rely on euphemism, with wary participants famously referring, for example, to 'the substantive issue' rather than more explicitly to the morally tainted word 'abortion' during the 1990s (Smyth, 2005 p. 13).

The opening of the borders following the X case, to allow women and girls to leave the state in order to end pregnancies elsewhere without fear of prosecution, can be understood as a refusal of citizenship, a form of punishment for those nationals who breach the honour code. Non-nationals have of course been treated differently (Luibhéid, 2006; Mullally, 2005). Women facing impossible pregnancies, regardless of the circumstances, have been left with little alternative but to emigrate, albeit temporarily, and find medical help elsewhere, usually in Britain (Rossiter, 2009). Some women recounted feeling 'like a criminal', as they stole away (e.g. Irish Women's Abortion Support Group, 1988, p. 65). The experiences and actions of the three women involved in the 2010 case of *A, B and C v. Ireland* were clearly shaped by the fear and shame of violating the 'pro-life' honour code (European Court of Human Rights, 2010).

Stories of having abortions abroad, mostly in England, published by the *Irish Times* in 2012, emphasise the shame and silence of women and their partners as they went through the experience and returned home to quietly resume their lives. Even when a woman didn't feel a personal sense of shame, the 'chilling effect' of the ban, as the European Court of Human Rights (2010) described it, has tended to have important consequences. As one woman reportedly commented, 'I'm not ashamed of my decision, but It's Just Not Something To Talk About' (Sheridan, 2012). Rachel, interviewed by journalist Kathy Sheridan in 2012 about her experience of going to Liverpool for an abortion following a diagnosis of a fatal foetal abnormality, reflected on how the barriers blocking the easy flow of health information and care 'makes you feel like you're doing something wrong [...] like you're being judged' (Sheridan 2012). Another woman, recalling the termination of her already dead foetus, said that 'we really felt that we were exporting our dirty little secrets ...' (Sheridan 2012), while another commented that the experience of having to travel in secrecy, without the support of health professionals or follow-up health care on return, 'must make a woman feel so rejected by her country' (Sheridan 2012). These stories and reflections highlight the personal impact of an honour code that has dismissed, isolated and criminalised those who violate it, regardless of how they feel about their actions, as they go through the trauma of seeking out essential health care in another country, often paying large sums of money and acting in secrecy, away from the ordinary solidarities of friends and family, and returning home without the prospect of follow-up care or emotional support.

PRESSURES ON THE HONOUR CODE

How is it that a code of national honour, which has exerted such strong emotional and moral influence over decades, has itself become the source of expressions of national shame? What follows explains the processes involved as a consequence, firstly of shifting gender norms, and secondly, a change in the state's perception of its status in the international 'honour world' of democratic states and political institutions, particularly following the death of Savita Halappanavar in October 2012.

a) Individual or collective pride?

Firstly, the dependence of the abortion ban on strong gender norms has slowly undermined its legitimacy, as expectations about the distinction between women's and men's lives, and the character of family life, have changed. In particular, the increased participation of women in the labour market, including married women and mothers, has unsettled the gender regime of Irish nationalism, with its central, self-sacrificial figure of 'Mother Ireland', and its reliance on a deeply gendered narrative of familial Irishness (Fortin, 2005; Innes, 1993; Thapar-Björkert et al., 2002). A norm of individual choice and fulfilment has, at least to some extent, and especially during the prosperous years of the 'Celtic Tiger', come into conflict with that of strong gender difference (Ging, 2009; Negra, 2012). The reliance of the anti-abortion lobby on gendered, traditionalist, nationalist rhetoric and imagery has consequently offered fewer guarantees of popularity in this context.

b) The honour of being 'pro-life'?

Against this background of normative conflict and change around gender, the meaning and status of the 'pro-life' honour code has itself directly and repeatedly become the focus of intense personal trauma and public debate, particularly since events of the early 1990s. A series of high-profile court cases involving rape victims, wards of court, women experiencing health crises, and those carrying fatally malformed foetuses, have repeatedly generated moral crises, characterised by public expressions of shame and efforts to re-think collective morality and identity. The association between national pride and 'pro-life' morality, established by the early 1980s' Pro-Life Amendment Campaign, has been reversed time after time, as specific cases came to the attention of news media and campaigning groups (Fletcher, 2005; Smyth, 2008).

This process of reversal was initiated and most intensely dramatised through the events of the X case in 1992, when a fourteen-year-old girl, pregnant as a result of repeated rape, was prevented from leaving the state to end her pregnancy in Britain. The national and international media attention this case received led to multiple and lasting individual and collective expressions of intense shock, anger and shame at the way the 'pro-life' code was operating, by those who felt themselves to be implicated in it (Smyth, 1992; Smyth, 2005). The cartoonist, Martyn Turner, encapsulated the dynamics of this pervasive emotional reaction very well in his front-page depiction of the case as a young girl holding a teddy-bear and standing on the territory of the state, where the chain-link border fence is locked shut, with the caption '17th February 1992 ... the introduction of internment in Ireland ... for 14 year old girls ....' (Turner, 1992). The cartoon suggested a parallel between the activities of the Irish state in this case and the deeply resented actions of the British administration in Northern Ireland in the early 1970s, when internment of suspected terrorists without trial was introduced in response to the eruption of political violence. In drawing this parallel, Turner's cartoon presented an unmistakeable image of national shame at the actions of the High Court against a forlorn, pregnant fourteen-year-old girl.

The final Supreme Court decision in this case, which lifted the injunction against X leaving the state to seek an abortion (ILRM 201), can be understood as a response to the public reaction to the case. The centrality of the 'ordinary' Irish family in this case, in the figure of a middle-class girl and her parents being pursued by an aggressive state as they sought to respond to the consequences of rape, was crucial to the emotional and moral responses. Many public comments at the time reflected an identification either with X herself, or with her parents, as they sought to alleviate their daughter's trauma. It seemed to many that the state was violating the integrity of the family, constitutionally recognised as the 'primary unit' of Irish society, upon which the nation is built (Government Publications Office, 1937). More specifically, the state's actions were perceived as having infringed the authority of the father, who had actively supported his daughter in seeking an abortion, and who had himself brought the case to the attention of the state by enquiring from the Gardaí about whether foetal DNA could be used as evidence in the rape trial. This sense that the Irish family itself, in its 'traditionally' gendered form, had become a victim of the 'pro-life' honour code was crucial in generating the anger and shame that overwhelmed the news media of the time.

The Supreme Court's decision in that case interpreted the constitutional ban as requiring some balance to be struck between the right to life of the 'mother', in this case a suicidal fourteen-year-old, and that of the 'unborn'. The court allowed for legal abortion in cases of suicidal intent, while calling for legislation to give substance to this interpretation. Subsequent political efforts to reverse this decision through successive referendums were unsuccessful, and the lack of legal certainty concerning how to balance competing rights to life continued to occupy the courts, the media and public debate over subsequent decades. The uncertainty and moral conflict over the operation of the 'pro-life' honour code culminated most recently in the appalling death of Savita Halappanavar in 2012, an Indian dentist who was refused medical assistance while miscarrying her much-wanted, second-trimester pregnancy, and consequently died from sepsis (Berer, 2013; Lancet, 2013; Qadir, 2013). The refusal of health professionals to provide essential medical assistance, reportedly on the grounds that 'Ireland is a Catholic country', generated yet another wave of intensive national and international shock and shame, and has been an important motivation behind the introduction of the Protection of Life During Pregnancy Act, 2013.

THE HONOUR CODE IN REVERSE: THE SHAME OF THE ABORTION BAN

Appiah (2010) argues that honour depends on both comparison with and claiming recognition from significant others. As he explains, '[w]hether you have done well by the standard appropriate to your group will depend on what the normal expectations are about how members of that group should behave' (2010, p. 63). Individuals tend to inhabit multiple, sometimes conflicting 'honour worlds' (p. 87), some of which they have deliberately joined, others of which they simply find themselves in, for instance by virtue of birth. Thus, one can deliberately become a member of an honour world of feminists, boxers, or experimental musicians, while at the same time finding one's self simply recognised as occupying the honour world of Italian people, Muslims, or a member of this or that family, regardless of how much one may have tried to leave. We act and interact with others in these reference groups in relation to more or less shared codes of expected behaviour, and we are caught up in evaluating whether and to what extent each of us lives up to these codes, not all of which we have deliberately affiliated ourselves with.

Honour rewards those who are particularly valued by their social group, while those who break honour codes are treated with contempt, and/or are subjected to punishment, whether formal or informal. Being part of an honour world, whether composed of individuals or institutions like states, carries no guarantees that one will receive the honourable status one seeks, and failure results in reduced status among one's significant others, or worse. In the case of nation-states, political actions are often motivated by seeking esteem from the honour world of the 'international community'. Ireland, a post-colonial state which has struggled to remain economically viable over decades, continuously strives to be recognised as an equal and valued participant in this honour world (Luibhéid, 2006).

The actions of the Irish state, both in supporting the abortion ban over decades and failing to introduce interpretive legislation following the X case, had the consequence of shifting both internal and external evaluations of the honourable state of the nation. The actions of the state have been repeatedly criticised in an international context where norms of democracy and gender equality circulate with some authority (Weeks, 2007). The response from elsewhere, far from being one of admiration for Ireland's moral stand against abortion, has been repeatedly reversed since 1992. Furthermore, this international critical attention has not been unimportant in shaping evaluative responses at home, as public expressions of shame at being Irish in response to the death of Savita Halappanavar indicate (see Pollitt, 2012).

Ireland's moral revolution?

According to Appiah, long-standing moral and religious challenges to the association between the honour-coded practice and its moral standing is what ultimately leads to a moral revolution, when honour eventually shifts sides as its pursuit becomes itself a source of collectively felt shame (2010, p. 162). Has the pursuit of national honour through the continued operation of an almost absolute ban on abortion become a collective source of shame? Can we understand the passage of the Protection of Life During Pregnancy Act, 2013 in this light?

There is much in this act which continues to present problems for reproductive health and justice, not least the continued criminalisation of abortions which do not threaten the life of the mother. Indeed, the act confers no authority on women to decide the future of their pregnancies, concentrating this entirely in medical hands. Thus, it cannot simply be regarded as a progressive piece of legislation which revolutionises the status of women in relation to reproductive decision-making.

However, there are a number of noteworthy features in this legislation. Firstly, the framing of arguments during the formal political debates in the Oireachtas (Ireland's parliament) was carefully managed to foreground matters of health and law, while curtailing the more morally based arguments of interest groups (Joint Oireachtas Committee on Health and Children, 2013). This can be viewed as an attempt to de-moralise political debate, following a relatively long-established trend (Smyth 2005, pp. 125–30). Indeed, this de-moralisation went further, as it sought to move the debate away from understanding abortion law as necessarily adjudicating between conflicting rights, and instead to frame abortion access solely as a health issue (Ferree et al., 2002, pp. 105–8). As the 'Explanatory Notes' to the publication of the General

Scheme of the bill introducing the legislation put it,

> Essentially the decision to be reached is not so much a balancing of the competing rights – rather, it is a clinical assessment as to whether the mother's life, as opposed to her health, is threatened by a real and substantial risk that can only be averted by a termination of pregnancy. (Government of Ireland, 2013, p. 12)

This effort to re-frame abortion as a health matter in this way constitutes one important signal that the long-established association between the 'pro-life' abortion ban and national honour has been broken, not least in reaction to the death of Savita Halappanavar. This effort to disassociate abortion law from moral views and arguments, as well as from rights politics, reflects the wider reversal in the status of the ban.

A second important sign of disconnection between national honour and the abortion ban is the growing phenomenon, beginning in the wake of the D case in the mid-2000s, of women speaking or writing publicly about their experiences of abortion (de Barra, 2007; Smyth, 2008), something that was unimaginable during the 1980s, or even following the X case in the early 1990s (e.g. Irish Women's Abortion Support Group, 1988; Sheridan, 2012a; 2012b). Ferree et al. (2002) argue that the inclusion of personal narratives in political debate about a morally contested practice such as abortion is a sign of a thriving, participatory democratic culture, where ordinary citizens are sought out by journalists and included in the debate, in their own words. Unlike a culture where an honour code operates to generate conformity to a single moral norm, this feature of public talk instead assumes moral diversity and disagreement. The growth of this phenomenon in Ireland is an important signal of a shift in this more morally pluralist direction.

The third important sign of a reversal in the honour status of the abortion ban is the government's apparent sensitivity to how members of the international community evaluate the moral quality of its actions, particularly in relation to human rights and abortion access. This may be one important driver of the official effort to move the debate away from matters of rights towards a more welfare-oriented health frame. This sensitivity has been sharpened by the death of Savita Halappanavar, which occurred just prior to the state's election in November 2012 to the United Nation's Human Rights Council for the first time (RTÉ

News, 2012). Furthermore, the state's response to the judgement of the European Court of Human Rights in the 2010 case of *A, B, C v. Ireland* (ECHR, 2032) was placed under the 'enhanced supervision' procedure of the Council of Europe over the three years it took to respond with legislation, and the council had expressed concern at the delays involved (Irish Family Planning Association, 2013). Weighed against the potential value of achieving international honour for its defence of human rights, the government was even prepared to withstand anti-abortion invective, for example when Taoiseach Enda Kenny was labelled 'Ireland's first pro-abortion Prime Minister' (Ertlelt, 2013) by a lobby group in the US.

CONCLUSION

The slowly loosening grip of the abortion ban on the collective moral imagination during the two decades since the X case, culminating in the death of Savita Halappanavar and the introduction of legislation providing for limited abortion access, suggests that the pursuit of honour in this way has finally become a source of shame, not least as the operation of the ban has violated the Irish nation's reputation in the wider world.

Nevertheless, efforts to portray the nation as 'pro-life' do continue, albeit in a more muted form than in the early days of the abortion ban. For instance, official justifications of the Protection of Life During Pregnancy Bill relied on 'pro-life' arguments, namely that the intention was to 'protect the life of the mother and her unborn child' (O'Regan, 2013). The bill was defended as merely introducing procedural changes to pregnant women's health care, as required by the decision of the European Court of Human Rights (Government of Ireland, 2013, p. 16). The act confers no right to abortion for women in the state, even in circumstances of rape, fatal foetal abnormality, or risk to health. Furthermore, seizures of abortion-inducing medication at the borders continue, although at a much-reduced rate (Gartland, 2013).

The introduction of a legislative framework which provides for legal abortion in Ireland, albeit in very limited and highly medicalised circumstances, is not unimportant. The ways in which this legislation has been justified does suggest a change in the official perception of the nation-state's position in the international honour world, which it is committed to belonging to. This is a context where norms of gender and sexual equality are often used to distinguish 'Us', enlightened democracies, from 'Them', authoritarian regimes, something which the US invasion of Afghanistan clearly demonstrated (Cloud, 2004). There is a much-diminished sense that the abortion ban provides a primary source of national honour in a liberal, secular world. In fact it has been a repeated source of shame.

15

After Savita: migrant m/others and the politics of birth in Ireland

RONIT LENTIN

O N 14 NOVEMBER 2012 the *Irish Times* reported the death from septicaemia and E. coli on 28 October in University Hospital Galway of seventeen-weeks pregnant Indian dentist, Savita Halappanavar. Her husband, Praveen, says they asked repeatedly for a termination after her amniotic fluids had broken but were denied because the foetal heartbeat was still present and because, they were told, Ireland is 'a Catholic country'. Her death rekindled Ireland's ongoing abortion saga, even though this was not abortion. Halappanavar was miscarrying and her foetus had no chance of surviving. Because the neck of the womb was open, there was an opportunity for bugs to travel into the womb, spreading infection and causing shock and multi-organ failure, leading to her death (Houston, 2012). Halappanavar's mistreatment, the latest episode in Ireland's (bio)politics of birth, was described by the coroner as a 'medical misadventure', by a Health Information and Quality Authority (HIQA) report as due to serious 'clinical mismanagement', and by her husband as 'horrendous, barbaric and inhumane' (Cullen and Holland, 2013a; 2013b).

Savita Halappanavar's death deeply shocked Irish society, rekindling the abortion debate and renewing demands for the long-promised legislation regarding the equal right to life of the unborn and the mother, as voted for in a 1983 abortion constitutional referendum; it also strengthened Ireland's 'pro-life' movement's resolve to oppose any legislation for abortion. Both sides staged emotive demonstrations, with the pro-choice lobby using the potent slogan, 'Never again'. Her death also brought to mind the inadequacies of Ireland's maternity care. My argument in this chapter is that besides being a pregnant woman who died unnecessarily, Halappanavar was a migrant woman who died in the heteronormative racial state of Ireland (Goldberg, 2002; Luibhéid, 2013). I locate Halappanavar's story within the broader narrative of women's reproduction in Ireland, and within the recent history of casting migrant m/others' birthing practices as threatening the 'integrity of Irish citizenship'.

Ireland has a long history of maltreating birthing women. Apart from several women whose babies died as a result of Ireland's illiberal abortion laws (Holland, 2012), the Irish government is only now considering compensating 200 survivors of the 1,500 women who in the 1960s underwent symphysiotomy (sawing a labouring woman's pubic bone in half to open the birth canal that left the majority permanently injured, with incontinence and difficulties walking) (Griffin, 2013). Between 1974 and 1998, obstetrician, Michael Neary, performed 129 needless caesarean hysterectomies in Our Lady of Lourdes Hospital in Drogheda before he was struck off by the Medical Council. By 2013 some of Neary's victims had still not been included in a government compensation scheme (O'Regan, 2013). And in 2010, another pregnant migrant woman, Bimbo Onanuga, died of cardiac arrest after being induced with the controversial ulcer medication Misoprostol, following the death of her foetus in the womb in Dublin's Rotunda maternity hospital (Naughton, 2013). However, her death did not receive significant public attention, probably because, unlike Halappanavar, her pregnant African body was the epitome of illegality, a narrative employed before the 2004 'Citizenship Referendum', as argued below.

Historically, Ireland's biopolitics of birth involved incarcerating thousands of 'fallen women' in Magdalene laundries run by religious orders between 1922 and 1996 with full knowledge of the state in what Ireland's premier called in his public apology 'a cruel and pitiless

Ireland' (*Irish Times*, 2013). In 2004, responding to moral panic about migrant women 'childbearing against the state' (Luibhéid, 2004), the government held a constitutional referendum that resulted in depriving migrant children of *jus soli* citizenship entitlement, and migrant m/others of residency entitlement. The intention was to banish migrant m/others from the remits of Irish citizenship, maintaining Ireland's racial homogeneity.

Because abortion dominated the debates following Savita Halappanavar's death, I begin by briefly outlining the ramifications of what became known as the X case, discussed elsewhere in this volume. I then make three interrelated arguments. Firstly, birthing Irish m/others have always been policed, controlled and abused. Secondly, as the racial state is also a 'state of exception' (Agamben, 2005), where minority and migrant populations are cast as what Giorgio Agamben calls *homo sacer* or 'bare life', at the mercy of sovereign power, birth and reproduction cast women in Ireland as *femina sacra*, devoid of state protection. Thirdly, I follow Eithne Luibhéid in arguing that Ireland's heteronormative regime centres the pregnant migrant as a figure of illegal immigration and combines with racism to shape the allocation of migrants' legal status (Luibhéid, 2013).

ABORTION IN IRELAND: THE X CASE AND ITS RAMIFICATIONS

Abortion had been illegal in Ireland since the British 1861 Offences against the Person Act, which remains on the Irish statute books (IFPA).[77] In 1983, the anti-abortion 'pro-life' camp initiated a constitutional referendum to tighten Ireland's anti-abortion legislation. The initiative backfired: after a bitterly contested campaign, 54 per cent of the electorate voted in favour of inserting into the Constitution article 40.3.3 that guaranteed the equal right to life of the unborn and the mother. Having discursively controlled women's reproduction by referring to 'women' as 'mothers' and 'foetuses' as 'babies' (Smyth, 1992a, p. 8), this amendment inadvertently facilitated the 1992 X case, when a fourteen-year-old girl, raped by a neighbour, was prevented from leaving Ireland to obtain an abortion in Britain. An Garda Siochána (Irish police) referred the case to the High Court, which issued an injunction against the journey, later reversed by the Supreme Court, which ruled that as X was reportedly suicidal, she was entitled to an abortion in Ireland.[78] Ailbhe Smyth writes about the X case:

> Women in Ireland are living in a police state ... the reproductive activities of women in Ireland are being subjected to a process of 'regulation, discipline and control' carried out by the police in accordance with state policy and laws. (1992b, p. 138)

Abortion has always been central to defining Irishness. In 1992 there was another constitutional referendum when the population voted in favour of the right to travel outside the state for abortion and to obtain information on abortion services outside the state; also in 1992 the people of Ireland voted in favour of the Maastricht Treaty only due to the insertion of Protocol 17, which provided against abortion; and in 2002 Irish voters rejected another attempt by the pro-life camp to constitutionally outlaw abortion.

Yet Irish women continue to seek abortions abroad: according to British statistics, between 1980 and 2011 at least 152,061 women living in Ireland travelled to Britain for abortions. This is probably an under-estimation as some women would not give their Irish addresses. The numbers peaked in 2001 (6,673, including twelve under-fifteens); in 2011, 4,149 Irish women (including thirty-seven under-sixteens) sought abortions in the UK; additionally, between 2005 and 2009, 1,470 women from Ireland sought abortions in the Netherlands.[79] It is important to remember that abortion is both a class and a race issue: having an abortion in the UK costs about €1,000 – many women can ill-afford it. Furthermore, asylum seekers have to apply for visas and some have been told that if they travel for abortion, they may forfeit their asylum application. Due to cost and legal difficulties, health workers have been detecting an increase in the number of asylum seekers resorting to illegal abortions in Ireland (Barron, 2009).

Had the Irish government legislated after the X case, Savita Halappanavar might arguably not have died. It was her death, as much as pressure from Europe, that brought home to the Irish government the urgency of legislating for abortion in Ireland, twenty-one years after the X case. In December 2012, after a strong reprimand by the Council of Europe, the government announced plans to introduce legislation to finally make abortion legal in certain circumstances. After lengthy emotive debates between the so-called 'pro-life' and 'pro-choice' camps, on July 2013, twenty-one years after the X case, the Dáil (Irish parliament) finally passed the minimal Protection of Life During Pregnancy Act 2013 on a vote of 127 to 31, guaranteeing the equal right to life of the unborn and the mother, though not making abortion freely available in Ireland (Holland, 2013a). Though abortion, like other 'unspeakable' aspects of female sexuality and sexual behaviour (Smyth, 1992b, pp. 143–4), is no longer a taboo topic, Ailbhe Smyth had argued already in 1992 that 'reproductive freedom' for women in Ireland remains problematic in a society where only m/others are 'real women'.

The Republic of Ireland has a long history of pitching 'good (Catholic, married) mothers' versus 'bad (unmarried) mothers' (Meaney, 2005). However, Savita Halappanavar died, not merely as a woman whose reproductive practices are controlled by Irish patriarchy, but as a migrant woman, planning to give birth in a country that only eight years previously legislated against migrant children's access to citizenship. The othering of migrant women's pregnant bodies, as emerged from the debates surrounding the 2004 Citizenship Referendum, made gendered (black) bodies central to the re-articulation of Irishness as white supremacy (Lentin and McVeigh, 2006, p. 98). Since mothering carries a property of otherness, I frame migrant women as m/others, denoting their otherness (Lentin, 2004).

A MIGRANT DIED

In the 1990s, Ireland, historically marked by emigration, became an immigration destination, resulting from the economic boom euphemistically called 'the Celtic Tiger'. In 1996 Ireland reached its 'migration turning point' when in-migration exceeded emigration for the first time (Ruhs, 2005, p. 109).[80] Since the establishment of the Irish Free State in 1922, all people born on the island of Ireland were granted automatic *jus soli* citizenship, also enshrined in, the 1937 Constitution and the 1956/1986 Nationality and Citizenship acts. Prior to 2004 a series of Supreme Court cases granted, and then denied, migrant parents of Irish citizen children the right of residence to give 'care and company' to their citizen children. In 2003, anxious about migrant m/others birthing children in Ireland, the minister for justice removed the process whereby migrant parents could apply to remain on the grounds of having a citizen child. This resulted in some 11,500 migrant parents becoming candidates for deportation. Despite robust lobbying, deportations went ahead, including at least twenty citizen children (Lentin and McVeigh, 2006, p. 53).

Following the tradition of intersecting gender and nation and entrusting women with the national 'common good', the government's anti-immigration rhetoric focused on migrant (particularly asylum seeker) m/others subverting the integrity of Ireland's immigration, asylum and citizenship regimes. A Department of Justice briefing document described migrant m/others being 'pregnant on arrival' in large numbers, intent on giving birth to secure Irish citizenship for their children, and residency for themselves (Lentin and McVeigh, 2006, p. 103). The government's claim was that migrants with no legitimate basis for their presence in Ireland entered by claiming asylum and then, through birthing an Irish citizen child, transformed themselves into legal residents and potentially future citizens (Luibhéid, 2013, p. 17). The 2004 Citizenship Referendum was the government's response; 78.9 per cent voted in favour of *jus sanguinis* citizenship, granting citizenship only to children born in Ireland, one of whose parents is a citizen.

FEMINA SACRA IN IRELAND'S HETERONORMATIVE RACIAL STATE

Goldberg (2002) argues that all modern nation-states are racial states intent on constructing homogeneity. I argue that the racial state is also, as Agamben (2005) argues, a 'state of exception' in which the sovereign reduces some population categories to 'bare life' (*homo sacer*) whose destiny is legally determined by sovereign power, which puts itself above the law (Agamben, 1995, p. 10). The racial state employs governmental technologies such as constitutions, border controls, population censuses, and the education and welfare systems to construct national homogeneity and categorise the population, often suspending the law and constructing unwanted categories of people as 'bare life'. Agamben's *homo sacer* is an excluded being, whose life is devoid of value; therefore killing or deporting a *homo sacer* is not a punishable offence as his/her life is deemed to be outside the remit of the nation. The racial state is also always gendered. However, as Agamben does not dwell on the gendered meanings of *homo sacer*, I engender his 'homo sacer' and the link he makes between birth and nation, deriving from *nascere* – to be born (1995, p. 128).

In Ireland the link between birth and nation is palpably obvious through explicitly positioning Irish women as the carriers of the nation's honour and 'common good'. Thus, article 41.2.1 of the Constitution of Ireland declares that 'the State recognises that by her *life* within the home, woman gives to the State a support without which the common good cannot be achieved'. Thus too, generations of women considered sexually deviant – particularly women who became pregnant out of wedlock – were committed by their families and incarcerated in Magdalene laundries run by religious orders, where they performed unpaid slave labour, often for years. This was part of a culture of incarceration: Ireland locked up one in 100 of its citizens in Magdalene laundries, industrial schools, mental hospitals and 'mother and baby' homes, where women pregnant out of wedlock were locked up and forced to give their babies up for adoption (O'Sullivan and O'Donnell, 2012). As O'Toole (2013) argues, the confinement of Ireland's 'flighty' daughters benefited families and society, and created deep habits of collusion, evasion and adaptation, which is why Irish people largely did not question the targeting of migrant m/others and voted in large numbers for changing Ireland's citizenship laws.

Examining what she calls 'the making of the illegal migrant', Eithne Luibhéid posits heteronormativity as enabling white supremacist ideologies to use the state to regulate sexuality. Thus, 'sexual subalterns in a heteronormative order usually include not just diverse lesbians and gay men, but also poor and racialised women who birth children'. This analysis, she argues, invites us to address the impact not only of sexuality, gender, race and class, but also legal status in creating complex regimes of privilege and subalternity (Luibhéid, 2013, p. 5).

As the body of woman creates and contains birth-nations, nation-states are moved to strictly control female sexuality and in Ireland 'womanhood and motherhood are represented as synonymous realities' (Smyth, 1992, p. 143). Moreover, 'women's heterosexualised bodies easily become sites of knowledge production that is used for immigration control' (Lubhéid, 2013, p. 48). Just as Irish women's pregnant bodies were sites of incarceration and control, migrant women 'were reduced to their vaginas and pregnant bellies ... The minister's planned solution ... involved reconfiguring normative heterosexuality along more obviously racialised lines and as an explicit technology of border control' (Luibheid, 2013, p. 52). Targeting sexually active Irish women was the preamble to banning and controlling migrant m/others as the producers of future generations of the racially 'inferior', leading me to posit migrant m/others as the female version of *homo sacer – femina sacra*.

It is important to caution, however, that the concept of 'bare life' – *homo sacer* or *femina sacra* – is problematic, as Walters argues, as racialised / gendered / colonised subjects are never just 'bare life': 'vesting subaltern subjects with the mark of exception reterritorialises their underprivileged place in language', and imagines them as 'subjects to whom all manners of things are done ... but who are rarely agents in their own rights' (Walters, 2008, p. 188). In view of this critique, it is worth remembering that migrant m/others are never just the victims of racial state govern-mentalities, as the history of campaigning against their positioning as *femina sacra* by the Irish state attests. Thus in 2003, reacting to some 11,500 migrant parents of Irish citizen children receiving deportation letters, an initiative by AkiDwA – the African and Migrant Women's Network[81] – led to the establishment of the Coalition against Deporta-tion of Irish Children (CADIC) campaigning to reverse the decision according to which migrant parents of Irish citizen children were no longer granted the right of residency. In 2005, after a two-year campaign, and six months after the government had won the Citizenship Referendum, the minister for justice announced new administrative arrangements for migrant parents of citizen children born before January 2005 to apply for residency in Ireland (Lentin and McVeigh, 2006, pp. 53–4). However, the very choice of some migrant women to birth children in Ireland while it was still possible to obtain citizenship for the children and residency for their parents is an illustration of agency, enacted by m/others aiming to overcome their racial otherness.

Migrant m/otherhood, just like Irish m/otherhood, is the lynchpin of the intersection of gender and nation. Furthermore, the positioning of migrant m/others as both *femina sacra* and active agents for change is at the heart of the intersection of victimhood and agency. This is illustrated, inter alia, by the CADIC campaign and by other campaigns led by migrant women in Ireland – most notably AkiDwA's success in bringing about a bill outlawing female genital mutilation in Ireland[82] – but also other initiatives in advocacy, social policy and support services for migrant women. The intersection of victimhood and agency is also exemplified by the successful campaign for the long-promised (even though ultimately limited) legislation on abortion in the wake of Savita Halappanavar's tragic, but avoidable death; some ramifications of which I turn to in the conclusion.

Conclusion

The HIQA report on the death of Savita Halappanavar identified 'significant deficiencies in the care of critically ill women in Ireland's maternity hospitals' and pointed to thirteen 'missed opportunities' that, had they been identified and acted upon, could have resulted in a different outcome for Halappanavar (Holland, 2013c). As former HSE regional manager Jackie Jones argues, it is time to reform the medical model of maternity care. Despite a new 'National Strategy Plan for Maternity Services' launched by the minister for health, Jones cautions that the difficulties in cutting through 'power and complacency will ensure things stay as they are for years to come' (Jones, 2013).

This is interesting in view of the claim by two separate ministers for justice (John O'Donoghue and Michael McDowell) around the time of the 2004 Citizenship Referendum that the initiative was necessitated by migrant m/others overcrowding the Dublin maternity hospitals (even though this was later rebuked), blaming migrant m/others for the short-comings of the system, creating what Balibar (1991, pp. 217–18) calls 'crisis racism'.

Furthermore, the Health Service Executive's official report on Halappanavar's death found that there was 'an overemphasis by hospital staff on her unviable foetus and an underemphasis on her deteriorating health' (Holland, 2013b). I argue that Savita Halappanavar's health and her very life were sacrificed to her foetus's heartbeat and she was thus *femina sacra*, who was 'made die' in order to 'make live' her unborn foetus (Foucault, 2003), her life sacrificed at the altar of Ireland's church-inspired strict abortion regime that privileges the life of the unborn over the life of the m/other.

As a legal migrant, Savita Halappanavar did not decide to have a baby in Ireland in order to subvert the integrity of Irish citizenship – after the 2004 referendum this option was no longer open. However, her death, which may be regarded as enabling the life of those considered 'truly Irish' (white, Catholic, settled), tipped the balance of Ireland's anti-abortion regime, forcing the government to table the long-awaited legislation on abortion.

What happened to Savita Halappanavar illustrates the complex ways in which processes of globalisation and migration and the sudden presence of non-ethnic Irish citizens has changed the relationship between the state and its m/others and created conditions for understanding Ireland as a heteronormative racial state, where Irish anxieties about m/others who disrupt 'nationalist heterosexuality' become the foundation of 're-nationalising the nation' (Luibhéid, 2004). It also reminds us that migrant m/others are never only *femina sacra* at the mercy of sovereign power: in the very act of 'childbearing against the state' (Luibhéid, 2004), they demonstrate agency and resistance, alas, no longer available to Savita Halappanavar.

16

Water, Water Everywhere ... exploring education geographies of abortion

AIDEEN QUILTY

IT IS THE 1980S, a time 'routinely viewed as a period of moral divisiveness in the light of the confrontational constitutional campaigns on abortion and divorce' (O'Sullivan, 2005, p. 307). I am in secondary school in the Presentation Convent, Waterford City, one year after the High Court rules that 'The availability, to women in Ireland, of information on abortion, outside the State is in breach of the Constitution, as under the 1983 amendment it undermines the right of the child to life'. And in this place of learning, this educational institution, I experienced my first encounter with abortion as an abomination, a horror that no 'good' student, 'good' girl, would ever inflict on herself, her unborn, her family, her God. I was one of thousands of young girls in state-sanctioned, yet Catholically owned and managed, schools subjected to the 'Abortion Video' as we called it – and the problem was that though I recall the horror, the black bags, what I don't recall was the debate, any debate, any conversation. This was the story, the only story. It was a truth, The Truth, told in a classroom full of impressionable teenagers, girls, where there was no option other than to stay and watch what I now understand to have been part of the pro-life propaganda machine.

For me personally the sadness and intense anger of realising what I, and the 100 or so other Catholic girls in the 'Pres' that year had been subjected to was an abuse of institutional, religious power, came only some years later. And it came in another educational place, another religiously infused place of power and control – this time involving control of our minds. The place: St Patrick's Teacher Training College, Drumcondra where I was training to be a primary schoolteacher. I didn't know quite so fully at the time that in fact I was being trained, some might say inculcated, into becoming a Catholic Teacher.

It was there in that place of religious power and influence that I started to see, to understand, that there was something incongruous about a system that called on Dewey and Freire and Piaget, to teach us about educating minds (fostering independence of thought, through opening minds to multiple positions, multiple stories) and the 'Pat's' environment that made certain conversations, some people's stories, all but impossible. Sexuality. Abortion. These were invisibilised. I was in St Pat's College in my final year in 1992. The X case was happening somewhere else, to someone else. The questions I had looming were nowhere near being answered in the Catholic bosom of that particular place.

And so it was that seeking answers and a place to ask questions I first encountered the Women's Studies Programme in UCD (then called Women's Education Research and Resource Centre, WERRC) and Ailbhe Smyth. Lacking the science-fiction-like innovation that would become Google, I discovered this place towards the back of the, *Irish Times* in the 'What's on Today' section ... all of this attesting to age and years and change and yes, unfortunately, stasis. Off I went to hear someone blatantly, boldly speaking about abortion in a packed lecture hall in the Arts Building of UCD, not as an abomination but as a woman's right. And in this other educational place of UCD, this woman was not only telling the story another way, offering another one of multiple possible truths, truths given legitimacy and validation within this 'university' place, she was also leading me, though I didn't know it then, to another way of teaching.

And so my third place reflective of a 'now reality': one of adults and feminist theory and women in a different sort of learning place. Where real lived lives and stories and memories of places (physical, emotional, joyous, tragic) are all present.

And in these learning and educational places the pro-choice politics and writing of bell hooks (2000), some might say role model feminist educator, and her explicit call that you cannot be feminist and therefore anti-sexist and not be pro-choice, is given breath, consideration and space. Here are spaces in which dissent, disagreement, insight, empathy, along with new stories and potential new positions, might emerge. And we all shared a moment in November 2012 just after Savita Halappanavar's death – we were referencing *The Abortion Papers* (1992) – and we experienced the profoundly frustrating moment of collective recognition that reading much of the excerpts blind, we might easily have been in 1992, 1993, that place of past, of memory. Yet we were here, now, with deep sadness at the loss of a life, and the clear evidence that this should not have been the case. In another place, perhaps, this would have been a different story. In another place, else-where, this loss of life would not have been tolerated. In another place, this woman might not have paid the ultimate price of exposing, albeit unwittingly, a legacy of disregard, a legacy of silencing and denying Irish women's reproductive needs, rights and choices.

INTRODUCTION

It is the relationship between the subject and place of abortion I wish to explore in this chapter where 'subject' infers both the topic of abortion taught within the context of the 'subject' of religion as in the opening story and the woman as 'subject' who has had or may have an abortion at sometime in her life. In an attempt to explore what I believe to be an important relationship between the subject of abortion and our education institutions, I found myself returning to my particular educational places as I remembered imposed, biased, sometimes brave, controversial stories of abortion.

Why this return to place? There are multiple analytic frames or interrogative lenses through which we seek to challenge historic and contemporary discourses and practices in relation to abortion: mine, in foregrounding questions and considerations of place, might be called a spatial or geographical frame. Reflecting my subjective positionality, it is also feminist – as it is educational. This framing reflects a prioritising of the place of place within our efforts to make sense of our worlds, personal, political, ethical: we might locate these places as part of the broader geographies of our lives. I am not the first person to argue for this particular disciplinary fusion where we actively set out to mine the geographical terrain, its concepts, theories, methods, as it relates to, and impacts upon, our understanding of the world. There is much to guide us in this work. Such thinking can be seen to reflect a broader 'spatial turn' or the importation of geographical terms and concepts into, and across, a host of other disciplinary areas (see McDowell, 1999; Blunt, 2007; Crang and Thrift, 2003; Hubbard et al., 2005). The attraction of the spatial within the human sciences has resulted in volumes of work being generated, as Blunt observes:

> More than ever before, scholars working in other disciplines in the humanities are thinking and writing in explicitly spatial terms, most notably in terms of imaginative geographies and the multiple and contested spaces of identity, which are often articulated through spatial images such as mobility, location, borderlands, exile, home. (Blunt, 2007, pp. 75–6)

PLACES OF ABORTION

The lived reality of abortion in Ireland is that quite obviously it is drenched in questions of place, or more appropriately the place of elsewhere. For women who have told and shared their stories of leaving, travelling, having to go somewhere else, as women who simply wanted to have choice and control over their bodies, their stories are always about their bodies in places: the boat, plane, taxi, the clinic, a sense of place that makes you feel fear, anxiety, aloneness, where you feel relieved, supported, lighter. We can understand place in this context as space invested with meaning in the context of power and what begins as undifferentiated space becomes place as we get to know it better and endow it with value (see Cresswell, 2004; Li-Fu Tuan, 2007; Massey, 2004; Philo, 2003). Importantly, this relational understanding 'prioritizes analysis of how space is constituted and given meaning through human endeavour' as people at once constitute, and are constituted by, the very spaces they inhabit (Hubbard et al., 2005, pp. 13–14). Beverley Skeggs' work reveals the centrality of place awareness in the ways in which we are placed into systems of social classification or positions. She suggests that 'recognition of how one is positioned is central to the processes of subjective construction' with some living 'their social locations with unease' (Skeggs, 1997, p. 4) and others being privileged through these same positionings. It seems clear that by virtue of living in Ireland, there is a privileging of other women's bodies over ours whose state and legislature imposes restrictions on how we might make choices for ourselves in the very construction of our-selves.

In this way, place extends beyond architecture, beyond the physical structures that delineate it, becoming both a way of knowing and of being in the world (Creswell, 2004). This epistemological and ontological potential of place has particular resonance educationally. And it speaks to my reflections on educational places as they have impacted on and spoken to my understandings and experience of abortion as concept, as practice, as sin, as contested, as choice.

In considering abortion within an Irish context, its marginal position, its exported reality, its temporary exiling of bodies, the relevance of this spatial turn might seem obvious. Adrienne Rich has described the body as the 'geography closest in' (1984, p. 212) and in this sense we might consider body geographies as integral to how we come to know the subject of abortion. And yet our geographies, the ways in which we inhabit place, constitute and are at once constituted by place, are anything but obvious. Our subjective realities are marked by their specificities, by difference as well as shared moments. Our being in place is complex, fluid and unstable. Holloway and Hubbard, reflecting the complexity and organic meaning of place, note:

> Places always have multiple identities. Different social groups engage with places in very different ways, so that places can be experienced in different ways according to person's gender, social class, ethnicity, and so on. (Holloway and Hubbard, 2001, p. 112)

STORIES OF ABORTION

The abortion 'place' too has multiple identities, an interesting, complex geography, a place and at once a no-place or place-less-ness within our national discourse. One of the reasons we know of the complex history of Irish women's relationship to abortion in Ireland is because women have chosen to tell and to share their stories so that greater understanding, empathy and choice might become a reality, as the stories held within this collection attest. And these are stories of bodies having to negotiate, unfortunately and in often profoundly distressing ways, other places, as they carve out new geographies, new biographies. Our experiences of 'the same place' cannot be assumed to reflect the same experiences, emotions, stories of all those present as so wonderfully reflected in Melissa Thompson's film *Like a Ship in the Night*.[83] Our stories, like our geographies, are subjectively articulated and given meaning differently across time and place. As Cousins argues, our subjective positioning means that 'our knowledge of the world is always mediated and interpreted from a particular stance and an available language' (Cousins, 2010, p.10). It is often the case that this mediation and interpretation process happens through stories.

Unsurprisingly therefore, the abortion story in Ireland is comprised of multiple, often competing, voices, stories, observations and emotions. Reflecting this complex and contradictory reality of women's highly nuanced abortion experiences, Maya Pindyck suggests that 'bringing together all abortion narratives would most likely offer a messy, ideologically confusing assemblage' (2013, p. 46).[84] Nevertheless, as she goes on to argue, what this confusing assemblage manages to achieve is a rupturing of the 'life/choice binary which continues to dominate and thereby shape the subject of abortion' (2013, p. 46). Such a binaric lens can obfuscate the fluidity, temporality, sociality and emotionality characteristic of our body stories. Gill Valentine speaks to this in her observation of the body as that which:

> … marks a boundary between the self and other, both in a literal physiological sense but also in a social sense. It is a personal space. A sensuous organ, the site of pleasure and pain around which social definitions of wellbeing, illness, happiness and health are constructed. (Valentine, 2001, p. 15)

Social definitions of the body, as articulated for example through the state's moralistic and legalistic stories and definitions, continue to be written on women's reproductive bodies. And these constructions can result in Sara Ahmed's notion of discomfort, which she describes

> … as a feeling of disorientation: one's body feels out of place, awkward, unsettled … the sense of out-of-placeness and estrangement

involves an acute awareness of the surface of one's body, which appears *as* surface, when one cannot inhabit the social skin, which is mapped by some bodies, and not others. (Ahmed, 2004, p. 148)

Ahmed's writing on this feeling of discomfort references queer subjects, or queer bodies. We might also read this disorientation on and through the female body subject, the body that knows abortion and the places in which abortions happen and the disorientation associated with the return to a place which denies the presence of these particular female bodies, their emotions and their stories.

Stories matter, as do the places in which our stories unfold, are housed, are memories, are living as they involve transforming a lived experience into language and constructing a story about it drawing 'on taken-for-granted discourses and values circulating in a particular culture' (Riessman, 2008, p. 3). And as Burke and Jackson note these experiences, these stories, our personal biographies are heavily influenced by our relationships with place where not only 'individuals and structural conditions impact onto our identities, but so too do our roots and the routes that we tread' (Burke and Jackson, 2007, p. 120). And so often in our contemporary world such roots and routes reflect broader societal inequities. Wendy Luttrell observes that stories can serve to highlight such societal inequities:

People tell stories in ways that explain and justify social inequalities related to privilege, power, or respect as we, each in our own way, search for personal recognition and esteem in a society where some people count more than others. (Luttrell, 1997, p. xv)

POWER-KNOWLEDGE AND ABORTION

We might infer from Luttrell that some bodies count more than others. And a state that sends women elsewhere, beyond the various waters that surround this state, tells a story of neglect and a lack of importance, to the extent that we might interpret these actions as promoting the idea of a hierarchy of bodies where some women matter more within a nation state than others. For Foucault, such a hierarchy was related to the disciplining of bodies, 'a political anatomy of detail' (1991, p. 139), maintained through the meticulous attention to the 'little things', 'through the meticulousness of the regulations, the fussiness of the inspections, the supervision of the smallest fragment of life and of the body' (1991, p. 140) in the context of school, barracks, hospital or workshop. Within such disciplining tendencies there emerges a hierarchy of bodies where 'certain types of body are preferable to others as the result of power struggles between different groups, with the state seeking to impose its ideas about what was right and wrong by disciplining the body-subject' (in Hubbard et al., 2005, p. 107). Recalling my opening story, both the X case and Savita Halappanavar's experience within an Irish medical institution offer profoundly distressing examples of the body disciplined. A more subtle example might be read through the sustained disciplining of the student body and the student's body, within our education institutions through a series of powerful practices played out in, and through, space and ultimately through the control of knowledge as the opening story based on my educational experiences referenced.

I share the view of Hubbard et al. and that of many educationalists (including Armstrong, 2003; Apple, 1982, 1996; Burke, 2002; Pinar, 2004; Freire, 1979; Greene, 2005), that 'knowledge production is not a neutral and objective pursuit, but rather it is embedded in the practices and ideologies of its creators and the contexts within which they operate' (Hubbard et al., 2005, p. 10). This position challenges in concrete ways the notion of disembodied knowledge, recognising that knowledge is not neutral but always socially situated: there is no 'God's eye view', no 'knowledge from nowhere' (Haraway cited in Barr, 1999, p. 40). Context is clearly important because 'all geographic knowledges are situated, and location matters' (McKittrick and Peake, 2005, p. 43).

What is at stake here is the need for an expanded understanding of knowledge that moves beyond the assumption that knowledge is made through rational processes but that it is also produced at the intuitive level, involving feelings, emotion and subjectivity (Burke and Jackson, 2007, p. 151). Knowledge understood in this way cannot be devoid of the interplay of power relations understood through Foucault's power-knowledge nexus and played out educationally across a range of institutions. Rather, 'the rules and policies of any institution serve particular ends, embody particular values and meanings and have identifiable consequences for the actions and situations of the persons within or related to those institutions' (Young, 1990, p. 211). The rules or norms governing our educational institutions, these places of social-isation through processes of knowledge-making and circulation, are also heteronormative. They promote the culturally engrained notion that heterosexuality is the marker of normalcy against which queer differences in sex, sexuality, gender, desire and expressions are to be gauged and judged (Grace and Hill, 2004). Ahmed observes that the power of such social norms means that they 'not only have a way of disappearing from view, but may also be that which we do not consciously feel' (Ahmed, 2004, p. 148). Yet, such norms matter. This heteronormative educational culture has much to say/comment on the subject of abortion, both body subject and topic subject. Berlant and Warner (2000) argue, 'national heterosexuality is the mechanism by which a core national culture can be imagined as a sanitised space of sentimental feeling' (in Ahmed, 2004, p. 147). The heteronormative, in an Irish context, is imbricated so powerfully with what might be termed a 'dogma-norm', a catholically and religiously infused multispatial context, it could be argued that it results in a failure to move substan-tively from a position where not only does sexual pleasure 'remain tied in some way to the fantasy of being reproductive' (Ahmed, 2004, p. 163) but that reproductive 'transgressions', including abortion, become markers of 'badness', of 'shame', tied as they are to norm-breaking practices. While these lessons are pervasive across society, they gain a particular articulation within an Irish education context. As Fintan O'Toole notes:

> Ireland, almost alone among developed societies, allows basic social services to be run by a secretive, hierarchical organisation that has repeatedly been seen to regard itself as accountable to no one – not even to the law. (O'Toole, *Irish Times*, 6 June 2009)

THE SUBJECT OF ABORTION

Currently in Ireland, 96 per cent of primary schools are owned and under the patronage of religious denominations, with approximately 90 per cent of these state-sanctioned schools owned and run under the patronage of the Catholic Church.[85] O'Sullivan observes that given this majority ownership by religious authorities we might understand the Irish education system as 'largely an aided rather than state system'

(2005, p. 212). Nevertheless, for parents seeking school opportunities for their children, unless in possession of significant financial resources and school choice afforded by city or major suburban locations, the reality is that this aided system becomes synonymous with a de facto system of state provision. The implications of this situation within an increasingly multi-ethnic, multi-denominational, non-denominational Ireland are aggravated further when placed in relation to the religious exemption clause known as Section 37 (1), which allows for discrimination against teachers whose lifestyle is perceived as undermining the religious ethos of the school.

Given this reality, the capacity to silence particular subjects such as abortion on the one hand, while providing guided moral teaching in relation to abortion on the other, remain distinct possibilities. O'Sullivan (2005, pp. 206–11) highlights two particular Irish education programme interventions that support this position: the Stay Safe programme for primary schools introduced nationally to schools in the early 1990s; and the Relationships and Sexuality Education (RSE) programme (1996). Importantly this latter programme was developed following the establishment of an Expert Advisory Group in 1994 following what Tom Inglis described as the 'grotesque, bizarre, unprecedented and, most of all, unacceptable discovery of two dead babies within a month' in that year (Inglis, 1998, p. 1). Both programmes generated significant debate and criticism, much of it generated from religious bodies, as the following response to the RSE programme in Catholic schools – A Resource for Teachers and Boards of Management (1995) – highlights:

> The Catholic school in the formulation of its policy should reflect Catholic moral teaching on sexual matters. Even more fundamentally, it needs to be specific in excluding approaches which are inconsistent with the foundations of Catholic moral thought. (cited in O'Sullivan, 2005, p. 209)

There are unfortunately many contemporary examples to highlight knowledge/subject inclusion and exclusion based directly on religious dogma. As detailed in *The Guardian*, a UK school in 2012 facilitated the Society for the Protection of Unborn Children (SPUC) in their use of 'abortion' videos as part of their broader campaign for a ban on what they describe as 'explicit' sex education in schools.[86] Sadly this is occurring decades after my own experience, highlighting critical questions as to what constitutes important knowledge, questions of curriculum, questions of power.

As we look closer to home we note a similar abuse of this 'power-knowledge nexus' played out in a Dublin Catholic primary school (one of the 90 per cent) in June 2013. As reported by Conor Feehan, children as young as five were given leaflets promoting a 'Vigil for Life' rally to be held in Dublin on 8 June 2013.[87] Sparking outrage from parents, the leaflet featured a photograph of a woman and baby on one side with the message 'National Vigil for Life' and on the reverse it stated: 'Right now our Government proposes dangerous and unjust abortion legislation. Abortion for a suicide threat means abortion on request.' As reported through the blogspot Clerical Whispers, the chairman of the school, Mr Eddie Shaw, a former spokesman for Cardinal Desmond Connell and whose idea the leaflet distribution was, resigned.[88] However, as one parent observed, by way of explanation Mr Shaw said that he should have put the leaflets in an envelope, which is surely to miss the point entirely!

One could read this as the politically motivated and utterly unacceptable exploitation of children. The scaremongering vis-à-vis the then proposed Protection of Life During Pregnancy Act (PLDPA) is also evident. While the coalition government, as boasted by the then minister for health, James Reilly, did not become the seventh government to leave the issue of abortion untouched, the legislative intervention fell far short of what was and continues to be required. As Cora Sherlock (9 January 2014) has commented, this particular coalition government 'will be remembered for having introduced a piece of legislation in direct contravention of international medical and psychiatric evidence, and do not have the bravery to realise they were wrong'.[89] Suicide on request this legislation can simply never be.

DEBATING ABORTION

There is a danger that this conversation about the no-place for propaganda material in primary schools could be hijacked and used to dismiss the important role of our education system in effectively providing age-appropriate, sensitively taught, unselfconscious sex education: a sex-education programme motivated by a desire to inform, and thereby protect, our children and teenagers, through the liberation of knowledge about bodies and sexuality and relationships and reproduction that eschews the life/choice binary. Pindyck, writing from a US context, outlines the ideological divide that seems to surround the debate as to whether or not the subject of abortion should be included within a broader sex education curriculum. On the one hand there is the 'dominant conservative position' that promotes the absence of abortion from sex education, a position guided by political, religious, moral and cultural beliefs, all of which converge around the idea that teenagers should not be having sex. On the other hand there is a more common-sense, liberal viewpoint that suggest the silencing of abortion in schools is the 'consequence of an oppressive taboo that leaves teenage girls uninformed and silenced' (Pindyck, 2013, p. 47).

The power of the religiously infused power-knowledge nexus, characteristic of many of our schools, should not, however, be under-stood to reduce school subjects to Foucault's 'docile bodies', to the realm of powerlessness or deterministic control. As Brookfield notes, it would be a 'mistake to think of power in wholly negative terms, as only being exercised to keep people in line' (2005, p. 47). Youdell makes a similar point, noting that within the power-knowledge nexus of the school as a disciplinary institution we 'cannot automatically infer that students (and teachers) are successfully or permanently rendered docile bodies – resistances, dissonances and ambiguities (however momentary, quickly recuperated, mundane) can also be found' (2006, p. 59). An example includes the teachers who 'forgot' to hand out the propaganda leaflets, or blatantly refused to do so in the Dublin school cited above. Thus, though the mechanisms of power discipline are strong, there is also a productive force, a dynamism which Brookfield defines as 'a sense of possessing power – of having the energy, intelligence, resources and opportunity to act in the world' and which he names as a precon-dition of intentional social change (Brookfield, 2005, p. 47).

And yet it seems that challenging power imbalances, knowledge gaps and abuses within our educational institutions remains problematic. O'Sullivan draws on O'Carroll's (1991) observations in the context of the abortion referendum debate of 1983 to highlight the inadequacy of the public sphere in supporting public engagement and informed dialogue vis-à-vis the cultural politics of education. Their relevance, some thirty years later, speaks its own story:

The argument was tightly locked into the occasion with no room for manoeuvre, and protagonists found themselves reduced to declaiming their truths or abusing their opponents. This tendency is also an example of a consequence of the failure to externalise thought ... Ideas are seldom if ever used apart from the concrete occasions to which they refer. The result of this tendency is a limitation of the growth of the public sphere in many domains. (cited in O'Sullivan, 2005, p. 554)

To work towards a more informed, open engagement with the reality of power-knowledge dynamics and processes within our educational institutions, William Pinar is useful. He calls for a process of intellectual engagement through what he refers to as 'complicated conversations', which represent 'a curriculum in which academic knowledge, subjectivity and society are inextricably linked' (Pinar, 2004, p. 11). This is a challenging task, one that demands from us new stories, new conversations, all the more so as we consider the proposed relinquishing of Church educational power and school ownership and the concomitant changes to the very structure and nature of educational provision and, therefore, knowledge.

CONCLUSION

We are embedded and enmeshed within the stories and story structures we have created, and which have been created around us. (Bolton, 2006, p. 206)

Perhaps it is finally time for new abortion stories, new ways of considering the state's responsibilities to all citizens, all of the state's subjects, to an education process and place that acknowledges openly the profound relationship between power, knowledge and place. Grunewald reinforces the need for such a 'rich and badly needed conversation about the relationship between the places we call schools and the places where we live our lives' (Grunewald, 2003, p. 624). This would presume, however, an educational system centred on ensuring the critical skills and capacities necessary for students to pave their own way and to reach decisions about their bodies, their lives, their worlds. Such an educational world would be one free from the dictates of dogma. Perhaps this might wilfully support Meaney's desire, over two decades ago, that women's bodies might no longer represent territory over which power is exercised; rather, women, in exercising power, may re-define the territory, the territory of their bodies (Meaney, 1993, p. 243).

This chapter took as its starting point the very early story-like thoughts that formed my contribution to the Abortion Papers Symposium, which in turn served as the genesis for this publication: story-like thoughts about place, the place of place within our efforts to make sense of our worlds, personal, political, ethical; the place of place in how we think, contest, agitate, theorise and politicise the topic and reality and injustice of the abortion regime in this island, Ireland place. And, just as on that day, as I conclude, I think of those women who are not here, who are elsewhere, because they are not allowed to be here, on this day, on any day, if they are to access a legal abortion service. Because this island place, this place of saints and scholars, is one where we continue to find ourselves seeking abortion rights and justice for women and girls.

17

Every Child a Wanted Child[90]

LIA MILLS

WHEN I WAS SEVENTEEN I WAS RAPED by an older man I knew. We were at a party. He gave me cocktails, fun to look at and easy to drink. I wasn't used to drinking and drank too many, too fast. He offered to bring me home, but once I was in his car he brought me somewhere else instead. I thought that night would never end, but morning came, as it does, and he let me go.

You probably have opinions about whether an experience like that constitutes rape or not, and that, right there, is one of the reasons I didn't tell anyone what had happened to me. I had those confusions too. I blamed myself enough to satisfy the entire nation, and then some. But I'm not here to write about rape, I'm here to write about what happened next.

I bled for three days, but kept it hidden. I didn't look for help because I was humiliated and ashamed and because I didn't have words for what had happened to me. In any case, because I was seventeen and no-one had ever told me otherwise, I thought I deserved the damage. And I really, really, really did not want anyone to know. No amount of hot baths or pumice-stones could wash the memory of that night away, or scrub the reek of it from my skin.

On top of all that, I was afraid I might be pregnant. There was no doubt in my mind that if I was, I'd have an abortion. I wouldn't have told anyone that, either.

I didn't want to have an abortion, but I knew that a pregnancy from that night would destroy me. I needed to scrape every trace of the experience off me, root it out from every pore and crevice. I'd have bathed in acid if I thought it would scour my body clean and free. The only thing that kept me sane in those first few days was thinking I had the option of abortion. I'd been stupid at that party, but I was savvy enough in other ways. I knew where to look for information, how to get out of the country, where to borrow the money I would have lied to get. I was the opposite of proud of myself, making these plans, but I was desperate to wrest my body back from the force that had stolen it.

Would I have been suicidal, if I'd been pregnant and unable to end that pregnancy? I think it's likely. My revulsion and loathing – self-loathing and the other kind – were so strong, I'd have done anything, and I do mean anything, to escape them. Lucky for me, there was no pregnancy. When the waiting was over and I knew for sure, I took a deep breath and got on with my life, more or less.

A wanted pregnancy, in very different circumstances, was a revelation to me in all its physical and emotional intensity. It was the most extraordinarily intimate and powerful experience I'd ever known. It was obvious and secret, ordinary and sacred, banal and deeply thrilling, all at once. There was magic in it. Every day I felt its power grow and embed itself more deeply in every cell of my body. You might think this would convince me that abortion was absolutely wrong, but it had the opposite effect. It convinced me that no one has the right to force that intensity on anyone who doesn't want it, or isn't ready for it. I couldn't begin to imagine the nightmare of going through such seismic physical and emotional changes against my will.

I didn't want to have an abortion, when I was seventeen, but I would have done it if I had to, to save myself. I think that sentence is at the heart of the current arguments about legislating for suicidal feelings. The argument as to whether abortion can be a valid treatment for a psychiatric condition is a distraction. There's a big difference between mental illness and the suicidal feelings a person might have in response to an overwhelming situation.

In the early stages of pregnancy there are two lives in the balance, but one of them is a potential life; it can only become viable over time and at the expense of the other. Only that mother knows what the cost to her will be and whether she can afford it or not.

I defy anyone, male or female, to look my seventeen-year-old self in the eye and tell her that they feel personally entitled to deny her the right to regain control of her own body, that they will force her to endure an extension of that rape for the sake of their world-view. But that's what it means to pass laws that frame the kinds of restrictions our legislature are discussing right now. Where will the pundits and the politicians or the panels of experts be during the long, frightened nights and days of an unwanted pregnancy, or during the storms of labour? Will they be the ones to cope with the consequences, to the mothers, to the children, to the families? Will they be the ones to mind those babies, bring up those children, minute by minute, day by day, year on year?

Abortion is a highly charged, difficult subject. It sparks so much passion, fury and hatred that many women are afraid to speak out privately, let alone in public. I was afraid to write this. But on balance, I think I'm more afraid of living in a country where I'm afraid to say what I believe and why.

18

Embodied Truths: women's struggle for voice and wellbeing in Irish maternity services

JO MURPHY-LAWLESS

HOW WOMEN MUST NEGOTIATE BETWEEN MYTH AND REALITY

I F WE ACCEPT THE JUDGEMENT of the anthropologist Rayna Rapp that 'reproduction lies at the heart of a culture's representations of itself' (1999, p. 317), we also accept that ours is a culture in deepest conflict. We know that our representations of reproduction in Ireland remain mired in the issue of women's agency and control of their bodies. On one side is a dominant culture which continues to thrive on what Pat O'Connor refers to as the 'patriarchal dividend' (2000, p. 82) – that is, the reality of unequal gender relations. Among other outcomes, this entails male-dominant elite groups determining policies and practices about women's bodies. We know too painfully that these practices have negative impacts on women's lives. On the other side and despite the appearance of a somewhat more liberal regime since the 1970s, stand women who must learn to assert themselves about their reproductive needs, generation after generation. For some, the struggles are considerably greater. Thus we are forced to read from Rapp's general observation the reality of Irish culture: with a stone weight of knowledge and sadness, we can see how our society continues to disempower women about their bodies and their wellbeing. The very phrase, Irish women's reproductive experiences, invokes memories that at times feel unbearable: what worse or more overwhelming than Ann Lovett's lonely birthing of her dead baby son, followed by her own death in the small midlands town of Granard in 1984? This is why our absolute determination must be to continue to disrupt this order which speaks so disingenuously to women. Memory and determination are why the X case itself has been a locus of extraordinary activism from 1992 onward and why Savita Halappanavar's death in 2012 renewed that activism for a wider public and for younger women who had known little or nothing about the X case.

With very different personal circumstances, all three women shared one common need: safe, secure medical care *in situ*, which was denied to them; legally, in the case of X because termination was not available to her; socially and culturally for Ann Lovett, who as a result of becoming pregnant in a society rife with hatred of young women in such circumstances, was forced to deal with her pregnancy alone; and legally and medically in respect of Savita Halappanavar, where the lack of legislation and the maternity care system itself failed her outright, leading to the coroner's verdict of death by medical misadventure. All three women attempted to exercise agency about their circumstances in one way or other, but ultimately their courage and their actions were not met by an acceptance of the truth of their circumstances. Their embodied truths were denied. That acceptance should have been instantly forthcoming, followed just as quickly by the skilled, compassionate responses they required, including legislation. Instead, denial at multiple levels in our society meant that two of them died, while the third anonymous woman, now in her thirties, lives on with that symbolic X summarising a continuing story of agency that the state and its official organs seek to obfuscate.

MATERNAL MORTALITY IN IRELAND: WHAT WE DO AND DO NOT KNOW

At the apex of cumulative denials is a government, replete with its 'patriarchal dividend', which refuses to meet or even acknowledge the courage of women in their truth-telling. It sets an example of deceit and dishonesty for the professional elite groups it protects against women's best interests. The issue of maternal mortality perfectly encapsulates this deliberate failure.

In October 2012, two maternal deaths occurred within two days in Dublin's Coombe maternity hospital. These were not publicly reported at that time. When the news of Savita Halappanavar's death became public in November 2012, the minister for health and children, politicians, Health Service Executive (HSE) representatives and senior clinicians endlessly repeated the canard that we have one of the lowest rates or even the lowest rate of maternal mortality in the world. This lie has been perpetrated for so long as to become ubiquitous in any official description of Irish maternity services. For decades, it has appeared in the statements and reports issued by politicians, medics, health service administrators, policy analysts and research midwives as an uncontested 'fact'.

Irish consultant obstetricians have had no compunction in continuing to promulgate this 'fact'. They have excellent reason to do so. In the twentieth century, private consultant obstetric practice proved hugely lucrative for ranks of consultants who successfully persuaded Irish women that their personal care was vital for healthy, fit women who did not need specialist care, women unaware that obstetrics is meant to provide for the minority of more complex cases only. Thus in 1996, four decades after the defeat of Noel Browne's Mother and Child scheme by doctors alert to their financial interests – as much as by churchmen alert to their own control (Ferriter, 2004, pp. 203–204) – and five years after free universal maternity care had finally been established, 37 per cent of all pregnant women chose some form of private obstetric care, or that care combined with GP care (Wiley and Merriman, 1996, p. 108). Astonishingly, 66 per cent of university graduates sought private care (ibid., p. 109) despite a resurgent international movement in feminist and midwifery philosophy emphasising the normality of birth. Here, this endorsement of private consultant care by women was due in no small measure to an effective gagging of Irish midwives – who were most often referred to as nurses – within a strict hierarchy of consultant-led care and the continuing obstetric ideology that consultants' presence conferred safety. This was the working reality even though given their frequent absence at the point of birth, it was state-employed and state-remunerated midwives who did most of their work at birth. The consequence of so many professional women accepting this argument and therefore the logic of private obstetric care was to contribute to a total lack of national policy about what best care in pregnancy and birth should comprise. In those same years, the 1990s, professional middle-class women in the UK campaigned vigorously for changes in the maternity services to become more midwifery-led and woman-centred, resulting in major shifts in official maternity care policy, using first the process of parliamentary select committees and subsequently national framework documents (House of Commons, Health Committee, 1992; England and Wales Department of Health, 1993). We never had such processes in Ireland. It was as if how women gave birth in this country simply did not matter, although Ireland continued throughout the twentieth century and into the first decade of the twenty-first century to have the highest fertility rate of any EU country (Murphy-Lawless, 2005, pp. 130–131).

Apparently, it did not matter much if women's maternal deaths were even fully counted. The inadequate statistical base which lay behind the claim about low rates of maternal mortality was part of that same policy lacuna. For many decades, the Central Statistics Office collected data about maternal deaths from a system of death registrations which permitted no classification of death as a result of pregnancy (Burke, 2012; Shannon, 2010). This led to consistent under-reporting, especially outside Dublin where comprehensive standardised figures were not kept. Again, this presents a stark contrast with long-standing UK policies to take the tragedy of maternal deaths seriously, where there has been an official triennial national confidential enquiry on maternal deaths since 1952 in an effort to understand how and why women died in order to reduce the rates of maternal mortality (Mander and Murphy-Lawless, 2013). The 'fact' of low Irish maternal mortality (because no one counted properly) even found its way into the joint 2007 WHO/UNICEF/UNFPA/World Bank international report on maternal mortality (WHO, 2007).

In 2007, a piece was published stating that our maternal mortality statistics should carry a 'health warning' because of 'significant under-reporting', attributable to the flawed data collection process (Murphy and O'Herlihy, 2007, p. 574). At last, in 2008, a maternal death enquiry team, the Maternal Death Enquiry (MDE), was set in place to run as part of that same triennial UK national confidential enquiry cited above. In 2010, the chair of the MDE stated, 'We believe that that situation is not as rosy as it would appear to be. In fact, we are certain that it is not as rosy' (cited in Shannon, 2010). A first report on Irish data was issued in 2012 (Maternal Death Enquiry Ireland, 2012). That report states that data collection continues to be incomplete due to the following factors: an 'inconsistent' approach to data classification on the part of coroners, the lack of a 'national approach to the notification of deaths'; the failure to include a question on pregnancy status at time of death on the coroner's certificate, 'uncertainty' about who has the responsibility to report to the MDE, and incomplete 'engagement' with the MDE on the part of some hospitals, because of concerns about 'data protection, potential litigation, and anticipated review of cases by other agencies outside the MDE process' (Maternal Death Enquiry Ireland, 2012, pp. 3–4). The MDE authors added that 'in some hospitals' it was 'occasionally difficult' to access data (ibid). Given what are serious problems of validity, the composite figures on maternal deaths from 2009 to 2011 can be viewed at best as preliminary. The twenty-five maternal deaths the MDE has pinpointed over that three-year period give an approximate rate of 8 per 100,000 maternities. This compares with 11.9 per 100,000 maternities in the UK for the period 2006–2009 and, on another scale of comparison, 8 per 100,000 live births in France, 7 per 100,000 live births in Norway and 5 per 100,000 live births in Sweden (ibid.).

The MDE is funded by the HSE, the operational body for all health services in Ireland, on behalf of the government's Department of Health and Children. It is an official body. Notwithstanding its status and its report, in December 2012 the minister for health and children, in response to a direct question put to him by an elected member of the Dáil (the lower house of the Irish legislature), Mick Wallace TD, stated that:

In the most recent World Health Statistics Annual Report (2012), Ireland had the 13th lowest rate of maternal mortality out of 178 countries reporting data. Maternal mortality is a rare occurrence in Ireland. It must be understood that since there are usually fewer than 5 such deaths per year, rates can appear to fluctuate significantly from year to year and reports based on data from different years *can appear to be contradictory* (Dáil debates. 19 December 2012, 57136/12)

We are forced to assume that this contradictory appearance is troubling because it disturbs the claims about our record made by those who are least comfortable in responding to the realities that lie behind the data. It is certainly not about the substantive issue that women are dying: nowhere in his reply did the minster state that any maternal death is one too many. The myth of low maternal mortality, that we are one of the safest countries in the world where women can give birth, continued to be circulated throughout the months of public debate on the Medical Treatment (Termination of Pregnancy in Case of Risk to Life of Pregnant Women Bill 2012).

THE POVERTY OF OUR MATERNITY SERVICES

At the root of this mythmaking is a blanket denial about our continuing poor maternity services, despite a growing body of Irish midwifery research data critiquing our system, despite the recommendations of the few officially sanctioned reports we have, and even despite criticisms from some of the hospitals themselves. Warnings on the inadequacy of our services date back to the early 2000s when there was a substantive push to establish midwifery services in line with emerging international evidence (Devane et al., 2007; Donnellan, 2003; O'Connor, 2002; Haughey, 2001). There have been further warnings since then, amid a barely contained sense of crisis and the admission that 'the midwife-to-patient ratio in Dublin is half what it should be' (Siggins, 2013; Hogan, 2011; Donnellan, 2011; O'Regan, 2007). This ought to have rung alarm bells at official level, yet has not done so.

From 1998 to 2008 we experienced a 37 per cent increase in the total annual birth rate, while between 2009 and 2012, annual births topped 75,000, placing massive pressure on an impoverished hospital infrastructure (Murphy-Lawless, 2011; ESRI, 2012). Our antiquated and costly form of state-funded antenatal and intrapartum care, the Maternity and Infant Care scheme, designed in the early 1950s to suit dominant medical interests and private medical practice, has never been evaluated, although the core element, antenatal and postnatal care by a private general practitioner, who is reimbursed by the state, is neither best practice nor cost-effective (see Begley et al., 2011; Brocklehurst et al., 2011, Devane et al., 2010).[91] With the exception of two pilot midwifery-led units, we have high rates of routinised interventions in nineteen consultant-led hospital units. The caesarean rate was 29 per cent in 2012 (AIMS, 2014; Brick and Layte, 2011). The 126 obstetric consultants maintain private practices in state-funded hospitals and produce highest intervention rates for private patients (Lutomski et al., 2014; Murphy and Fahey, 2013). They have strongly resisted the incorporation of rigorous international evidence from which to develop national guidelines.

The impact since 2008 of the economic crisis has led to severe curtailments of existing public maternity services, with budgets cut by more than 20 per cent, and further midwifery staff shortages, taking us well below internationally recommended ratios to maintain clinical safety (HSE Chief Medical Officer, 2014; O'Regan, 2014; O'Brien, 2013; KPMG, 2009).

Midwives have had to deal with this complexity in their daily working lives, many still trying to retain a caring space for women and a supportive teaching environment for students. Many have given up, accepting the logic of consultant obstetric care and rejecting the meaning of midwifery as an autonomous professional practice. For midwives trained under the new direct entry education syllabus, called for as long ago as 1998 in the Commission on Nursing, and only instituted in 2006, the strains have been especially evident as they struggle with the medicalised system with all its adverse consequences, the exact opposite of current evidence (Mander et al., 2009). All midwives have endured severe cuts to their wages as well as increased direct taxation and regressive indirect taxation measures, stemming from the state's agreement with the EU and IMF to 'solve' the economic crisis. Under such morale-sapping conditions just getting through one's shifts, without undue jeopardy to oneself and others, can be viewed as a major accomplishment. The experience described by Georgina Sosa (2009) of staff feeling safe, being nurtured and supported by one another and thus able to nurture each woman, to have that 'special connection' with a woman, so that her care is part of a trusting and respectful relationship, becomes an unattainable luxury, whereas it should form the bedrock of safe practice for and with women.

Our consultant-driven model of birth provision focused on an interventionist birth culture impedes the voices and actions of women and midwives alike. It is notably sustained by a continuing deference to professional, male-focused authority, in line with the power of the 'patriarchal dividend'. It cannot be stated strongly enough that it is not safe, cost-effective, or evidence-based and that it cannot stand up against international data (Hodnett et al., 2013; Sandall et al., 2013; Devane et al., 2012; Begley et al., 2011; Brocklehurst et al., 2011).

CONCLUSION: THE NEED FOR TRUTH-TELLING

The HIQA report on the death of Savita Halappanavar was published in 2013, three weeks before the anniversary of her death and just before the final two days of the inquest for Bimbo Onanuga. Ms Onanuga was a thirty-two-year-old Nigerian woman from Lagos State who in the midst of treatment for a late intrauterine death collapsed in the Rotunda Hospital on 4 March 2010 and died later that evening. Bimbo's partner, who was with her that day in the Rotunda, and Bimbo's family in Lagos pressed for an inquest about her death to discover and under-stand the unfolding train of events that led to yet another maternal death and which created unease in the Nigerian emigrant community in Dublin around the circumstances of that death (Reilly, 2011). The unrest echoes statistics that show that non-national emigrant women die almost twice as frequently as women born in either the UK or Ireland (CMACE, 2011). The inquest for Ms Onanuga, which took three years to obtain, raised yet more questions about how easily women with uncertain social status are marginalised in Ireland, never more so than in relation to their reproductive care needs (Murphy-Lawless, 2014). In efforts to establish the truth of the circumstances behind maternal deaths, we now realise that ethnicity as a problem and the shadow of racism must be entered into our frame of understanding of how women are being dealt with in our maternity hospitals (Tobin et al., 2014).

And, we need to add other names, to our list of women about whose deaths we must think politically: Tania McCabe, Jennifer Crean, Nora Hyland, Dhara Kivlehan, Bimbo Onanuga, Savita Halappanavar (HSE, 2008; HIQA, 2013).[92] We speak of them familiarly as if in the face of their deaths, the use of their first names brings us closer to honouring them when official institutions for the most part have preferred to forget them altogether. The widower of Dhara Kivlehan still awaits a full and fair inquest (McDonogh, 2014).

The HIQA (2013) report on Savita Halappanavar represents a small break in that official history of continuous forgetting. Not alone did it observe that Savita Halappanavar lacked 'basic, fundamental care' but that 'the most basic means of identifying' a woman at risk of deteriorating health was lacking (2013, p. 10). This was an official report which finally acknowledged what women know, namely that our services do not conform to international best practice in their so-called models of care.

It may be something of a record in western European countries to have retained an unreformed maternity care system for six decades, against the run of evidence, with no national framework assessment or evaluation. That is how little women's lives matter, women's lives as mothers matter.

We have the cast-iron evidence to prove that the approach to care matters very much, matters for the outcomes for women and their babies, for their longer-term wellbeing as members of families, and for the wider community. In the wake of Savita Halappanavar's death, and in the ensuing intra-professional battles on the need for legislation for the X case, Irish obstetricians failed to step forward to say that our services are in need of urgent reform from the top down, starting with the consultants themselves. Many obstetric consultants in Ireland are very wealthy indeed as a result of their generously paid public contracts, which historically have left considerable scope for a lucrative private practice. Yet it is as if the standards of care have little or nothing to do with them, even though it is their interests and their decision-making which most determine our services. The HIQA report cited a situation that makes it 'impossible to assess the performance and quality of the maternity service nationally' (2013, pp. 15–16).

The report concluded by saying there is a 'need to ensure that all pregnant women have appropriate access to the right level of care and support at any given time' and that the HSE must conduct a review of the national maternity service to 'implement standard, consistent models for the delivery of maternity services nationally in order to ensure that all pregnant women have access to the right level of safe care and support on a 24-hour basis' (2013, pp. 132–3). That might be a goal in the midst of the current roll call of centenaries about Irish independence. One might hope that women of reproductive age could access 'safe care and support' but we will need to push very hard to achieve this goal, given entrenched interests and beliefs.

In April 2011, during a lengthy debate in the Dáil on the Nurses and Midwives Bill, meant to update the legislation in line with changing professional developments, the junior minister for health, Kathleen Lynch, defended the need not to make any further amendments to that bill in favour of midwifery autonomy and made this statement about our maternity services:

I believe being pregnant and having a baby is not a medical condition. I hope as many women of a particular age as possible can meet with the joyous experience of this natural condition. We need to make it clear that it is not something to be terrified of. Although I do not believe our maternity services are in crisis, having had some interaction with them recently, I accept they may be a little overstretched. That can happen when there is an influx of people having babies at a particular time, for example. It is dangerous to use the word 'crisis', especially when one is talking about people who are vulnerable as they prepare to have babies. I do not think we should encourage women to panic. I believe in telling them the truth, but not in causing them to panic. (Dáil Éireann Debate, 2011)

Truth is what we need most urgently, but not this version of 'truth', which is part of what Foucault terms the 'coercive power', which sustains regimes that seek to deny the experiences of women, as the officials and politicians in the Department of Health and Children, the HSE and the hospitals themselves have consistently done. It is worth noting that during the inquest into the death of Savita Halappanavar, the HSE legal team tried to argue that in respect of the nine hours between Tuesday night and Wednesday morning, when there was no regular recording of Savita's vital signs, it would be incorrect to say that 'no vital signs' had been taken as her temperature had been taken on two occasions (Holland, 2013). If that passes for good quality clinical care, women in Ireland should feel a sense of dread in having to enter a maternity unit at all.

More astonishing was the interview on the RTÉ *Prime Time* programme, 10 October 2013, with the HSE National Director of Quality and Patient Safety, Dr Philip Crowley. Quizzed about the safety of our maternity services, he stated that 'our maternity services produce results that are internationally best practice', 'comparable' to international best outcomes. He proceeded to quote the very CSO figures on our 'low' maternal mortality that have been disavowed as vastly under-counting maternal deaths by the MDE (RTÉ, 2013).

In 1983, Foucault wrote that the process of truth-telling has certain requirements. For the person who would be a 'truth-teller', it is a fundamental requirement both that the speaker is 'sincere' in her belief *and* that the belief is also the truth (Foucault, 2001, p. 14). This differs significantly from a 'regime of truth' which is the way coercive power reinforces a series of what are actually deep untruths. The truth-teller is invariably less powerful than those whom she confronts, but she has a duty to articulate the truth, to not keep silent, even if in speaking she exposes herself to the risk of retaliation: 'you risk death to tell the truth instead of reposing in the security of a life where the truth goes unspoken' (ibid., p. 17). Inadvertently, this group of women who have died in our maternity services have become *parrhesiastes*, truth-tellers, and to them we owe an enormous debt of witness.

Twenty-one years ago, in *The Abortion Papers Ireland*, I wrote, about women who had lost their lives to a particular clinical regime repre-senting a particular ideological anti-woman stance in the nineteenth-century Rotunda hospital (Murphy-Lawless, 1992). It is immeasurably painful to know that women's lives are being lost still to regimes which purport to be about truth and care, but which are really about outsize power, greed and indifference. However we respond as women and feminists to these terrible challenges, I hope that in another twenty-one years, we will have overturned the weight of that patriarchal dividend, and that our current circumstances can be seen as a history we have left behind us. Just think: a maternity service that truthfully, respectfully, and caringly responds to women's felt needs when pregnant. That is a worthwhile legacy from us as activists.

19

Abortion Stigma: a health service provider's perspective

MAEVE TAYLOR[93]

MUCH PUBLIC DISCOURSE IN IRELAND constructs abortion as criminal, undesirable and contrary to the public good. The Constitution fosters stereotypical notions of motherhood as the natural and principal role of women and of women who choose to end a pregnancy as unfeminine, unnatural and deviant. Access to information about abortion services is framed in law as a conditional right, the information itself treated as odious and hazardous and those who avail of this information – and those who provide it – are stigmatised. The Irish Family Planning Association (IFPA) has worked since 1969 to promote and protect basic human rights in relation to reproductive and sexual health, relationships and sexuality. At various times the law in Ireland has restricted our ability to provide services to our clients. This, in turn, has led to our involvement in high-profile legal cases, including landmark cases such as *McGee v. AG*,[94] in 1973, which established the constitutional right to avail of contraception. The IFPA has also supported cases in relation to the ban on the sale of contraceptives and censorship of family planning leaflets. Most recently, the IFPA gave counselling and practical support to three women, whose case, *A, B and C v. Ireland*, led the European Court of Human Rights in find Ireland in breach of the European Convention on Human Rights for its failure to give effect to the constitutional right to abortion where a woman's life is at risk ([2010] ECHR 2032).

As an organisation that provides state-funded pregnancy counselling and post-abortion counselling and medical services, the Irish Family Planning Association can be said to work at the intersection of abortion law and abortion stigma. Our experience is that the state's reliance on the rights to travel and to obtain information in relation to abortion services is inadequate to give effect to women's human rights and results in cruel, inhuman and degrading treatment by the state of many women. This chapter discusses the impact of law and stigma on women's access to health services, with a particular focus on the barriers to access to abortion that women asylum seekers face and on the possible intersections of stigma and law in the operation of the Protection of Life During Pregnancy Act, 2013, which commenced on 1 January 2014.

THE LAW, STIGMA AND VULNERABLE WOMEN

The role of abortion stigma in the social, medical and legal marginalisation of abortion care worldwide is coming under increasing scrutiny internationally as well as in Ireland. Abortion stigma is produced, reproduced and reinforced at individual, community, institutional, cultural and legal levels. Stigma attaches to women and girls who seek abortions or who have had an abortion – who are frequently ostracised and discriminated against, shamed and silenced – and to those who help women and girls to access abortion. Abortion stigma is pervasive even in countries where abortion is lawful and readily accessible; in Ireland, stigma interacts with and is exacerbated by the provisions of the law and the necessity to travel outside the state to access services that are not only denied, but are criminalised. Abortion stigma and abortion law intersect also with unequal power relations, patriarchal norms and systems of discrimination, so that accessing safe abortion services is even more difficult for groups living in vulnerable situations.

The state relies on women travelling for abortion as a means of avoiding the public health crisis of unsafe and clandestine abortion that would otherwise ensue. But not all women can travel at will. The exercise of the right to travel is only a real option for those who have or can access the financial means to do so and who can travel freely between states. The IFPA sees many women and girls in circumstances of extreme vulnerability; indeed increasingly our services are used by women who experience multiple forms of disadvantage and for whom access to the right to travel is onerous and complicated, and in some cases, is impossible. Caught between two state systems – the direct provision system and the law on abortion – whose denial of basic human dignity has repeatedly been condemned by human rights bodies, those who face the most daunting barriers to accessing legal abortion services are women asylum seekers. At best, the need to raise funds and to organise the practical details of travelling abroad – including weeks going through administrative hurdles – means they experience significant delay in accessing services, and this can have serious health consequences, particularly where there is an underlying health condition. Some women resort to illegal and risky methods, such as acquiring the abortion pill online, or self-administering other substances to induce abortion. And some women ultimately have no option but to parent, regardless of their wishes, their personal situation or the circumstances of the pregnancy.

This situation violates women's human rights. The European Court of Human Rights in *A, B and C v. Ireland* recognised that travelling for abortion involves physical, financial and psychological burdens that interfere with women's rights, but accepted that women in Ireland can avail of abortion in other states. The court acknowledged that stigma is a significant aspect of women's experience, one that adds to the psychological burden of travelling outside the state to access abortion. And the court cautioned that if a case presents of a woman who could only avail of abortion by travelling outside the state, but was unable to travel or experienced extreme hardship, a ruling could be made that Ireland violated the European Convention on Human Rights. In July 2014, the UN Human Rights Committee found that the abdication of state responsibility in providing for abortion services in Ireland discriminates against women without the resources to travel to another state.[95] Less than a month later, in what has become known as the Ms Y case, a young woman who had been raped and had repeatedly requested an abortion, and who became suicidal during her pregnancy, underwent a caesarean section to enable the early delivery of a twenty-six-week foetus. The full facts of the case, including when her right to a lawful abortion was engaged, are not known at the time of writing and may never be known. But we do know that in every other European country, except Malta and San Marino, she would have had access to a local health service provider for the service she needed at the point when she requested it, and well before the risk to her life presented.

ASYLUM SEEKERS AND TRAVEL FOR ABORTION

All women who travel from Ireland for abortion incur costs and delays, and women who lack the means to travel immediately incur additional costs and lengthier delays. A woman who cannot travel freely in and out of Ireland will become mired in paperwork, wait weeks for responses from embassies and government offices, and face costs amounting to multiples of the weekly allowance of €19.10 that is issued to those in reception centres.

There are two stages to obtaining travel permits: in order to get an entry visa to a country where abortion is lawful, a woman must be able to present a passport. She also requires a re-entry visa to Ireland. If she is undocumented, she must obtain a temporary travel document. The fees for a re-entry visa and a temporary travel document are €60 and €80 respectively. So the woman's first task is to raise €140 and to apply in person to the Department of Justice. She must wait around three weeks for these documents, the latter of which can only be obtained with the assistance of a non-governmental organisation.

If the Department of Justice issues the documents, the second, much more complex, stage begins. The fee for an entry visa to the Netherlands is €60 (slightly more than three weeks' allowance for an asylum seeker); for the UK it is €100. In order to be eligible for a visa, a woman must lay out a substantial amount of money. The Dutch and UK embassies also require at least ten separate pieces of documentation before a visa can be issued, including: an application in English, a copy of a registration card of the Garda National Immigration Bureau; an up-to-date bank account statement showing adequate funds; a copy of medical travel insurance; confirmation of a clinic appointment; details of booked accommodation; and return tickets (which can only be secured by making a credit card payment). Most women asylum seekers travel to the Netherlands for abortion services; the British embassy does not, in our experience, issue visas to women with temporary travel documents. The British embassy also requires a woman to have an email account so that she can receive and send a ten-page application form.

The complications mount. Actions that are unproblematic for most people, such as walking into a Garda station to have photographs signed, are far from easy for women who live in reception centres. All of the relevant offices are based in Dublin city centre, whereas the Refugee and Integration Agency has a policy of dispersing asylum seekers to locations at some distance from the capital. A woman – any woman – living in a rural area who requires the signature of a Garda on her application and a bank draft for the fee may well find that there is no longer either a Garda station or a bank in her local area. Bus fares eat significantly into the weekly €19.10 allowance, as does phone credit.

Some support is available for the costs of travel and accommodation from, for example, the Abortion Support Network, a UK-based group about which the IFPA gives information to clients who have no financial resources. Some abortion clinics waive their fees where a woman has no means to pay. Some women have been able to access emergency special financial assistance from community welfare officers or from charitable organisations, sometimes in the guise of, for example, a clothing grant. But such payments are discretionary, and help with funding for an abortion is sometimes refused. And in order to make her case, the woman must expose a deeply personal and private situation over and over again to strangers: to translators; embassy staff; counsellors; government officials; and reception centre staff. And, perhaps against her wishes, to friends, family or partner. Such disclosures can expose women to hostile and judgemental attitudes and comments and make it impossible to conceal their situations, regardless of their wishes and their right to confidentiality and privacy in accessing health care. Women's dignity is violated at every step.

ROLE OF PREGNANCY COUNSELLORS

The IFPA has twelve pregnancy counselling centres. Pregnancy counselling is regulated by the Abortion Information Act.[96] The IFPA is clear that while we will always comply with the law, we will do nothing that steps beyond compliance and impedes women's access, or doctors' or counsellors' good practice, or the IFPA's conscientious commitment to our clients.[97] This commitment has drawn opposition from those opposed to abortion, including a campaign of clandestine recording by agents provocateurs from an anti-choice organisation and an associated smear campaign. All our counsellors are experienced and accredited therapists. Sessions include information and a therapeutic aspect and can last anything up to two hours. To comply with the Information Act, if a woman requests information about abortion, she must also receive information, counselling and support in relation to all the options open to a woman in her particular circumstances.

IFPA counsellors see women who are in extreme distress because of the circumstances of their pregnancy, women whose physical or mental health is seriously compromised, women who are desperate to end a pregnancy, and on rare occasions, women who are suicidal. IFPA counsellors have experience in recognising suicide risk and have protocols in place to refer women appropriately where there is such risk, or where treatment might be available in Northern Ireland, where the threshold is that a woman is likely to become a 'physical or mental wreck'. For a lawful abortion in Ireland, the Protection of Life During Pregnancy Act applies only where a woman's life, as distinct from her health and wellbeing, is at risk from a life-threatening physical condition or from suicide. Reliable human rights analysis of the act[98] suggests that the provisions relating to certification of risk to life because of possible suicide potentially involve violations of human rights.

The IFPA works from an understanding of women as agents and decision-makers who are experts in regard to their particular circumstances; if a woman rules out any option but abortion, a counsellor will work with her to support her in giving effect to her decision. In the case of asylum seekers, the support needs are particularly complex. IFPA counsellors must give women information about which country is most likely to grant a visa, about the documentation she needs if she is to travel, how to get to the embassies and the Department of Justice, and about opening times, bus routes etc. They can help her fill out forms. They give information about clinics in different countries, about abortion procedures, risks and aftercare. All of this information is given in the context of a number of counselling sessions for which the counsellor organises a professional interpreter.

But there are limits to the support that can be given. The counsellors are precluded by the Information Act from making appointments or arrangements on the client's behalf. The IFPA can provide interpreters only for the counselling sessions. Unless she has someone else to support her, the woman or girl, new to the country, perhaps unable to speak English, unable to ask for help, and unfamiliar with the practicalities of getting around an Irish city, must navigate these processes largely by herself.

However, we know that if a woman presents at an early gestation stage, it is possible for her to gather all the documents and access financial supports and make her way to an abortion clinic. When the alternative is to parent against their wishes, far from home and in a reception centre, many women are willing to do whatever they can to make the journey. IFPA counsellors give all the support and information they can. They can explain the process she needs to go through, give her all possible emotional and practical support in their role as pregnancy counsellors, but they can't accompany her through it all and they can't disguise the difficulty or take the burden away (Fletcher, 2005). Yet, the IFPA is not in a position to do more than fill a counselling and information gap, and we have always maintained that counselling and information cannot mitigate the lack of lawful abortion services or alter the fact that the law stands in the way of women exercising their considered, conscientious choice about their pregnancy. But in the absence of any institutionalised system of state supports or funding, we work closely with other non-governmental organisations (NGOs) and health service providers to create care pathways for women and to ensure women have access to financial supports. These pathways and supports are delicate constructions, almost entirely reliant on the good will and conscientious commitment of individuals, e.g. numerous NGOs, counsellors and volunteers. And it is on these shaky and impermanent supports that the state relies to ensure that women can exercise their right to travel out of Ireland for an abortion. This shambles, which is entirely of the state's creation, is an appalling derogation by the state of its duty to ensure women's dignity and human rights.

The case of asylum seekers stands out as the most egregious example, but any woman in Ireland who seeks abortion services that are denied by the state is stigmatised, and treated in discriminatory and degrading ways by the state. Much of what asylum seekers face is also experienced, albeit in other ways, by other women who must travel for abortion. Through our counselling services, particularly post-abortion counselling, which is part of the continuum of care for all clients who request it, the IFPA is acutely aware of the psychological hardship associated with denial of abortion services. For some women, the most difficult aspect can be the abdication of responsibility by the health service and the way this makes women and their partners feel stigmatised 'like criminals' or 'like a displaced person'. Indeed the image of statelessness recurs a number of times in the testimonies of women documented in the IFPA's 2000 publication, *The Irish Journey* (Ruane, 2000). This sense of being relegated to a category of people who fall outside the law can be very painful. For many women, the financial, physical and emotional burdens of travelling for termination is exacerbated by the often clandestine and secretive nature of the journey. Where women do not disclose their situation to friends and family, the sense of isolation and secrecy adds to the burden and deprives them of the support networks that they would otherwise have.

Many women express outrage and disbelief that a modern health system, whose medical personnel are highly regarded as experts at the cutting edge of their practice and which makes repeated claims about the excellence of maternity care, cannot provide medical treatment that is available in other highly developed countries. Many women feel anger at the experience of being expelled and exiled from a health service they trust – and pay for through taxes – yet which obliges them to organise and pay for health care in another country. State policy stigmatises the choice to end a pregnancy by women who have financial resources in other ways, for example through the lack of financial assistance or tax relief such as is granted on the cost of other medical treatments obtained outside the state and lack of coverage by private health insurance policies.

HEALTH CARE PROFESSIONALS AND ABORTION STIGMA

The IFPA knows from our experience of delivering training courses on reproductive health that health professionals' understanding of the Constitution, the criminal law and the Information Act, the specific provisions that apply to their work and the sanctions and penalties for breach of law tends to be of a general nature, vague or incorrect. Many health care professionals assume or fear that they are precluded from discussing abortion and that to allude to termination of pregnancy would be considered as advocating or promoting such a course of action.

In the IFPA's experience, in cases where a woman's medical history gives rise to concerns about possible complications in her treatment, it is not the norm for the Irish health institution to proactively communicate with the doctor who is to carry out the termination (although this does happen in some cases). Unlike any other medical treatment situation, the continuum of care is broken: the onus shifts to the patient to make contact with a doctor outside Ireland and to provide her medical history; this doctor is then deprived of the option of discussing her case with the treating doctor involved in her antenatal care prior to the abortion. Health care professionals are aware of the stigma and opprobrium that attaches to abortion in much political and media discourse. Doctors working in small and, especially, rural communities may fear that publicity linking them with abortion in any way will affect their livelihood and reputation (through loss of patients) and lead to personal harassment. Many health care professionals evade the potential or perceived repercussions of falling foul of the law by declining to discuss abortion or to provide information to their patients.

STATE POLICY AND PRACTICE AND THE STIGMATISATION OF WOMEN'S REPRODUCTIVE CHOICES

The denial of abortion services under Irish law and the associated chilling effect in regard to information provision mean that information that would in other countries be given by medical care providers is only available to women in Ireland who are referred or self-refer to an agency that is permitted by law to give 'Act information'. Most women who decide to seek abortion services do so in early pregnancy and make their decision alone, or in consultation with a general practitioner or pregnancy counsellor. However, many women whose pregnancy involves a fatal foetal anomaly are already receiving antenatal care within the hospital system and receive the diagnosis during a routine scan. If they want to discuss ending the pregnancy, they are frequently referred to pregnancy counselling. As appropriate and sensitive as such counselling is – and IFPA counsellors specialise in dealing with clients in these circumstances – a referral by a hospital to an NGO involves an abrupt and sometimes insensitive cessation of the state's care continuum. For some women the expulsion from state care into the care of an organisation, such as the IFPA, that is also associated with unplanned and unwanted pregnancies and with abortion, reinforces the sense of stigma.

The prohibition and criminalisation of abortion in Ireland, the equal right the Constitution affords to the life of the unborn with that of a pregnant woman and the pervasive stigma that surrounds abortion combine to impede understanding abortion as a regular medical procedure and a part of many women's reproductive lives. This has prevented the development of proper guidelines, protocols and processes of accountability in relation to abortion such as are in place in relation to other aspects of health care. The clinical guidelines on the implementation to the PLDPA do not give cause for optimism that the state has any regard to the issue of stigma in relation to abortion within this legislation, enacted to give effect to a constitutional right to lawful abortion. In a phrase nowhere to be found in the statute itself, the guidelines state that the purpose of the Act is to restate the general prohibition on abortion while regulating access to lawful termination of pregnancy. The message to practitioners appears to be that nothing has changed. The chilling effect is not to be addressed and secrecy and shame continue to be the lot of women who seek abortion[99], Department of Health (2014).

CONCLUSION

The failure to provide abortion services within Ireland is cruel, inhuman and degrading. In failing to provide such services and, in their absence, failing to articulate a positive duty of care to women who avail of abortion services outside the state and to hold health care institutions accountable for such a duty of care, the Irish state falls short of its obligations under international human rights law. Until the law and health service policy recognise this and acknowledge that abortion needs to be taken out of the criminal law and addressed as part of an integrated approach to women's reproductive health, women in Ireland who make this decision will continue to be stigmatised, shamed and isolated. They will continue to carry the unjust, inequitable and discriminatory psychological, financial and physical burdens of travelling to another country for services that are criminalised in Ireland – burdens that the European Court of Human Rights have recognised as interfering with their right to privacy under the European Convention on Human Rights.

20

The Fragility of Respectability for Lone Mothers

CATHERINE CONLON

COMING TO KNOW EMBODIED WOMEN IN PREGNANCY

THE PREGNANT BODY as a resource for knowing 'woman' as a social construct, feminine identity and the female body has been a contentious site to mine. In the legitimate concern within feminism to demonstrate the full extent of women's capacities, the attendant concern to avoid the equation of woman with her reproductive capacity has left the pregnant body under-theorised. Ironically, in a cultural moment when pregnancy is highly visible, researching women encountering women who had 'concealed pregnancy' (Conlon, 2006) revealed critical insights regarding how pregnancy is carried by an individual woman and framed or understood by a society. Women's concealed pregnancy stories narrated discursive formations of (hetero)sexuality, ('crisis') pregnancy, abortion, adoption, mothering and motherhood. They illuminated 'blindspots' in how we know pregnancy and suggested alternative formations that dominant ways of knowing pregnancy had concealed.

RESEARCHING CONCEALED PREGNANCY

The research reported here was initiated as a Crisis Pregnancy Agency funded study commissioned to gain a better understanding of 'concealed pregnancy' to inform policy and service development. The study set out to generate an understanding of the factors and processes entailed in the concealment of pregnancy and to consider how services could respond to women concealing a pregnancy. The research methodology involved a retrospective analysis of case notes of fifty-one women identified as presenting with a 'concealed pregnancy' by maternity social work and crisis pregnancy counsellors in two Irish hospitals over an eighteen-month period during 2003 and 2004. Thirteen of the women agreed to participate in an unstructured, qualitative research interview. A research report based on this data, *Concealed Pregnancy: a case study from an Irish setting* (Conlon, 2006), was published by the Crisis Pregnancy Agency. A set of guidelines were developed for staff working in maternity settings to enhance their capacity to recognise, respond appropriately to and have understanding and empathy for women who present concealing pregnancy (Conlon, 2009).

Between 2006 and 2010 I undertook a further iteration of analysis of the interview data women contributed to this study as part of a doctoral thesis. This inquiry sought to draw out the 'discursive formations' of women, fertility, sexuality and pregnancy I perceived within the data. This analysis first articulated out my position on what qualitative interview data represents to appreciate the kind of knowledge it can generate. The qualitative interview entails a woman transforming her lived experience into language and constructing a story about it (Riessman, 2008). These stories or narratives draw on taken-for-granted discourses and values circulating in a particular culture at the moment of their telling (2008, p. 3). From this perspective then, when we tell a 'story' we are not simply recounting events, but how we can recount them is constrained, who we are recounting them to is critical to how or what we tell and the culture in which we are located during the telling both shapes and is revealed in the narrative. Narratives or stories allow us to consider the social and cultural dimensions of an event – the relations and in particular the power relations as well as the ideologies underlying the story. A method of qualitative interview data analysis directed at revealing these multiple dimensions in the narratives entitled the Voice Centred Relational Method (VCRM) (Doucet and Mauthner, 2008) was followed in this iteration of analysis.

Four listenings/readings are involved in the VCRM method of interpretation. A first listening/reading asks 'what is happening here?' This focuses on plots, subplots, key characters and captures the researcher's response to the story being told. The second listening involves 'tracing narrated subjects'. This listening/reading attends to the particular subject or narrator, in this case how the woman narrated herself and the parameters of her social world. Attention centres on the active 'I' telling the story, amplifying the terms in which the woman sees and presents herself while also highlighting where she might be emotionally or intellectually struggling to say something. The third listening attends to the 'relational narrated subject', listening for talk about the woman's social networks, close and intimate relations to reveal how she narrates her self-in-relation. Finally, the fourth listening/reading attends to 'structured subjectivity' focusing on the structured power relations and dominant ideologies that shape the woman's narrative.

This chapter considers the narration of one woman, who will be called Eileen here, whose story of concealing her pregnancy portrays how the respectability a woman mothering alone builds for her family is a fragile thing.

Eileen's Story: 'The Fragility of Respectability for Lone Mothers'

The first listening in this method of analysis seeks out the essence of the story. Eileen's central story line or plot is the incompatibility of pregnancy as a result of casual sex for a good (lone) mother.

> She just made me feel like, as if I was a slut that was after arriving in pregnant after a one-night stand. She had misunderstood everything. [Eileen, lines 140–2]

Eileen was born and has lived all her life in a town in the mid-west, with a population size of just over 3,000 people and a very rural hinterland. We met and carried out the interview in Eileen's home in a small council housing estate on the edge of the town, where she was living with her seven-year-old daughter. Eileen had concealed a pregnancy and given birth to a child she placed for adoption less than two years prior to when we met. Eileen's daughter was five years of age when Eileen became pregnant. She is a lone parent and had lived with her parents until after this pregnancy, indicative of the kind of support Eileen got from her parents. Now Eileen and her daughter live in their own home and while their relationship is not a strong feature of the interview, seeing them together at home gave the impression of a close, strong relationship with Eileen drawing deep pride from her daughter. Her daughter has a good relationship with her father, which Eileen prioritises and seems to have had to work hard at to get established. Eileen is also in paid employment as a manual worker in a local small business. Eileen's pregnancy was the result of a single sexual encounter she enjoyed after which she used the morning-after pill for contraceptive effect but it did not prevent the pregnancy.

Eileen told how she denied her pregnancy to herself for the initial months and then concealed the pregnancy from family, friends and work colleagues as she prepared a place to give birth alone after which she would bring the child to a hospital for 'safe-finding', imagining a positive adoptive placement for the child's future. Two weeks before giving birth, her sisters and mother confronted her. She reluctantly admitted the pregnancy and they all agreed to comply with her wish to continue concealing the pregnancy after she gave birth in hospital and placed the baby for adoption through an open adoption process she was fully engaged with.

Preserving the Status of 'Good Mother'

In the first sequence of her story Eileen says of her pregnancy that she did 'know' of it but was not able to accept it.

> R: I suppose when I missed my periods
> I just knew,
> I knew straight away I was.
> Do y'know?
> [I: Yeah]
> But em, every pain or cramp I got
> I said this is, this is my period coming now whatever. [I: Yeah]
> I just couldn't accept, that I was pregnant
> even though I knew at the back of my mind I was
> I couldn't accept it.

So I just kept denying it to myself
and I'd go into work and I'd just kill myself working, you know.
If the fridge needed moving I'd move it. [I: Yeah]
D'you know?
And I never ate a thing in the hope that I'd, miscarry, the baby
    y'know?
And I never told anyone
I just kept saying I'm not, its not really happening, d'you know?
[Eileen, lines 9–32]

Eileen describes knowing at levels of both the body and mind, but interestingly depicts each level differently. Knowing at the corporeal, bodily level is uncontested by her: '… I missed my periods I just knew, I knew straight away I was.' But knowing at the mental level is more qualified: 'I knew at the back of my mind I was, I couldn't accept it.' Eileen placed her mental knowing at the back of her mind, relegated there by her inability to accept the pregnancy. Certain practices can define or undermine a woman as a 'good mother'. Sexuality and mothering represent discordant discourses when that sexuality is given expression outside the confines of a recognised/regulated relationship. For Eileen, concealing the pregnancy and maintaining a non-pregnant identity would avoid her being 'tainted' by her unregulated sexual behaviour. Not being able to accept the pregnancy, to assimilate the pregnant self into her identity, is the starting point for Eileen concealing her pregnancy. '*I denied it to myself.*' '*I never told anyone.*' '*I told myself I'm not.*' During pregnancy certain practices can define or undermine a woman as a 'good mother'. Adherence to an ever-growing regulatory regime of medical examination, diet and lifestyle consistent with medical scientific discourses of foetal wellbeing is central to good mothering in pregnancy (Rúdólfsdóttir, 2000). Women concealing pregnancy are 'suspect' in their behaviour for their failure to adhere to this regime in the first instance.

This evokes Bourdieu's concept of *habitus*, wherein perception and appreciation are proposed as mental schemata. Patterned after the social structure of the group, mental schemata are the *embodiment* of social divisions and collective representations of the external structures of society. Individuals internalise the extant social environment inscribing the constraints of the external reality on the body through *habitus*

(Bourdieu, 1977). For Eileen, not disclosing the pregnancy kept her identity intact, in 'denying it to myself' she sought convergence between Eileen the mother within the institution of motherhood (her self-in-relation) and her mother-self. At times that denial faltered and she sought to retain convergence between her concealing pregnant self and 'good mother'.

Eileen imagined this pregnancy would be resolved by birthing the child herself and bringing it to a place for safe-leaving and in her narration of that, care for the child is placed centre stage. Eileen's imagined account of how the pregnancy might have ended brings us close to the *habitus* of a woman who succeeds in delivering alone.

> I had this plan in my head that
> I had my own little house
> outside mammy and daddy's (house where I lived at the time)
> but I didn't stay in it much
> I always stayed with them
> and I had my plan then set in my head
> that when I would start labour I'd go down to the house
> and I had a baby grow and a little do you know the all-in-one thing
> to bring the baby to the hospital.
> I had the towels got and I said I'd boil the kettle, and the towel.
> Do you know? When you are reading this?
> I: Like something on the telly?
> R: Yeah.
> So I had all that set up
> and the one thing that was at the back of my mind was
> how was I going to get the child from [my town] to [nearest hospital]
> after I'd have it.
> I: Because you didn't have a car or … ?
> R: No, I had a car
> but how would I get it into the car without it falling down
> so even though I desperately wanted to lose this baby
> when I had it …
> I: You would be worried about it?
> R: Ye I'd be worried that it would fall in the car or something.
> [Eileen, lines 36–53]

Eileen portrayed an isolated place where she had arranged secretly for herself alone to attend to her body in labour so as to give birth without the pregnancy and child ever coming to be known by any others. Her intention was to bring the child to a place of 'safe-leaving-for-imagined-safe-finding' and this would represent the end of the pregnancy for her. Eileen orientates the telling to her concern for the wellbeing of the child after birth. Up to this point she had been telling how throughout the pregnancy her behaviour was constantly directed towards losing or miscarrying the pregnancy. In narrating the imagined concealed birth, Eileen carefully itemises out the clothing and equipment appropriate for a newborn and identifies where she intended to bring the child to demonstrate her intentions to ensure the child's wellbeing. While being pregnant and carrying the child is incompatible with her role as mother, caring for the child when born is critical for her to maintain coherence in her most treasured identity as (good) mother to her first daughter.

FROM GOOD MOTHER TO 'A SLUT AFTER ARRIVING IN PREGNANT'

Eileen's pregnancy was the result of a single sexual encounter she enjoyed after which she used the morning-after pill for contraceptive effect, but it did not prevent the pregnancy. The pregnancy brings two discordant discourses into embodied being for Eileen – a sexually autonomous woman and a good mother. Through Eileen's narrative of concealing pregnancy her subjectivity as lone mother and in turn the positionality of lone motherhood within the institution of motherhood are narrated.

In her narrative, this discordance is strikingly portrayed when she narrates herself presenting to medical professionals in the antenatal clinic of the hospital where she gave birth to her baby. Eileen first tells her presentation of herself to the doctor in her own voice. She then retells her story through the voice of a nurse who is telling it in a public area of the waiting room within the hearing of Eileen and, Eileen believes, the hearing of all of the other pregnant women and their companions as well as the staff in the clinic at that time. In this retelling Eileen is narrating herself-in-relation to both the nurse and all of those who (potentially) overheard her story in the clinic that day.

Eileen was making her first attendance to the antenatal care that day in the eighth month of her pregnancy.

R: We went to [maternity hospital] on the Monday.
And I had explained to him [doctor] that
I already had a child to [pause]
someone else.
I said the child's father is involved in its life.
And I said this is more or less a one-night stand,
you know?
And em …
He said right so.
And the next thing he sent me back out to the waiting room and
[Eileen's voice becomes animated]
a nurse just came out and announced it to the waiting room.
She said, 'Oh this girl isn't,
she needs to see a social worker,
she isn't happy.
Because she had a one-night stand
and it isn't her partner's child.'
The whole thing was [pause]
misunderstood.
I: And [she] said it to you?
R: Said it out to another nurse.
Now if I heard it in the waiting room,
everyone did.
Do you know what I mean?
That was [pause]
one thing,
I think if for girls in future
if they are going in
that they should be took away privately.
Because I could have just got up and walked out that day
and said,
'fuck the lot of you I'll stick to my own plan.'
You know what I mean?
I was just so mad with that nurse.
She just made me feel like
as if I was
a slut that was after arriving in pregnant after a one-night stand.
You know?

And the whole,
she had misunderstood everything.
[Eileen, lines 111–42]

In telling the story of her first appointment, Eileen illustrates vividly two versions of herself in the interaction. Firstly, her ontological self she presents to the doctor. Here Eileen tells of herself as a (good) mother to her daughter and her narration signals that she felt she had managed to preserve her identity as 'good mother' intact. She then performs the nurse retelling her situation to another nurse within hearing of occupants of the waiting room. This 'relational self', Eileen as narrated by one nurse to another and as heard by other attendees at the antenatal clinic fatally ruptures Eileen's sense of herself as a good mother. Eileen draws on gendered discourses of (hetero)sexuality to portray how in this telling of her pregnancy she was sexualised within a discursive construction of 'slut' that is counter to ideologies of femininity, respect-ability and motherhood (Lees, 1993; Hollway, 1984; Hollway, 1996; Skeggs, 1997). In the absence of a partner to have/hold her, such sexualisation has no recourse to legitimacy and so Eileen's respectability is critically undermined.

In the first telling to the doctor, Eileen is doing the telling and situates herself as a mother already from a different relationship but whose co-parent (her daugther's father) is involved in her daughter's life. Eileen invokes discourses that emphasise the child–father relation-ship. In doing so Eileen attempts to forge out a position of respectability for herself as a mother, to assert a 'good mother' position or claim cultural capital within the field of mothering. In turn she frames this pregnancy as a 'crisis' with reference to the unlikelihood of the prospect for a child–father relationship. This pregnancy is the result of 'a one-night stand', the implication being that there is no prospect the father of this child will be involved in its life. Eileen is the active voice here and the doctor adopts no position on what Eileen has told him in his narrated response to her.

However, the circumstances of this pregnancy threaten to destabilise her respectability as lone mother. When Eileen hears her story retold through the nurse, she perceives herself as heard as 'a slut', a fatal threat to Eileen's respectability.

In the retelling, Eileen saw her situation as recast into what she terms 'a slut arriving in pregnant after a one-night stand' when she narrates her self-in-relation to the nurses and the other occupants of the waiting room. Rúdólfsdóttir (2000) notes that implicit in the regulation of the health of mothers-to-be are normative ideas or 'certain expectations' about proper motherhood, such as, who should be mother, who should not, who should be given extra care, what qualities new mothers should have, and so on (Rúdólfsdóttir, 2000, p. 339). Through Eileen's narrative we hear how sexual autonomy is placed in opposition to proper/good motherhood. Skeggs (1997) argues that women are key points of reference in how the family is constituted as moral, particularly in relation to their role as wives, mothers and sexual beings. Women's subjectivity is constructed through sexual categorisation, and discourses of maternal care and sexuality are often in contradiction with each other, enabling motherhood and sexuality to be represented in opposition (Skeggs, 1997, p. 119).

Within Eileen's *habitus* as a lone mother, this pregnancy signified her embodiment as a sexual being. By virtue of being outside the context of marriages sexual autonomy converged into the position of 'slut'. As a lone mother then, her family's respectability is bound up in high levels of self-surveillance and restriction of her sexuality to demonstrate attachment to the moral order.

FROM CONCEALING TO BIRTHING

Two weeks before Eileen would go into labour, one of her three sisters confronted her saying there were 'rumours in the town' that she was pregnant. Eileen narrates how this generated acute distress for her but in the end she would reluctantly admit the pregnancy, but only to her mother and sisters. Eileen continued to conceal the pregnancy from everyone else, including her father and daughter, as well as from 'the town'. Her mother and sister's coming to know of the pregnancy impelled Eileen into attending for antenatal care. Eileen's plan had been to leave the baby in a safe place in a hospital. She now decided she would place the child in foster care in the hospital where she was due to give birth. Her mother and sisters did not all support her in this, but she persisted with her plans.

Eileen's narrative features strong discourses of maternal bonding and the essentialism of motherhood after birth is evident in her narrative with dominant discourses deployed through the voices of others.

> I got [to the hospital] at two o'clock
> and the baby was born at twenty past two
> so I just made it and no more
> and as soon as she was born
> I said to the nurses, 'I want to go home now.'
> …
> I cried and I cried and I never slept the whole night from crying.
> I asked myself what I'd done and telling them to take the baby
> that I didn't want to see the baby or anything.
>
> I: Did they put the baby in the room with you?
>
> R: No, they didn't.
> I didn't,
> the minute the baby was born they put her on me
> and all that
> and she was lovely
> but at that time I didn't care.
> So then early Sunday morning
> I asked for the baby to be brought up so
> I fell in love with it then.
> But I didn't know what was going on
> I couldn't stop crying
> and this midwife came in then
> and she asked me did someone give out to me?
> Because I was in such a state
> and I couldn't answer her
> and the baby
> I had the baby all the time then with me
> and it was lovely
> but I still didn't know what was going on in my head.
> I just wanted to get home.
> [Eileen, lines 188–217]

The practice of placing the baby on the mother's breast and the baby being cared for by the mother from the moment of birth has evolved in (hospital) maternal care practices in line with child-centred discourses of optimum maternal bonding. Eileen initially resists this, wanting to leave the baby and not caring when the baby was placed on her immediately after birth. Later when alone, Eileen questions her behaviour through a relational voice chastising herself for 'telling them to take the baby'. Eileen's voice is contradictory: 'I fell in love with it then. But I didn't know what was going on'; 'It was lovely but I still didn't know what was going on in my head.' The period of uncertainty between the birth of the baby and meeting the foster parents is characterised by Eileen being rendered incapacitated by emotional distress manifested through constant crying. Neither she nor anybody else knows what is to be the outcome. Meeting the baby's prospective foster mother marks the end of that period in Eileen's story.

> R: I hid it for so long and then in two weeks' time it was
> the family had known and it was all over.
> And I was on my way home from [maternity hospital].
> So for Monday and Tuesday I cried and I didn't
> I cried for the two days solid
> mammy was up the walls
> she didn't know what was going on or anything.
> I went back to [maternity hospital] on the Wednesday then
> and I met [the baby]'s foster parents for the first time and she was lovely
> just wonderful.
> [Eileen, lines 223–30]

Given the dominance of the expectation that mothers will take their baby home and mother them that prevails within maternity care settings and beyond, Eileen's strategy to adopt the position of the inactive I, too distressed to make a decision, saved her from having to confront those discourses directly.

MOTHERING-IN-ADOPTION

As Eileen continues to tell the story of placing the baby in foster care which then evolves into adoption, her narrative formulates a relationship between herself, the birth mother and the adoptive family within which mothering is performed in novel ways. In this way Eileen is striving to reconcile her ontological self and her structured subjectivity as 'good mother' through a process I argue to be generative agency.

> R: [The foster mother] was just [voice tails off] …
> I: You were so confident about her?
> R: Ye she was just so wonderful,
> d'you know?
> I: Did [your social worker] give you the option of meeting her?
> R: Ye.
> I: And that was a good thing?
> R: That was a good thing ye.
> …
> When she brought [the adoptive mother] in it was …
> It was like myself and my sister was there,
> it felt the four of us just like
> we had grew up together or something
> you know?
> [Eileen, lines 253–82]

Eileen narrates identifying immediately with the foster mother. It is as if they've known each other all their lives. She adopts a position of actively selecting her and her family to become her daughter's adoptive family. Through placing the baby for adoption with that specific woman, Eileen practises the maternal through fulfilling another woman's maternal aspirations and hopes. Later Eileen even depicts an embodied transference of the maternal bond to the adoptive mother.

> She used to pray [to St Anne]
> that she would be blessed with a child of her own
> and [my baby] was born on St Anne's day.
> Something in that is telling me
> that everything was meant to be
> and she used to tell me
> the first time she brought [the baby] home
> she had [the baby] since she was three days old,
> she just got this little flutter

in her stomach
when she brought her home that night
and was feeding her.
[Eileen, lines 444–50]

This resonates with Teman's (2009) analysis of the relationship between women involved in surrogacy who described how through verbal communication and through practices of disembodiment and vicarious embodiment, the women construct a 'shifting body'. This process which Teman calls a 'dyadic body project' is used to designate the social label of pregnancy, in identity-building processes associated with pregnant embodiment, and even in constructing the lived experience of pregnancy.

While the choice of adoption is very much a minority choice as a pregnancy outcome in Ireland today it remains an option within the Crisis Pregnancy Agency's 'Options' discourse. Discourses relating to the maternal and the child have marginalised adoption and biological motherhood has become essentialised. Eileen forges a discourse of mothering-in-adoption in her narrative through a range of practices she describes that mark this/her adoption process apart from dominant images of adoption. Eileen narrates her agency in the process by endorsing the mother and family with whom the child is to be placed and in relating the many opportunities she has foregone to withdraw from adoption.

R: Definitely I could still bring her home tomorrow
if I wanted
but I'm happy now.
For the first time in a long time I'm happy.
And I know the day will come
going up to the court
and it will kill me
but still
she's going to have a better life than I could ever offer her.
[Eileen, lines 976–980]

Placing her daughter with an adoptive family through an open adoption process has been taken by Eileen as a way for her to forge an active form of 'mothering-in-adoption' of both her daughters and further extending this to involve 'grandmothering-in-adoption' and 'aunting-in-adoption', that allows Eileen integrate 'good-mothering-in-adoption' into her 'good mother' habitus. Eileen invoked dominant images of adoption wherein the child is 'wondering about her [mother] for eighteen years' and contrasts her involvement in her adoptive daughter's life with how uninvolved other adoptive mothers are in the lives of their children.

FRAGILITY OF RESPECTABILITY IN *HABITUS* OF LONE MOTHER

Through normative discourses of the family Eileen narrates her structured subjectivity as lone mother, reveals her lone mother *habitus* and in turn how lone motherhood is located within the institution of motherhood. A family comprising a lone mother without the involvement of the child's father represents an ideologically diminished family and one that is structurally at greater risk of poverty. In the absence of the ideologically ideal of a two-parent, marriage-based family, negotiating a good child–father relationship within which both parents co-operate in the raising of the child is a means by which lone motherhood can be made more 'respectable'. Eileen's existing family unit of herself and her daughter is saved from both disruption and consolidation as a lone parent family by concealing pregnancy. In this way then Eileen and her daughter can continue to be located closest to an imagined normative family status and aspire to attaining that status some day.

Historical analysis of the transformation of mothering within Western societies demonstrates how regulation of motherhood within marriage has always featured. De Silva characterises mothering as contingent, socially constructed and relational wherein lone mothering as an increasing feature of contemporary society both reflects changing sexualities in society as well as a general continuing process of redefinition of gender identities: the increasing autonomy of mothers and fathers (de Silva, 1996, p. 20).

Motherhood has been invoked as a discourse of symbolic domination in a very particular way in the Irish context as analyses of representations of womanhood in Irish identity illustrate how the nation has traditionally been symbolised by Irish motherhood (Inglis, 2003; O'Connor, 1998; Gray and Ryan, 1997; Valiulis, 1995; Meaney, 1993). At the foundation of the state in the 1920s, the family was placed at the centre of Irish culture and the nation came to be increasingly symbolised by Irish motherhood (Gray and Ryan, 1997). Women's behaviour was linked with the dignity and integrity of the nation. The images of women and mothers emanating from such symbolism incorporated messages about appropriate lifestyles of women and young girls and in particular the appropriate context for motherhood culminating in strict dictates prescribing women's sexual behaviour. While Gray and Ryan (1997) acknowledge the significant socio-economic changes that have occurred in Ireland since then, they demonstrate continuities in the use of such symbols and representations of women in the Irish context. The insertion of an anti-abortion amendment into the Constitution in 1983 continues in the vein of traditional symbolic images of Irish motherhood that have, according to Meaney (1993), served to obliterate the reality of women's lives and perpetuate an image of 'woman' far from the experience, expectations and ideals of Irish women and women living in Ireland.

GENERATIVE AGENCY IN EILEEN'S STORY

Eileen found herself pregnant as a lone mother of a (deeply loved) five-year-old daughter in a society where the normative, dominant family model is a two-parent, marriage-based family. As Eileen comes to know her body as pregnant, her perception and appreciation, her mental schemata or *habitus*, are shaped by discourses relating to feminine sexuality, lone motherhood and 'good' mother and crucially the intersection of these discourses with discourses of 'respectability'. Mothering as a lone mother, mothering in pregnancy and mothering through adoption are narrated by Eileen as subjectivities shaped by *habitus*. Eileen goes on to reimagine mothering-through-adoption so as to challenge the privileging of birth-mother as the only real mothering, and in turn the imperative to mother in a demonstration of *habitus* as generative. Eileen's story of concealing pregnancy, which would often at first glance be construed as pathological, is constitutive of generative agency if fully listened to.

21

A Holy Alliance?
Obstacles to abortion
rights in Ireland
North and South

GORETTI HORGAN

INTRODUCTION

O NE INTERESTING QUESTION about debate on abortion in Ireland is why, although the law in the North is significantly more liberal than that in the South, is the policy discourse in both jurisdictions so similar – about saving women's lives only? This chapter argues that, while in the South the Eighth Amendment to the Constitution has restricted debate to the question of life-saving abortions, in the North it is a 'holy alliance' of evangelical Protestantism and fundamentalist Catholicism that has kept the debate so limited.

Since the late 1970s, the island of Ireland was held up as a 'beacon' by the anti-abortion movement internationally. Initially, it was the South that was seen as standing 'alone in her fight to defend the Judeo-Christian moral code of sexual behaviour and the sanctity of life', as promoter of natural contraception and Knight of Columbanus, Prof John Bonnar, argued in 1978 – when contraception was still illegal. But in 1979, Ireland got its 'Irish solution to an Irish problem' when

Charlie Haughey legalised contraceptives for 'bona fide married couples'. In the same year, Pope John Paul II used his visit to Limerick to rally the Catholic troops against abortion: 'May Ireland never weaken in her witness, before Europe and the whole world, to the dignity and sacredness of all human life, from conception until death' (Kerrigan, 1983).

The campaign for the Eighth Amendment to the Constitution referred frequently to the importance of Ireland's role as a world leader against abortion. Dr Julia Vaughan, chair of the Pro-Life Amendment Campaign, spoke about how the constitutional amendment would mean Ireland will 'once again become a beacon' that would 'turn the tide in the Western world' against abortion. The notion of Ireland's key role spread across the border with the advent of Precious Life (PL) in 1997. Modelled on Youth Defence (YD) in the South, Precious Life looked to the USA for campaign ideas. It denied firebombing the Ulster Pregnancy Advisory Association's offices in Belfast, but its founder, Bernie Smyth, got huge cheers at 1998's YD conference when, in front of TV cameras, she started her speech with 'one down, two to go'. PL raised unknown amounts of money in the US to 'keep Ireland abortion-free' and promoted the idea that 'Northern Ireland is a pro-life beacon to the world'.

In order to maintain the fiction that the island of Ireland is 'abortion-free', the anti-choice movement North and South has had to ignore the thousands of women who travel to England each year for abortions and to pretend that the relatively few abortions that take place in Northern Ireland are either illegal or 'not abortion'.

THE LAW ON ABORTION IN NORTHERN IRELAND

The law on abortion, North and South, is based on the same piece of Victorian legislation, the 1861 Offences Against the Person Act, which criminalises abortion and endorses life imprisonment as the punishment. In Northern Ireland, the law has been updated somewhat by the 1939 'Bourne judgement' – the acquittal in England of a doctor who had performed an abortion on a fourteen-year-old girl who was pregnant as a result of multiple rape. The core of the judgement is that abortion is legal if continuing pregnancy would leave the woman 'a mental or physical wreck'. The Bourne judgement, like the judgement in the X case in the South, is notoriously unclear, which is why the 1967 Abortion

Act had to be introduced in Britain. Both the (Westminster-appointed) Standing Advisory Commission on Human Rights and the UN committee overseeing the Convention for the Elimination of Discrimination Against Women (CEDAW) have criticised Westminster for allowing the lack of clarity to persist in the North and for not acting to end the current situation which amounts to one law for the rich, another for the poor.

The lack of clarity in the North was demonstrated when, between 1993 and 1995, four cases on abortion were considered by the Northern Ireland High Court. These judgements suggest that abortion is legal in Northern Ireland in many more circumstances than is generally realised. It may be that, if they were willing to go to court to prove it, a large proportion of the women who travel to England for abortions would have a legal right to obtain them within Northern Ireland – after all, most travel because they feel that continuing the pregnancy would leave them 'a mental or physical wreck'. The law in the North is the same as that which applied in England until 1967. In 1966, there were about 10,000 legal abortions in England, but these were only available to women who had enough money to pay for private treatment (Francome, 2004). As a result of court cases taken by the Family Planning Association, the Department of Health for Northern Ireland was forced to issue guidelines to clarify to medical staff when abortion is legal in the region. After several years of prevarication, draft guidelines were issued in January 2007, allowing abortion when a woman's mental or physical health is in 'grave' danger of 'serious and permanent damage'. In autumn 2007, the NI Assembly rejected these as being too liberal, with only a handful of MLAs (Member of the Legislative Assembly) from the UUP and Alliance voting to accept them (Horgan and O'Connor, 2013; Bloomer and Fegan, 2014). The Department of Health now agrees that 'Guidance is required to ensure that medical professionals are empowered to make decisions within the law and based on the medical circumstances that they face. It also ensures that women, no matter where they are from in Northern Ireland, are able to access services to which they are legally entitled' (Hansard, 2013a).

Three different sets of guidance have been issued for consultation since 2007. The most recent, from DUP Health Minister Edwin Poots in 2013, are so restrictive that legal experts argue that the NI Department of Health 'has acted beyond its powers in seeking to change, rather than clarify, the existing law on access to abortion in Northern Ireland' – a view shared by Alliance for Choice. So, instead of the view of the courts that a woman has a right to an abortion if continuing the pregnancy would leave her 'a physical or mental wreck', the 2013 version of the guidance says that 'The circumstances where a termination of pregnancy is lawful in Northern Ireland are highly exceptional'. In fact, as the response to the 2013 guidance from the Royal College of Nurses points out, 'the language used to illustrate this point escalates from "limited" in the title of the document to "highly exceptional" in the first sentence of paragraph 1.3 to "very strict and very narrow" in the second sentence and then to "very limited" in the penultimate sentence of the same paragraph'. One can only conclude that the point of all this is to scare doctors from providing abortions to women who need them and to maintain the current situation where abortions in Northern Ireland are carried out mainly at home, without medical supervision or where women are forced to travel.

The North's Department of Health has acknowledged that, until the mid-2000s, between 70 and 100 abortions were carried out in the North every year. Most of these were because the woman's life or health was in danger or for reasons of foetal abnormality. However, the chilling effect of the various draft guidelines issued by the Department of Health since 2007, together with the fact that abortion for reasons of foetal abnormality has been declared illegal, has brought the number of such abortions down to around forty each year. Some abortions for reasons of foetal abnormality continue but are hidden, while some couples from the North seeking abortions on grounds of foetal abnormality are forced to travel to England, like their southern counterparts.

PRETENDING IRELAND IS 'ABORTION-FREE'

Although the law in the North was confirmed as allowing abortion in potentially quite wide circumstances, Minister for Health, Poots has done everything to suggest that this is not the case. Why is he doing this when all the opinion polls show that: two-thirds of people think that abortion should be available to women pregnant as a result of rape; when three quarters think it should be available in cases of severe foetal impairments; and over half think it should be available either if a woman's physical or mental health is in danger or if the woman decides she wants an abortion. Poots and his fellow evangelical Protestant DUP members are every bit as fundamentalist in their approach to abortion as the most right-wing Catholics and provide a level of support to anti-abortion activists of which their equivalents in the South can only dream. For example, Bernie Smyth of PL has an Assembly pass, usually only available to political party advisers. Small wonder then that Poots' appointment as health minister in May 2011 was welcomed by the Society for the Protection of the Unborn Child (SPUC) with a plea to him to tighten the law on abortion even further.

Precious Life, like Youth Defence, is desperate to maintain the myth that 'Ireland is abortion-free' and to deny that any abortions are taking place. It argues against the need for guidance on when abortion should be provided within the law on the NHS by insisting that 'abortion is never necessary' to save a woman's life, ignoring that the law allows it to protect a woman's *health* from serious, long-term damage. Precious Life's *No Medical Necessity* pamphlet argues that there 'are NO medical conditions when the life of a pregnant woman can only be saved by abortion ... for example, it is now possible for women with heart defects to carry a baby to term with expert health' (PL, no date). While the first statement is a lie, the second has long been true. However, such women risk taking years from their lifespan and, while many choose to do that in order to have a much wanted child, the law in the North is clear that they have a right to an abortion in order to protect their health. Despite this, women in this situation all too often have to travel to England and pay for an abortion.

This anti-abortion insistence that abortion is never necessary is partly strategy, to protect the view of Ireland as the 'pro-life beacon', which helps bring in US money, and partly theology. Again and again, PL and YD insist that life-saving abortions are not abortions, drawing a medically and legally meaningless distinction between 'direct' and 'indirect' abortion: '... there are no medical circumstances justifying direct abortion, that is circumstances in which the life of a mother can only be saved by directly ending the life of her unborn child' (PL, *No Medical Necessity*). This is an attempt to impose Roman Catholic dogma which teaches that 'indirect' foetal destruction (for example, in the course of a hysterectomy) is not abortion, although medically it is. (This is what is known as 'double effect'.) This theological intervention in health care even found its way into the Poots' draft guidance issued in 2013. Paragraph 1.1.: 'Intervention cannot have as its direct purpose the ending of the life of the unborn child' (DHSSPS, 2013).

In the South, this distinction was raised by anti-abortionists in the course of Oireachtas hearings but was derided by most of the doctors who gave evidence to the hearings because it is not a medical concept. This is an example of how, although the anti-abortion arguments are similar North and South, there are real differences in the way they are received, as evidenced in the different tenor of parliamentary debates.

ACTIVIST POLITICIANS 'IMPLEMENTING GOD'S LAW'

Political parties in most jurisdictions tend to address abortion only reluctantly (Halfmann, 2011). This has been the case in the South since 1983, and especially since 1992. It has been argued that 'morality issues never reach a prominent place on the political agenda' in the UK (Engeli et al., 2012*)*. But Northern Ireland's politicians, especially DUP politicians, have been very pro-active in trying to restrict reproductive choice. Within three weeks of devolution in 2000, the Assembly had its first debate on abortion when the DUP's Jim Wells introduced a motion opposing 'the extension of the Abortion Act 1967 to Northern Ireland' (NIA Debate, 20 June 2000).

The influence of religion on government in the North largely explains this willingness to rush in where others fear to tread (Whitaker and Horgan, 2014). Several DUP ministers, including Health Minister Poots and Social Development (responsible for housing and social security) Minister Nelson McCausland are members of the Caleb Foundation, an organisation set up in 2009 to promote law and government in line with biblical thinking. Those associated with the Caleb Foundation refer to themselves 'jokingly' as 'The Caleban'. The *Belfast Telegraph* pointed out, 'Where the Taliban is pushing for an ultra hardline version of Sharia law based on its own reading of the Koran, Caleb wants to see a Bible-based society with every law measured against scripture' (*Belfast Telegraph*, 2010a).

The *Belfast Telegraph* published an investigation into the Caleb Foundation, which it described as 'a highly politicised group of religious fundamentalists'. It quoted an unnamed member of Caleb who is also a member of the DUP and the Free Presbyterian Church, as telling it that 'the [Free Presbyterian] Church needs to be able to castigate the

DUP when it believes it is doing something that is not consistent with Biblical views. Big issues are coming up in terms of transgender rights, abortion, the whole equality agenda, and the issue of creationism in schools' (*Belfast Telegraph*, 2010b). While there is no nationalist equivalent of the Caleban, some members of the SDLP do their best to appear to be just that. Pat Ramsey of the SDLP is chair of the All-Party Pro-Life Group, to which Precious Life provides the secretariat. He frequently cites religion as part of his motivation: 'My culture, background and faith mean that I – not just politically, but personally – want to be a champion for the unborn child' (Hansard, 2013b).

Precious Life is far more open about its religious agenda than is Youth Defence in the South. This was seen most clearly at the Convention for Life 2014 in Dublin where Bernie Smyth repeatedly spoke of the power of prayer, while Niamh Ni Bhrian of Youth Defence played down any mention of religion. This reflects the discourse in the North where, as Jonathan Bell told the Assembly in the March 2013 debate, the 'leaders of our Roman Catholic Church, our Presbyterian Church and our Church of Ireland have all spoken out on the matter, as have many other Churches'. The church leaders also wrote a joint letter in 2008 opposing moves in Westminster to extend the Abortion Act to the North (Horgan and O'Connor, 2013).

The extent to which politicians in the North continue to bend the knee to clergymen, now discredited and lacking in any moral authority in the South when it comes to matters related to sexuality, was demonstrated in April 2014 when Sinn Féin sought to associate itself with the views of a Catholic bishop in relation to abortion. In the run-up to the European and local elections, Precious Life briefed its supporters to include Sinn Féin in the list of 'pro-abortion' parties, which previously had included only smaller, more left-leaning, openly pro-choice parties. In west Belfast, Sinn Féin sent a letter to those who had attacked them on this ground on the doorstep. The letter stressed that 'We are not pro-choice and we are not in favour of abortion', and went on to state that 'In cases where a pregnant woman's life is in danger Sinn Fein, in line with current legislation and practice, believes the option of termination should be available. This is a position shared by the SDLP and the DUP and Catholic Bishop John McAreavey.' This backfired spectacularly when the bishop complained about it to the newspaper and an apology had to be issued. But would such a letter have been issued in the South?

MISOGYNIST NATURE OF ASSEMBLY DEBATES ON ABORTION

While the politicians in Dáil Éireann (Irish parliament) can be as fundamentalist in their views on abortion as the DUP/SDLP, they have learned to be far more careful in their language and in particular to be respectful towards women. The emotive language that is no longer seen as acceptable in the Dáil continues to be the norm in the Assembly. In the debate on the first set of guidance issued by then Health Minister Michael McGimpsey in 2007, Pat Ramsey (SDLP) asked Iris Robinson, then chair of the Assembly Health Committee, 'Does she agree that, if the guidelines were introduced in Northern Ireland, in one part of a hospital, doctors would be aborting children – dismembering legs and arms – while in another part of the same hospital, doctors in an intensive care unit would be trying to bring children back to life?' (Hansard, 2007).

In most Assembly debates, abortion is compared with the Holocaust by at least one MLA. Again, in the 2007 debate, DUP MLA Thomas Buchanan argued: '... We cringe at the number of Jews who were gassed or murdered by Hitler, and rightly so, yet in today's so-called civilised society, we witnessed 200,000 abortions across the UK last year, which is 600 a week and 50 to 60 children an hour.' In the 2013 debate, Jonathan Bell, a junior minister responsible for equality, said, 'We have to face the truth that in the West, we have destroyed more viable human life than Hitler ever put into a gas chamber.' It's hard to know whether these comparisons are more insulting to those who died, or watched their loved ones die in the Holocaust or to the hundreds of thousands of women across the world who have abortions every year.

The 2013 debate came about when the DUP's Paul Givan and SDLP's Alban Maginness tabled a last-minute amendment to an unrelated bill seeking to close down Belfast's Marie Stopes sexual health centre by making it illegal to perform an abortion outside an NHS hospital. The debate again exposed the misogyny underlying the approach of many of the North's politicians, particularly the DUP. The amendment being debated was 276 words long. Not one of these words was 'woman'. This used to be able to happen in the Republic, but it would cause a furore now. Paul Givan mentioned 'vulnerable women' four times in the debate while Jonathan Bell (DUP) talked about 'our women' needing protection. It seems that Bell feels women need protecting from themselves since in that same debate he asked, 'Is it not a shame that, in our United Kingdom, the most dangerous place for a child is in its mother's womb?' (Hansard, 2013b).

Several speakers in the 2013 debate referred to Precious Life, which had been campaigning to have the Marie Stopes centre (MSI) closed. Unable to maintain anything more than a token (though quite disruptive) protest outside MSI in Belfast, Precious Life had turned to its allies in the churches and faith schools to help garner support. As a result, on the day of the Assembly debate it was able to deliver 'a petition, signed by a quarter of a million people ... concerned about the defence of the most vulnerable in our society – the unborn child' (Patsy McGlone, SDLP).

Again and again in the course of all the Assembly debates, MLAs speak about the law as if it does not allow abortion when a woman's health, as opposed to life, is in danger. It is hard to know whether this is wishful thinking or if they actually believe Precious Life's line that abortion is 'always illegal' in the North. So, while Sinn Féin played an honourable role in ensuring that the Givan/Maginness amendment was defeated, its speakers nonetheless promoted this view of the law: 'In the absence of proper guidance, there can be no other conclusion but that the amendment is aimed at ensuring that no other avenue will be open to a woman in a life-threatening situation ... Are we to wait until we have a repeat of the Savita Halappanavar case before we are shaken to our senses?' (Caitriona Ruane, SF); 'I state once again for the record that Sinn Féin has a clear policy on the termination of a pregnancy. That policy states that, when a life of a woman is in danger, she has a right to a termination' (Raymond McCartney, SF in Hansard, 2013b).

PRO-BIRTH, NOT PRO-LIFE REGIME IN THE NORTH

It is important to note that the Assembly parties that are most vociferous and united in their anti-abortion stance, the DUP and SDLP, are also parties that have had fewest concerns when it comes to implementing legislation that make it more difficult for *born* children to have a decent life. The Welfare Reform Act 2008 was introduced by an SDLP minister and given 'accelerated passage' in the Assembly – meaning that all parties agreed to it passing all stages in one day, with minimal debate.

Yet, this legislation required lone parents whose youngest child is over three years of age to seek employment and introduced changes to the Local Housing Allowance so that the poorest families pay a large proportion of rent from social security payments intended for food and other essentials. More recently, the Assembly allowed the Health in Pregnancy Grant, which gave all pregnant women £190 towards a healthier diet, to be abolished, and the Surestart Maternity Grant of £500 to be limited to the first child only (Horgan and Monteith, 2012).

The DUP 'Caleban' minister in charge of social security supported the Welfare Reform Bill that, as well as the Bedroom Tax, included a benefit cap limiting the total benefits available to families to £26,000 a year. This means that benefits would be paid only for the first four children in any family. There would be no family allowance, no tax credits, no account at all taken of the needs of the fifth or any subsequent children – despite the fact that children experiencing persistent and severe poverty are more likely to come from large families (Adelman et al., 2003).

CAMPAIGNING DIFFERENCES NORTH AND SOUTH

There is some evidence that the North lags behind the South in terms of public attitudes to abortion, but since there have been no large-scale representative surveys of public opinion in the North such as those carried out by the Crisis Pregnancy Agency in the South, this cannot be confirmed. It is not surprising that opinion in the North had not progressed as much as that in the South. The impact of the conflict meant that religion remained a key mark of identity in the North and that all issues that did not 'belong' to one 'side' or the other tended to be ignored. However, as well as the opinion poll evidence cited above, the limited information available from the representative Northern Ireland Life and Times (NILT) Survey indicates that public attitudes are far ahead of the politicians. The 2008 NILT Survey asked, as part of a module on religious opinions and observance, whether it is always wrong to have an abortion if 'there is a strong chance of a serious defect in the baby', only 25 per cent of respondents said it is 'always wrong'; asked whether it is always wrong for a woman to have an abortion if 'the family has a very low income and cannot afford any more children', 43 per cent said it is always wrong. On the latter point, many pro-choice people might have been part of that 43 per cent because it is wrong if a woman is forced to have an abortion because of poverty. In any event, it is clear that Northern politicians who claim that they speak for the majority when they say there is no desire for a more liberal abortion law are wrong.

Attitudes in the North are certainly changing in spite of the efforts of the 'holy alliance' and largely because women in the North now live their lives in the same way as women in the South or in Britain. Women make up almost half the workforce, although two of every five women workers are part-time, largely because childcare is so expensive. In 2012, 43 per cent of all births in Northern Ireland were outside marriage, while in the cities of Belfast (59 per cent) and Derry (56 per cent), well over half of births were outside marriage (NISRA, 2012). This reflects changed attitudes to sexual activity and where there is sexual activity, no matter how carefully contraception is used, there will be accidents and there will be some pregnancies that women will want to end.

In spite of this, it is clear that the Assembly will allow abortion only in the very limited circumstances evangelical Protestantism and conservative Catholicism allows. The question which arises concerns what can be done in this situation to advance the right of women in the North of Ireland to self-determination, to control over their own bodies, and to the same level of health care as women in Scotland, England and Wales.

In March 2013, Alliance for Choice published a letter in which over 100 women (and some men) admitted to having taken, or to having aided and abetted a woman in procuring, abortion pills for the purposes of causing a miscarriage – and invited prosecution. Although the police issued a statement saying they were investigating the letter, not one of the signatories was approached by the police or any other agency (apart from the media). It is clear that the political classes would prefer not to have a public debate about the reality of abortion in Northern Ireland. Pro-choice activists North and South may force the debate by presenting themselves at police stations and demanding that either the police or courts take action or concede that home abortions are legal, thereby giving women the confidence to approach their doctors for after-care when they've induced their own abortion.

The really vital difference between North and South has been the social movement for reproductive rights that has grown steadily in the

South since the early 1980s. The campaigns around the five referendums on abortion in the Republic between 1983 and 2002 brought onto the streets a social movement such as has not been seen in the North. The Pro-Life Amendment Campaign in support of the Eighth Amendment to the Constitution had at first been compared to the Mother and Child scheme. It anticipated being as victorious as in the Catholic right's 1950s' campaign against basic healthcare for expectant mothers and pre-school children. But, as journalist Gene Kerrigan pointed out, 'The Mother and Child debacle was a flexing of well-used muscles by the traditional forces, and opposition collapsed immediately. This time there was at least a fight' (Kerrigan, 1983). The fight saw the Anti-Amendment Campaign establishing action groups from Cork to Donegal and points in between. Of course, there were more troughs than peaks but by 1992, when the X case came to light, tens of thousands could take to the streets to support a woman's right to choose on a relatively spontaneous basis. The more than 25,000 people who demonstrated in Dublin on the Saturday after the death of Savita Halappanavar came to light were a further example of this social movement.

While there are proportionately as many women in the North who have had abortions and while the injustice in the North is more stark – we pay the same taxes as women in England, Scotland and Wales who can access abortion on the NHS – what has been missing in the North is thousands of people on the streets showing support for a woman's right to choose. In the South, no one could have predicted the reaction to the 1992 X case but the howl of anger from people no longer willing to live in a society that treats women and girls so badly broke the logjam of years of sexual repression and conservatism. We cannot predict how the grip of the holy alliance might be broken in the North but, if it is to happen, it will need the kind of mass action seen on the streets of the South.

22

Abortion as a Women's Health and Human Rights Issue:
National Women's Council (NWCI) activism on reproductive rights over the decades

ORLA O'CONNOR

NATIONAL WOMEN'S COUNCIL OF IRELAND (NWCI) is a feminist, non-governmental membership organisation of women's groups in Ireland with over 180 member organisations. Our vision is of an Ireland where there is full equality between women and men.

NWCI celebrated its fortieth anniversary in 2013. Though recent events have brought abortion back into the public domain, NWCI has worked on the issue consistently over the last thirty years. Our position on abortion has developed over time in recognition of the diversity and evolution of views in the area. Abortion is a significant contention in Irish society and one that remains unresolved. NWCI acknowledges the entrenched social, religious and political views on both sides of the debate.

Members have mandated NWCI to adopt a pro-choice position on abortion that is rooted in an analysis of gender equality, women's human rights and social inclusion. This position has developed very gradually over time and has involved much discussion and consideration.

Given the wide diversity of the NWCI membership and the status as the national representative organisation for women in Ireland, this mandate has been and continues to be critical with respect to our position within wider abortion debate. It is always the issue raised in media and political circles. Therefore, it is important that our policy on abortion will continue to be driven by our members.

OUR APPROACH TO AND ANALYSIS OF REPRODUCTIVE RIGHTS

NWCI approaches its work on abortion from a rights-based and equality perspective. Access to safe and legal abortion is indistinguishably linked to human rights values and principles that protect a woman's right to privacy, her right to bodily integrity, her right to self-determination, her right to be free from inhuman, cruel and degrading treatment and her right to accessible, appropriate and quality health care, as guaranteed by international human rights instruments. Failure to provide for safe and legal abortion in Ireland consistently contravenes these rights.

NWCI views access to safe and legal abortion in Ireland in an overall context of gender equality and social justice. Gender inequality significantly affects women's lives, and cuts across an intersection of socio-economic, political and cultural boundaries. Since the foundation of NWCI in 1973, Ireland has made considerable progress on women's equality. Despite this, full gender equality has yet to be achieved. Women in Ireland continue to work fewer hours, earn less and are under-represented in the Oireachtas and in local and regional authorities compared to men. Women are far less likely to be in the labour force and are almost twenty-five times more likely to be looking after home/family than men. In 2009, women's income was around 73 per cent of men's. Disposable income for households headed by a male continues to be significantly higher than that of households headed by a female: deprivation and poverty rates are higher for women and for households headed by a woman, compared with men or households headed by a man.

It is in this wider context that women with crisis pregnancies are denied access to safe and legal abortion in Ireland. The lack of access to reproductive health care, including abortion, intersects with other structural and systemic forms of discrimination against women and needs to be discussed within the framework of gender inequality. Abortion is too often isolated from issues such as socio-economic inequalities, health inequalities, barriers to active participation and inequality of opportunities and of outcomes – matters which directly affect an individual woman's decision-making process and are inextricably linked to gender equality.

NWCI views reproductive health and rights within a social justice framework, highlighting the right to have and not to have children and linking it to other fundamental human rights such as the right to decent housing, the right to access good education, and the right to have access to health care. Ethnicity, culture, social class, income poverty, location, sexual orientation, age, disability and other differences can all contribute to the inequalities in women's lives and impinge on decisions concerning their health and wellbeing.

NWCI believes that achieving access to safe and legal abortion in Ireland is critical to advancing the position of women in Irish society. Women must be able to make decisions about their own bodies and health care free from coercion, discrimination and threat of incarceration: this, crucially, includes the decision to carry a pregnancy to term or to seek an abortion and exercise these rights without discrimination.

NWCI ACTIVISM ON ABORTION

NWCI motions and policy development

Motions brought by members at our annual general meetings (AGMs) is a unique way in which our members can drive and influence NWCI policy and prioritise areas of greatest concern in the drive for equality between women and men. Over the years motions on abortion have been frequent and reflective of external events happening at that time.

NWCI motions from the 1980s referred to the need for research into the impact and effects of crisis pregnancy and abortion on women. This developed in the 1990s into motions highlighting the artificial distinction between the life and health of women in pregnancy. In 1995 members brought motions on access to abortion information. In 2001 a motion was passed calling on NWCI to conduct a full consultation with members to ascertain their views on the implications of the upcoming referendum and bill for all women in Ireland, in particular its implications for women with crisis pregnancies. Following extensive consultation undertaken, there was agreement that NWCI should call for a 'No' vote.

In 2002 a motion was passed in support of abortion being permitted in cases of fatal foetal abnormalities. The same AGM also passed a motion requesting that NWCI lobby the government to have article 40.3.3 removed from the Irish Constitution. In 2004 four motions relating to abortion were passed by members related to the grounds on which a woman can avail of abortion services in Ireland, for the government to legislate to provide for abortion in cases where a woman's life is at risk in cases of rape and a motion asking NWCI to take a pro-choice position on the issue of abortion and to lobby the government accordingly.

In 2009, members supported a motion which called for development of a policy seeking provision of safe, legal abortion for women in this state. This states our current mandate. In June 2011 an emergency motion was passed in the aftermath of the landmark 2010 *A, B and C v. Ireland* case to the European Court of Human Rights, asking that in line with its pro-choice position, NWCI strongly urge the government to implement the judgement of the European Court of Human Rights in the case of *A, B and C v. Ireland* without further delay, by providing legal certainty on when a physician may carry out an abortion in Ireland.

In this brief sweep of motions carried at our AGMs over three decades it is interesting to note that this policy development is hugely reflective of the shift in public attitudes to abortion seen in public opinion polls over the same period. For example in June 2013 an *Irish Times* / IPSOS poll reported that 89 per cent of people supported abortion in cases where women's life is at risk, 83 per cent supported abortion in cases where the foetus cannot survive outside of womb, 81 per cent said abortion should be allowed in cases of rape or incest and 78 per cent felt abortion should be allowed when women's health is at risk. It is clear that our members and the public at large consider our current law on abortion to be too restrictive and in need of urgent change.

Engagement of human rights monitoring bodies

Lack of access to safe and legal abortion affects the human rights of women: the right to bodily integrity; the right to equality before the law; the right to be free from inhuman and cruel treatment; the right not to be discriminated against on grounds of gender; the right to health;

and the right to life. These rights are guaranteed by a range of international instruments including the Universal Declaration on Human Rights, the International Covenant on Civil and Political Rights, the International Covenant on Economic, Social and Cultural Rights, the Convention on the Elimination of all Forms of Discrimination Against Women, and the Convention Against Torture.

Ireland's prohibitive regulation of abortion and the discriminatory nature of its application have been consistently subject to criticism by international human rights monitoring bodies. Since 2005 the UN Human Rights Committee, the UN Committee on the Elimination of all Forms of Discrimination Against Women, the UN Committee Against Torture, the Council of Europe Commissioner for Human Rights and the European Court of Human Rights have all criticised Ireland's regulation of abortion as being inadequate to fulfil Ireland's human rights obligations. At the Universal Review Process in 2011, nine countries asked questions or made recommendations to Ireland in relation to abortion – all critical of the existing law.

Over the years NWCI and other organisations have been consistently engaging with international human rights bodies and processes to highlight the impact of Ireland's restrictive abortion regime on women's human rights. Different UN committees have taken up the issue and incorporated it into their Concluding Observations, which has served to highlight the issue both nationally and internationally and to put pressure on different governments to be answerable to these concerns. This engagement has been critical in situating abortion as a human rights issue, taking it out of the moral national framework and integrating it into the international human rights framework.

NWCI convenes the Women's Human Rights Alliance (WHRA), a coalition of national organisations concerned with the promotion and protection of women's human rights and the translation of international human rights norms into the national context. Abortion rights in Ireland has been a strong focus of the work of the Alliance since its inception in 2001 and its activism directed at the UN Committee in relation to Ireland's report to CEDAW in 2005 led to a strong recommendation from the CEDAW Committee in relation to abortion.

More recently the Alliance secured speaking rights at the UN Human Rights Council as part of the examination of Ireland's human rights record under the Universal Periodic Review Process. The Alliance also submitted a complaint to the UN Special Rapporteur on the Right to Health in relation to the impact of Ireland's restrictive abortion regime on women's health rights. This low-key form of activism can be very effective in keeping abortion on the human rights agenda and making successive governments answerable to international human rights monitoring bodies and their peers.

Campaigning on abortion

In recent years we have adopted a stronger campaigning approach to all of our work including reproductive rights. In 2012 we launched an online campaign with regard to legislating for the X case. Some 76,000 emails were sent from more than 17,000 women and men, representing every constituency in the country, calling on TDs and senators to bring forward legislation as a matter of urgency to give effect to the X case. Our active participation at marches and rallies organised more recently and over the decades has been significant in making our position on abortion visible to policy makers and politicians. Through media and social media NWCI has been promoting discussion on abortion from a feminist perspective, clarifying myths and misinformation circulating in the public domain for our many members and friends.

NWCI has also recently produced a policy paper on abortion to give detail to our analysis and our approach to advancing reproductive rights which was circulated to all our members for comments. We have also established a working group of member organisations and individual members to drive the campaign side of the work and to ensure the membership is leading and advising the work on abortion. This working group has been invaluable in advancing our work on abortion. Working with other organisations and members to advance change has been hugely beneficial and has strengthened our cause when facing much opposition to the legalising of abortion in Ireland.

Our role and work is to give voice to the experiences of women in Ireland who remain largely voiceless in this debate due to the stigma that surrounds abortion in Ireland. This is done in a number of ways. We support new and emerging groups who are campaigning on liberalising access to abortion services. NWCI is called upon regularly to comment on or participate in media debates on the impact of abortion on women in Ireland and we are conscious to include the voice of women who have experienced the effect of current law and policy where possible. We believe that this is fundamental to changing policy in this area.

NWCI prepared its 2013–2015 Strategic Plan after extensive consultation with our members. Reproductive rights are one of the core priorities of the plan and of the campaign areas of NWCI over the next four years. Our focus will be on encouraging the government to initiate the constitutional reform and legislative changes necessary to introduce safe and legal abortion in Ireland.

23

Ireland's First Abortion Legislation

CLARE DALY TD

I N THE EIGHTEEN MONTHS following the death of Savita Halap-panavar in October 2012 there was more debate in Ireland about abortion than in the previous two decades.

In 1992 the Supreme Court ruled that it was lawful to have an abortion in Ireland where the life of a woman was at risk as a result of the pregnancy, including a risk of suicide. Justice Niall McCarthy described the political establishment's failure to legislate as 'no longer just unfortunate, it is inexcusable', and yet by 2002 all that Fianna Fáil could deliver was another referendum to attempt to roll back that X case ruling – an attempt that was again rejected by the people of Ireland. Another ten years passed and still nothing was done.

When in 2010, the Grand Chamber of the European Court of Human Rights unanimously found Ireland to be in breach of Article 8 of the European Convention on Human Rights in the case of *A, B and C v. Ireland*, it was clear that considerable international pressure was beginning to mount. The new government set up a so-called 'Expert Group' with representatives from the legal and medical profession, to examine what sort of regulations or legislation were necessary to give effect to a woman's right to abortion as outlined by the Supreme Court.

It was against this backdrop and conscious of the approach of the twentieth anniversary of the X case ruling that myself and my colleagues, Independent TD for Wexford, Mick Wallace, and fellow United Left Alliance TD, Joan Collins, began work in the winter of 2011 to prepare legislation to give effect to the X case ruling. Working with the pro-choice group, Action on X, we sought to ensure that this issue would no longer be allowed to remain ignored or long-fingered.

Coinciding with the-run up to the anniversary and preparation for our legislation, the Medical Treatment (Termination of Pregnancy in Case of Risk to Life of Pregnant Woman) Bill 2012, a major public meeting was organised for 21 February 2012 in Dublin – the first major pro-abortion initiative in the city for years. It is interesting looking back that in preparation for that meeting we discussed the possible need for security, knowing the intimidation exercised by the anti-abortion lobby. As it turned out, the protest was small and the meeting a great success, with a room packed full of young people, mainly women, who clearly were not going to sit back and wait another couple of decades for progress in this area.

The moving of the bill in private member's time on 18 and 19 April 2012 was the first time abortion was proactively discussed in the Dáil without a tragedy provoking it, but rather from the standpoint that it was an important health and human rights issue. The vote was lost twenty votes for, 111 against, with Fianna Fáil, Fine Gael, Labour and a number of Independents voting against the bill, while Sinn Féin, the United Left Alliance and seven Independents voted for it.

The large majority against the bill, however masked the quality of the debate and the subsequent open dialogue that took place around the issue in the media, with four women waiving their anonymity and telling their stories of making the journey to Britain for a recent abortion as their foetuses had fatal abnormalities incompatible with life. With 150,000 women travelling out of the state to access an abortion for so many different reasons over the past three decades, it is clear that no family has been untouched by this issue, whether they know it or not. The stories of mothers, daughters, sisters, wives, girlfriends were beginning to be told openly. The minister for health at the time, James Reilly, promised that his government would not be the seventh to ignore this issue.

While our bill restricted the provision of abortion to the limited circumstances where a woman's life was in danger, given the constitutional position, we were unapologetic in making it clear that we favoured access to abortion in any circumstances that a woman sought it. Ironic-ally, Labour deputies who argued against our bill on the basis that it did not go far enough later supported legislation that was far more restrictive.

It is clear that the problem with abortion legislation is not the public who consistently demonstrated an understanding of the many varied and valid reasons why a woman might need an abortion, but the political establishment, who lagged significantly behind public consciousness and who remained lethargic about touching this issue for fear of stirring up the well-organised, vocal minority in the anti-abortion campaign and the Catholic Church.

The March for Choice on 29 September 2012 saw thousands confidently take to the streets of Dublin, demanding abortion legislation. The mood of the participants and the response from shoppers and passers-by clearly showed a new generation in the ascendancy who would not tolerate the ongoing hypocrisy of it being legal for an Irish woman to have an abortion, enshrined in the Constitution by her right to travel and right to information, but being unable to access that treatment in Ireland. Years ago women with crisis pregnancies were hidden behind the walls of Magdalene laundries; now they are expected to take a Ryanair ticket out of our sight – an option that will be more and more difficult as austerity continues and people do not have the wherewithal to secure a minimum of €1,000. Non-national women, whose status in the country is precarious, do not even have the chance of making that journey. The March for Choice queried whether we had to wait for another tragedy, another X case, before legislation would be forthcoming.

Sadly that tragedy happened a month later with the death of Savita Halappanavar on 28 October 2012 in Galway University Hospital. Her death sparked an enormous movement of anger at another woman needlessly losing her life as a result of political inaction. Tens of thousands took to the streets demanding 'Never Again'. The issue of whether her life would have been saved had our bill been passed was openly discussed. To keep the pressure on, we again re-tabled that legislation on 27 and 28 November 2012.

Again the vote was lost, by 27 votes to 101, with the same forces voting as before, but this time to cut across the growing momentum the Expert Group report was published the day the debate started and we were told action would be taken. Hearings were convened into the report at the Health Committee, which came back early from the Christmas recess. The anti-abortion lobby swung into force as legislation was becoming an inevitability, with the battle on to restrict it as best they could. In the end abortion legislation, despite all the fire and brimstone speeches, was passed into law on 30 July 2013, with twenty five TDs voting against it for anti-abortion reasons – fourteen Fianna Fáil TDs who were given a free vote, six who broke the Fine Gael whip, one each from Labour and Sinn Féin, and three from the Independent benches. However, the reality is that the legislation introduced by the Fine Gael/Labour coalition government, the Protection of Life During Pregnancy Bill 2013, while being important symbolically in that it legislates for abortion in Ireland for the first time, in practice is so restrictive as to make it almost inaccessible to anyone.

Even women experiencing inevitable miscarriage can continue to be denied an abortion. Prior to the 2013 act, Savita's sad death had shown, as clearly stated by Dr Peter Boylan and by the HSE report, that in a situation of inevitable miscarriage, in which the death of the foetus is the inevitable outcome, the presence of a foetal heartbeat puts a legal restriction on what a doctor can do.

The legal situation on when a doctor could terminate a pregnancy to protect a woman's life was unclear. The 2013 act has not changed that. In fact the act now gives legal protection to the so-called 'unborn' from the moment of implantation in the womb until delivery from the woman's body. There is no legal provision for termination of pregnancy shortly after a woman's waters have broken (inevitable miscarriage) if there is still a foetal heartbeat.

This point was made by the consultant obstetrician who treated Savita. It informed the medical strategy of 'wait and see' that was adopted by her medical team. Yet this is the time when a woman is increasingly at risk of infection: the longer the delay in clearing the womb, the greater the risk of sepsis. But doctors are legally obliged to wait until the foetus dies, or until a woman develops sepsis to the extent that her life is at risk, before they can clear the womb and thus remove the source of infection. This is an outrage and a product of our

Constitution which puts a Chinese wall between a woman's right to life and her right to health.

We have now had three reports into Savita's death. Her inquest returned a verdict of death by medical misadventure. The HSE report listed the medical failings in the treatment of her infection. It also highlighted the fact that she was not offered one particular medical intervention: termination of pregnancy shortly after she was admitted to hospital and diagnosed as having an inevitable miscarriage. Savita herself asked for this but was refused. The HSE report highlighted the legal restrictions to terminations in such circumstances and called for legislators (the Dáil) to consider legal and constitutional change to deal with these restrictions.

The HIQA report highlighted thirteen 'missed opportunities' for medical intervention to treat Savita during her deepening illness and the development of the sepsis that killed her. But it did not mention that termination of pregnancy was an intervention that could have prevented the sepsis developing in the first place. By focusing on issues relating to management of infection, HIQA has let Fianna Fáil, Fine Gael, Labour and Sinn Féin off the hook regarding their responsibility to remove the legal restrictions to terminations which can prevent infection taking hold. Neither the consultant obstetrician nor the Galway hospital medical team, who may have made errors in the way they treated Savita, should be made scapegoats for the failure of politicians to remove legal restrictions on the treatment that doctors can provide to pregnant women.

So now after Savita's death, women in Ireland still face risks to their lives due to the state's denial of the right to an abortion. The 2013 act is so restrictive that none but the most desperate, or those in state care, are likely to benefit from it. This act, which is underpinned by article 40.3.3 of the Constitution, forces women and their doctors into situations where women's lives are threatened. It also denies women abortions in cases of rape or incest, fatal foetal abnormality or risk of permanent damage to health.

A number of senior government figures have said they support legislation to permit abortion in cases of fatal foetal abnormality and other specific circumstances. A strong legal opinion emerged during the debate of the past year that it could be possible to legislate for abortion in this instance without a constitutional referendum, as the right to life of the unborn, which has constitutional protection, could not exist in cases where its condition was incompatible with life. Labour in particular should stop hiding behind the supposed advice of the attorney general and move to legislate while they are still in office. Any notion that such a law would be unconstitutional could be tested by putting it to the Supreme Court.

The 2013 act effectively makes abortion unobtainable in Ireland. It also criminalises women who use abortion pills they buy over the internet – making it less likely they will go for aftercare. It denies women the right to choose when they wish to continue a pregnancy. These denials of access to abortion are why I and other pro-choice TDs voted against it.

During the debate on our bill in November 2012, the Minister for Equality and Justice, Alan Shatter, summed up very succinctly the consequences of Ireland's approach to abortion when he stated that 'It can truly be said that the right of pregnant women to have their health protected is, under our constitutional framework, a qualified right, as is their right to bodily integrity. This will remain the position ... This is a Republic in which we proclaim the equality of all citizens but it is a reality that some citizens are more equal than others.' He also described it as an 'intolerable cruelty' that a woman should be denied abortion in cases of rape or incest and fatal foetal abnormality, and proclaimed that 'a pregnancy that poses a serious risk to the health as opposed to the life of a woman, even where such risk could result in permanent incapacity, does not provide a basis of a termination in this state ... In the absence of constitutional change there will continue to be a British solution to an Irish problem.'

This explains the situation very well, but for the Minister for Equality to make such a statement and then shrug his shoulders as if the resolution of that inequality has got nothing to do with him demonstrates an appalling abdication of responsibility and political cowardice.

This is an approach that has prevailed for too long. In order to protect the lives and health of women the 2013 act must be repealed, as must article 40.3.3 of the Constitution. This discriminatory provision, which equates the life of a woman with that of the unborn has no place in today's Ireland, and indeed it never had. Irish abortion has always existed at pretty much the same level as in other countries, it is just that the state does not permit it to take place in Ireland. Instead, with breath-taking hypocrisy, the reality is hidden, and vulnerable women coping with a crisis pregnancy are exported to Britain and beyond with all of the extra expense and emotional cost that such a situation brings.

Hundreds of women spoke openly of their abortion experiences during the months following the death of Savita Halaphanavar, people such as Hazel who wrote to me saying, 'I protested tonight for the first time since I was in college. I never felt so moved to stand up and be counted in my life. I've just had my second child, a beautiful baby girl, and this is not what I want for her or my country, of which I am usually so proud.' And Alice: 'As a woman with grown-up children I thought I had lost the urge for the fight but since Saturday's march I have rediscovered it and will not let it go'. The task is to channel that energy and that determination into the broadest possible campaign to get a referendum to repeal 40.3.3. This should include not just those of us who are pro-choice but also those who support access to abortion on restricted grounds, be it in cases of rape or incest, fatal foetal abnormalities or where a woman's health is in danger.

Already the Union of Students in Ireland, Unite and SIPTU have called and campaigned for legislation that is less restrictive than the act that was passed. We need to build on that support to build a movement for change. We are the majority who have been silent too long. We owe it to the memory of Savita Halappanavar, to her husband Praveen, and to the many women who have suffered and died because they were denied abortion, to remove the current reactionary, anti-woman legislation from the statute books as soon as we can.

24

The Radicalisation of a New Generation of Abortion Rights Activists

CATHIE DOHERTY and SINÉAD REDMOND

I N THE SUMMER OF 2012, the virulently anti-choice organisation, Youth Defence, launched a new national billboard campaign. There were two posters with the same text, 'Abortion tears her life apart. There's always a better answer'. Youth Defence used two stock images for this campaign: one of a foetus at eighteen plus weeks' gestation and another of a woman crying. This campaign made it clear to those not already in the know that the anti-choice lobby in Ireland had vast financial resources at its disposal. The posters went up on hoardings, covering towns and cities throughout Ireland overnight. Commuter links seemed to be particularly targeted, with the posters plastered over much of the Dublin Bus fleet, huge billboards at many train stations, and even an animated version displaying on a screen in Heuston Station. This was a campaign clearly designed to shame and silence those who have had abortions and do not feel that their lives have been torn apart by them. It also wanted to shame and silence those who had abortions and felt that there was no 'better answer' available to them.

For the authors of this piece, born after the Eighth Amendment was inserted into the Irish Constitution and for many of our contemporaries, this was the first time we had experienced, as adults, the power, funding, and utter disregard for the health and wellbeing of those who have had abortions of the extremist anti-choicers. It's strange to say it now, with wide and opened eyes, but before that billboard campaign – despite the fact that both of the authors had in fact needed to access abortions before the summer of 2012 – neither we, nor many of the now radicalised abortion rights activists we work with, had really realised how virulent Youth Defence and their ilk are, or, despite their tiny size, how much power and access to those with power they still maintain. How bizarre, that even having needed to either seek abortion access legally outside Ireland, or illegally seek help from outside Ireland to access, hadn't brought home to us the utter disregard for the health and wellbeing of people like us held by the instigators of this tone-deaf display of moneyed misogyny.

We found ourselves far from alone in our outrage, shock and disgust. In fact, throughout Ireland, people expressed their anger at having their public space so invaded with such bile in a number of ways. Many took direct action, vandalising the posters. People used various methods including tearing the posters down, paint-bombing them, and in several instances, even doctoring the posters so that a pro-choice message remained plainly visible, literally overwriting the shaming that all that money had gone into putting up. Photos of these editings by members of the public were widely shared on social media outlets, the main among these outlets being Twitter and Facebook.

The rise of social media over the last decade is an interesting one. In Ireland alone, over 60 per cent of adults have a Facebook account, with 50 per cent of adults in Ireland using Facebook every day, and 25 per cent of adults have a Twitter account. This means that not only is a very large share of the population of Ireland directly accessible through social media, but also a large share of the population can now talk with and to each other about their concerns and opinions in a direct and immediate way, not bounded by geography or other physical limitations, in a manner never before possible. Thus, social media has become a tool used by activists to share information and ideas and to coordinate other forms of direct action and protest.

On the July night of first seeing the Youth Defence campaign posters and fuelled by the rage they had caused, one of us, Sinéad, used Facebook to create the page 'Unlike Youth Defence, I trust women to decide their lives for themselves' (UYD). It was surreal, but deeply soothing and vindicating, to watch the 'likes' pour in. Within an hour it had over 250 'likes' and by the end of a week, a thousand. The outpouring of frustration and outrage was palpable, and it was clear that plenty of people out there shared our desire to take physical action in the face of the silence of the majority of those in power. Through our conversations using UYD as a vehicle to share information, talk, discuss and organise, we (who had never so much as attended a major protest before, let alone organised one) put together a protest outside Leinster House for 11 July 2012. As part of the protest organisation, we also put together two poster and banner-making events, one in the Exchange Dublin[100] and one in Seomra Spraoi[101] that happened to coincide with a RAG Dublin[102] meeting.

This meeting and the protest that followed were the starting points of what later became the Abortion Rights Campaign. The protest was positive, well-attended and successful – in the region of 300 people were there, and it truly invigorated us, other fledgling abortion rights activists new to the foray, and the many long-term activists who said to us at the protest that they felt change in the air and were renewed by the large turnout. The weeks and months that followed were filled with a flurry of abortion rights events and activity, both online and off, which more and more people were joining. We were part of a group of people who organised an open meeting on abortion rights activism in Seomra Spraoi, out of which came the official founding of the Irish Choice Network (ICN). The Irish Choice Network was intended to be a banner organisation for the grouping together of pro-choice organisations and people, and existed in the interim period between that hectic July full of events and the December of 2012, when the Abortion Rights Campaign was formally announced.

Before the tragic news broke of Savita Halappanavar's horrific and unnecessary death, in November of 2012, there was a real buzz of excitement and joy around the newly galvanised abortion rights movement. We were part of the group who organised the first annual March for Choice, on 28 September 2012, to coincide with the Global Day of Action for Access to Safe and Legal Abortion, and we deliberately chose to have the mood of that march be a celebratory one: that despite all the obstacles in our way, despite our lack of funding to run national advertising campaigns, we were coming together to support the right of anyone who needs access to abortion. There was a turnout of around 3,000 at that march, a truly moving and inspiring sight.

In Northern Ireland, the Marie Stopes clinic began offering early medical abortions – but only within the current legal framework: that is, if a woman's life is at immediate risk or there is a risk of 'real and serious' long-term or permanent damage to her physical or mental health, and only on a privately paid-for basis. The Irish Choice Network organised a bus to travel from Dublin to Belfast to attend a rally in support of the clinic. Work on the set-up and structure of the Abortion Rights Campaign (to replace the ICN) was continuing apace, with meetings in the National Women's Council of Ireland (NWCI) and other locations with large groups of activists from around the country.

A week later, on 14 November, the news broke in the *Irish Times* that Savita Halappanavar had been denied a life-saving abortion for an inevitable miscarriage, and had died in University Hospital Galway of sepsis, at seventeen weeks' pregnant. Kitty Holland was contacted by friends of Savita and Praveen Halappanavar, friends who were outraged by the two weeks of utter silence that followed her death on 28 October, and broke the news to the country that in Ireland, a woman's life ranked below that of a foetal heartbeat, even a heartbeat destined to stop in the very near future.

It's not an exaggeration to say that for us and for the other abortion rights activists we know and work with, this news was shattering. We had known that women were being treated appallingly, their health and wellbeing neglected and their rights ignored when pregnant, but for a woman to be left to die in pain and fear in an Irish hospital in the twenty-first century because she was suffering an inevitable miscarriage was genuinely devastating. We were part of the groups that organised the rallies and marches in the following few weeks. In Ireland, what it takes for people to stand up in large numbers and say 'No more; never again', unfortunately, is the publicisation of the direst situations. Twenty thousand people marched in the Never Again march on 17 November, which was Diwali, the Hindu festival of lights. The activists who would later form the Creative and Direct Action branch of the Abortion Rights Campaign (ARC) made sure this festival of Savita and Praveen's faces was marked with huge banners embossed with Savita's face, encircled with lights that lit up as the sun went down on the march and left the 20,000 of us in darkness. When the march reached Merrion Square, most of those 20,000 people lit candles that we held in the dusk: for Savita and for our own failure as a country to enact a change that could have saved her. Two weeks later, the official launch of the Abortion Rights Campaign took place in the Gresham hotel.

25

Ireland's Handmaid's Tale

SINÉAD KENNEDY

There is more than one kind of freedom, said Aunt Lydia. Freedom to and freedom from. In the days of anarchy, it was freedom to. Now you are being given freedom from. Don't underrate it. (Atwood, 1996, pp. 32–3)

THE RECENT HISTORY AND POLITICS OF ABORTION in Ireland rehearses themes women living in Ireland are extremely familiar with: class, power and control. Abortion has been illegal in Ireland since the introduction of the 1861 Offences Against the Person Act. Over 150 years later, it is still illegal in almost all circumstances. Indeed, Ireland continues to have one of the most restrictive abortion regimes in the world, with abortion being prohibited in all circumstances except where there is a threat to the life of the pregnant woman. The narrative of that 150 years is largely unspoken, but it is haunted by the nameless, faceless women who have suffered, died or been forced into exile as a result of the Irish state's insistence on its right to limit the freedom of pregnant women living in Ireland. Nigel Rodley, the former

UN Special Rapporteur on Torture, probably most accurately articulated the experience of being a pregnant woman in Ireland when in his closing remarks during Ireland's Fourth Periodic Examination by the United Nations (UN) Human Rights Committee in Geneva in July 2014, he stated that Ireland's abortion laws treat a pregnant woman 'as a vessel, nothing more' (Holland, 2014c).

The Irish state has long enjoyed elevating itself as a protector and promoter of human rights internationally, campaigning vigorously for recent membership of the United Nations (UN) Human Rights Council.[103] Yet, this same state was incapable of explaining to the UN Committee why it was unable to develop a strategy to bring abortion law into line with international human rights standards. The state was asked by the committee to comment on how the stipulation that a pregnant woman, at risk of suicide, be examined by a series of doctors before being allowed access to abortion was compatible with its obligations to protect citizens from mental torture, and to justify the inequalities in the law that adversely affected poor women, asylum seekers, those in state care and women with disabilities. The response was to suggest that if a majority of people wanted to take away the rights of any group, they were entitled to, and the state had no choice but to comply. The ramifications of this position have been terrifying for Irish women whose bodies have become ideological battlefields between the 'private' choice of an individual woman and the 'public' interests of the Irish state.

THE REALITY OF IRELAND'S ABORTION REGIME

If, after the death of Savita Halappanavar, a further reminder was required of the lived reality of this ideological position, it was offered less than four weeks after the UN Committee meeting when a young rape victim, whose life was at risk from suicide, was denied an abortion and forced, under probable duress, to undergo a caesarean section. The young woman, known only as Ms Y, was a migrant and therefore was unable to travel abroad, lacking both the financial means to travel and pay for an abortion and the required visa to leave and re-enter the state. Her situation was no doubt further compounded by the fact that she was, in all probability, interned in one of Ireland's notorious direct provision centres, putting her outside of the informal networks that

Irish women rely upon to access legal abortion abroad or illegal abortion online using the abortion pill (O'Shea, 2014). Ireland is no different to any other country where abortion is illegal or restricted. Women need access to abortion and making it illegal does not reduce the number of abortions; it simply reduces the safety of abortion. According to the World Health Organization, twenty million of the forty-two million abortions performed every year are illegal and unsafe. In every country where abortion is illegal the result is the same: it is young, rural and working-class women who bear the most suffering from illegal abortion (see Kennedy, 2015).

So in some ways Ms Y's situation was unlike that of other women in horrific situations and in desperate need of access of abortion. What made her case particularly significant in terms of the history of Irish abortion debate was that Ms Y was one of the first women to apply for a legal abortion under the Protection of Life During Pregnancy Act 2013. This act was passed, in part, as a response to the public outrage directed at the government following the death of Savita Halappanavar, but also in order to fulfil the requirements set out by the 2010 European Court of Human Right's (ECHR) judgement in the *A, B and C v. Ireland* case. The ECHR judgement required the government to provide 'certainty' and 'procedural rights' to the question of access to abortion, which had remained ambiguous for the two decades since the 1992 Supreme Court ruling in the X case (Smet, 2010). The 1992 X case established the constitutional basis for abortion where there was 'a real and substantial risk' to the life of a pregnant woman, including the risk of suicide. This risk, Chief Justice Finlay acknowledged, did not need to be 'inevitable or immediate' (*Attorney General v. X*, IR 10[1992]). Two subsequent referendums, in 1992 and in 2002, saw the government attempt to exclude suicide as grounds for lawful abortion in Ireland but, on both occasions, the electorate conclusively rejected this option. However, due to the failure and political cowardice of six successive governments to provide a legal framework for the circumstances under which abortion is permissible in Ireland, a dangerous vacuum existed that would result in numerous women being dragged through the legal system and, ultimately, the death of Savita Halappanavar.

The X case was possibly the most defining moment in the struggle for abortion rights in Ireland, not just because the case itself was exceptional – a fourteen-year-old rape victim injuncted by the state from leaving the country to access an abortion – but because it changed the nature of the abortion debate in Ireland. Since the 1983 referendum which introduced a constitutional ban on abortion, the Irish abortion debate had been conducted in a highly dysfunctional manner. For the most part, women who have had abortions remain invisible, their actions concealed under a veil of hypocrisy and political cowardice, so that the myth of an abortion-free Ireland can be maintained. Women are free to travel abroad and have abortions abroad as long as they don't talk about them.

It is assumed, as a matter of course, that the abortion debate is different here; that it is too sensitive, too controversial for Irish sensibilities. On the limited number of occasions when abortion is acknowledged the terms under which the debate is managed are extraordinarily limited, conducted in abstract, ethical and philosophical terms. The X case changed the nature of the debate by clarifying precisely the argument on which the whole debate about abortion rests: Do you think that the rights of the woman, her life, her health, her hopes, her well-being should be considered paramount? Or do you think that a foetus, still invisible to the naked eye, should have rights that supersede those of the woman? In February 1992 Irish people were forced to answer those questions and overwhelmingly they sided with the woman. Thousands of people took to the streets and forced the hand of the judiciary, making abortion legal in Ireland for the first time where a woman's life was at risk.

Due largely to a deliberate strategy of political inaction among the mainstream political parties and to the presence of article 40.3.3 (commonly referred to as the Eighth Amendment) in the Irish Constitution, progress on abortion since 1992 has been stagnant. The Eighth Amendment created a constitutional prohibition on abortion stating that 'The State acknowledges the right to life of the unborn and, with due regard to the equal right to life of the mother, guarantees in its laws to respect, and, as far as practicable, by its laws to defend and vindicate that right'. In effect, these forty-three words mean that, in legal terms at least, a foetus is an independent entity whose rights must be protected regardless of the risk to the health or well-being of the pregnant woman. Its presence in the Irish Constitution for over three decades has resulted in over 160,000 Irish women being forced to travel abroad in order to access safe and legal abortion services; that represents an average of twelve women every day, or 4,000 women every year.[104]

However, within that thirty-year period a dramatic shift in attitudes to abortion has occurred with research and opinion polls consistently showing wide support for increased access to abortion services within Ireland.[105] Despite these levels of support, the Irish electorate has never been given the opportunity to make abortion less restrictive or, indeed, to offer legal abortion. Even after the enormous outpouring of anger over the death of Savita Halappanavar and the demands for political action, the legislation introduced by politicians to give effect to the X case was fashioned in the most restrictive terms imaginable, requiring a woman to have her abortion approved by between three and six doctors. Politicians also insisted on the introduction of a new criminal penalty of fourteen years imprisonment, criminalising women and medical practitioners who accessed or performed an illegal abortion on Irish soil.

WHAT IS TO BE DONE?

A whole new generation of abortion rights activists have been politicised by the death of Savita Halappanavar and the horrendous treatment of Ms Y and have begun to organise to repeal the Eighth Amendment and campaign for free, safe and legal abortion in Ireland through organisations and groups like the Abortion Rights Campaign, Galway Pro-Choice and Action for Choice. How this will be achieved continues to be the subject of much debate but there have been important steps forward. The establishment of the Coalition to Repeal the Eighth Amendment in the months following the Protection of Life During Pregnancy Act (2013) was one of these key steps. The Coalition is an umbrella organ-siation that has managed to bring together a diverse groups of activists, campaigners, NGOs, trade unionists and civil society organisations to campaign for repeal of article 40.3.3 in order 'to respect and protect women's lives, health and choices' (see www.repealeight.ie). This is an important first step but it would be a mistake to assume that simply removing the Eighth Amendment from the Constitution is the sole solution to the Irish abortion problem. We will also need to repeal the legislation enacted to enforce it – including the Abortion Information Act (1995) and the Protection of Life During Pregnancy Act (2013). In developing strategies to fight for abortion rights we also need to consider what meaningful access to abortion would involve and look at the variety of intersecting laws and policies – class, medical, immigration, child protection, mental health, among others – which shape women's access to abortion. This will involve challenging not only the Irish state but also the medical establishment who continue to exercise tremendous levels of power that contribute to the degradation and distress of Irish women and the deaths of Savita Halappanavar and Bimbo Onanuga (see Enright, 2014b). There has been a great deal of emphasis in the Irish abortion rights movement on legal solutions, yet the best possible solution would not be to just decriminalise and legalise abortion but to remove it from criminal law altogether and regulate it like other models of women's reproductive health care like, for example, the Canadian. To achieve this will require a large-scale, grassroots movement that can effectively intervene on the political terrain and force meaningful change.

Probably the biggest challenge of all facing the abortion rights movement more than twenty years after the X case and other such headline cases is that the too-often public debate on abortion continues to focus on the extreme cases: where a woman's life or health is at risk or where a woman is a victim of rape. Even some advocates of abortion rights can appear more comfortable on this terrain, as if somehow abortion is more justifiable in these cases because it is not really the woman's 'fault' that she is faced with this decision. However, reality again is very different. The vast majority of the 160,000 Irish women who had abortions in the last three decades did not decide to do so because their life was at risk, or they were suicidal, nor had they been raped. They chose abortions for thousands of different and sometimes complicated reasons. They made a decision. Sometimes it was a difficult choice, often it wasn't; but it was their decision to make. Instead of respecting and facilitating that choice the Irish state summoned all of its authority and power in order to deny them their autonomy, brand them as criminals or force them into exile.

We need to stop apologising for abortion and put it at the centre of women's reproductive lives and health. Access to abortion is a social good that contributes to a more equal and just society. One of the important political achievements of second-wave feminism was winning people to the idea of abortion as an essential choice for women. Indeed, in the past four decades women's lives have been transformed so dramatically through the legalisation of abortion that, as US author and activist Katha Pollitt notes, we are in danger of forgetting how things used to be: 'Legalising abortion didn't just save women from death and injury and fear of arrest, it didn't just make it possible for women to commit to education and work and free them from shotgun marriages and too many kids. It changed how women saw themselves; as mothers by choice not by fate' (Pollitt, 2014, p. 3). There is nothing more fundamental for a human being than autonomy over their own body. It is an essential component of what it means to be a free, rational human being. If Irish women are denied the fundamental freedom to make rational, informed and ethical decisions about their own lives, their own bodies and their own personhood, then all the other freedoms that we have fought for and continue to fight for really do not amount to very much at all and we are little more than handmaidens.

NOTES

BIBLIOGRAPHY

INDEX

NOTES

FOREWORD

1 The footnotes rev up in my head as soon as I start to write. Speaking on the barricades is different. Why? There's a hitch in there already. An earlier version of this appeared as a 'think piece' in *Estudios Irlandeses*, no. 10, 2015.

2 And carrying with it something of the spectacular, in Debord's sense.

3 Interview with the Bishop of Elphin, Kevin Doran, on *Newstalk 106*, 9 March 2015 (Doran, 2015).

4 Invited to speak at a political event a short while ago, the organisers told me (reinforced by meaningful glances and nods) that straying on to 'other' topics (i.e. abortion) wouldn't be welcome. The techniques of silencing here are indeed finely honed.

5 'Termination' is the preferred synonym, and even that is used economically. During the 1992 referendum campaign, abortion was called 'the substantive issue' by politicians and lawyers.

6 *Women have abortions every day. It's just one choice.* Video made by Katie Gillum for the Irish Family Planning Association. Available at: https://www.youtube.com/watch?v=R4SSHkgD73E

7 Euthanasia being the other exception.

8 The Guttmacher Institute estimates that globally between 30–40% of pregnancies end in abortion. The figures vary across different parts of the world and depending on whether abortion is safe and legal, prohibited or effectively unavailable. Guttmacher observes that highly restrictive abortion laws are not associated with lower abortion rates. The Irish abortion rate is somewhere between one in nine or one in ten.

9 Sadly, nearly half of all abortions worldwide are unsafe, and nearly all unsafe abortions (98 per cent) occur in developing countries. In the developing world, 56% of all abortions are unsafe, compared with just 6 per cent in the developed world. Available at: http://www.guttmacher.org/pubs/fb_IAW.html

10 The Protection of Life During Pregnancy Act 2013 legalised abortion where a woman is suicidal, although the act imposes a draconian interrogation regime which vests the power of decision in up to six doctors (gynaecologists /obstetricians and psychiatrists). The Eighth Amendment to the Constitution, which equates the life of the woman ('mother') with that of the foetus ('the unborn') remains in full force, requiring the woman's life to be saved only in so far as it is 'practicable' to do so. Failure to observe the law can result in up to fourteen years' imprisonment for the woman or for any person acting 'with the intent to destroy unborn human life'.

11 1983, 1992 and 2012

12　Technically, there have been five referendums as the 1992 referendum put three potential amendments to the electorate, of which two were passed, i.e. the rights to travel and to information. In both 1992 and 2002, the electorate rejected proposals to further narrow the grounds for abortion in Ireland.

13　At least 3,679 women accessed abortion in Britain in 2012, and over 158,252 women have had to make the journey since 1980. These statistics are for women who gave Irish addresses. It's not known how many women from Ireland gave UK addresses, or accessed abortion in other countries, such as the Netherlands. See Irish Family Planning Association, https://www.ifpa.ie/HotTopics/Abortion.

14　For many women, provision of the abortion pill (Mifepristone) would be a straightforward solution. However, it is illegal here.

15　Throughout her months-long ordeal, Ms Y had said she wanted an abortion.

16　Sheila Hodgers (d. 1983) died screaming in agony of multiple cancers. She and her husband had been repeatedly refused an abortion, induction or caesarean section throughout her pregnancy because, the hospital said, the baby would not survive. Their baby girl died immediately after birth. Sheila died two days later. Savita Halappanavar (d. 2102) was about sixteen weeks pregnant when she developed back pain and was admitted to hospital. She was found to be miscarrying but was refused an abortion as the hospital said 'the foetal heart was still beating'. She died a week later after miscarrying, contracting E.coli leading to septicaemia. Her husband maintained she would have lived had their request for termination been met. See Holland (2013a).

17　It is always about who has the power to control the means of reproduction.

18　This brings me back to my starting point. I can't answer that question. Maybe it's because, having been involved for so long, I've lost sight of the key to understanding. It isn't simple, in any case.

TIMELINE

19　This timeline was produced by the Irish Family Planning Association and is used with permission. The original version is available at https://www.ifpa.ie/Hot-Topics/Abortion/Abortion-in-Ireland-Timeline

CHAPTER 2

20　Author's discussion with Maurice Moynihan with whom Éamon de Valera worked on drafts of the Constitution.

CHAPTER 3

21　See the Irish Family Planning Association's website for comments by human rights commissioners and human rights committees on Ireland's abortion law. http://www.ifpa.ie/Hot-Topics/Abortion/Abortion-Human-Rights (accessed 8 August 2013).

22　Until 2013 criminal abortion was punishable under sections 58 and 59 of the Offences Against the Person Act 1861 and involved sentences of up to life imprisonment.

23   Figures collected by the UK Department of Health indicate that between
      January 1980 and December 2012 at least 156,076 women from Ireland had
      abortions in England and Wales. As many women do not give Irish addresses,
      the figure is known to be an underestimate. For statistics and links to UK
      documents see the Irish Family Planning Association website,
      http://www.ifpa.ie/Hot-Topics/Abortion/Statistics

24   See for example a 26 April 1970 *Sunday Independent* report, 'Senator attacks
      divorce prohibition', on Senator Mary Bourke's (later Robinson) assertion that
      the law should not uphold a particular church's position.

25   Printed matter advocating contraception and abortion had been banned
      since the Censorship of Publications Act passed in 1929.

26   Browne was subsequently censured by some party colleagues:
      http://www.irishtimes.com/newspaper/archive/1971/0301/Pg008.html#
      Ar00804

27   The other TD was Michael Kitt.

28   'Knits' is used in the sense of drawing together and creating.

CHAPTER 5

29   I have taken these three dimensions of equality from an equality framework
      developed by Baker et al. (2004).

30   The amendment predominantly affected Medicaid, the means-tested health
      programme jointly funded by the state and federal governments, which provides
      resources for healthcare to low-income families and individuals.

31   In 2011, the World Health Organisation reported that this figure stood at
      approximately 47,000 deaths per year (Department of Reproductive Health
      and Research, 2011). Furthermore, it was estimated that a total of 21.6 million
      women experience unsafe abortions worldwide (ibid.).

32   The death of Savita Halappanavar in 2012 has reinvigorated the debate
      around abortion as a life-saving health care service. Traditionally, however,
      feminists have drawn on broader definitions of health care in order to appeal to
      a medical framework.

33   The case is one that has become common knowledge to those who have
      struggled to achieve change in Ireland. In 1992, a fourteen-year-old girl known
      as X was prohibited by a high court injunction from travelling to the UK to seek
      an abortion (Smyth, 2005). Having become pregnant as the result of rape, she
      became suicidal following the injunction.

34   Ireland is an extreme case; however, in countries where abortion is legally
      available on request, such notions still prevail. In France for example, women
      have this access, but must still declare that they are in a 'state of distress'
      (Henshaw et al., 1999).

35   Such a critique has been noted in the application of the medical model to
      disability (Oliver, 1996). Disability activists have acknowledged that disability is

a social construction as opposed to a biological fact. What is disabling, they argue, is being situated in societies that are hostile to the specific needs of the less dominant group. Disability has shifted from an illness to a civil rights issue, from a bodily issue to one rooted in a social context of prejudice and discrimination (ibid.).

CHAPTER 6

36   It is worth noting that Savita is rare among the women listed in that we have a face to put to her name, a face which has been widely circulated and replicated by media and activist movements. The image is both conventionally beautiful and noticeably non-Irish. I believe these things matter.

37   Cissexism is prejudice or discrimination against people who are transgender, or whose gender identity does not match with the sex they were assigned at birth.

38   The Criminal Law (Sexual Offences) Act 2006 established a common age of consent to sex at seventeen for males and females whether it is a heterosexual or homosexual relationship.

39   In the medical area, the Non-Fatal Offences Against the Person Act 1997 (section 23) provides that a minor who has reached the age of sixteen can give consent to medical treatment.

40   The Criminal Law (Sexual Offences) Act 1993 makes it an offence to have or attempt to have sexual intercourse with a mentally impaired person unless they are married.

41   The Eighth Amendment of the Constitution Act 1983 introduced a constitutional ban on abortion in Ireland. The Thirteenth Amendment and the Fourteenth Amendment (both in 1992) were attempts to loosen the ban, by guaranteeing the right to freedom of travel and to information about abortion services available abroad respectively.

42   Irish adoption law currently only allows for applications to adopt children by married couples or single applicants. It is therefore not possible for a gay couple to jointly apply to adopt, but a single gay person or one partner of a couple may apply. Even though joint adoption by a same-sex couple is not possible, same-sex couples may submit a joint application to foster children.

43   A General Scheme of the Gender Recognition Bill 2013 which would provide for a scheme whereby transgender people could apply to change the gender marker on their birth certificates has been drafted. The scheme contains proposals which include a number of human rights violations. This process is currently with the Joint Committee on Education and Social Protection, awaiting enactment by Minister for Social Protection Joan Burton. Ireland is one of the last countries in Europe to enact such legislation, which represents a fundamental right for trans* people. See http://www.ihrc.ie/download/pdf/equality_authority_observations_on_the_revised_general_scheme_of_the_gender_recognition_bill_1.pdf

44 Trans* is an umbrella term which seeks to include the wide array of gender identities and expressions which differ from the sex assigned to a person at birth.

45 Individuals who were assigned female at birth, but identify more as male. This includes female-to-male spectrum trans* people as well as many non-binary trans* experiences. It is a myth that all trans-masculine individuals undergo hysterectomy or do not wish to bear children.

46 Cisgender people are those whose gender identities match up with the sex assigned to them at birth.

47 Female genital mutilation. While this is the commonly accepted term, it must be acknowledged that the term mutilation holds judgement for a certain set of practices, a judgement which strangely does not carry over when considering more Western-sanctioned genital cutting practices such as penile circumcision and surgeries performed on intersex individuals.

CHAPTER 7

48 Investigation of Incident 50278 from time of patient's self referral to hospital on the 21st of October 2012 to the patient's death on the 28th of October, 2012, Health Service Executive, June 2013.

49 Section 58 provides: 'Every woman being with child, who with intent to procure her own miscarriage shall unlawfully administer to herself any poison or other noxious thing or shall unlawfully use any instrument or other means whatsoever with the like intent, and whomsoever, with intent to procure the miscarriage of any woman, whether she be or not be with child, shall unlawfully administer to her or cause to be taken by her any poison or other noxious thing, or shall unlawfully use any instrument or other means whatsoever with the like intent, shall be guilty of felony, and being convicted thereof shall be liable to be kept in penal servitude for life.'
  Section 59 provides: 'Whomsoever shall unlawfully supply or procure any poison or other noxious thing, or any instrument or thing whatsoever, knowing that the same is intended to be unlawfully used or employed with intent to procure the miscarriage of any woman, whether she be or not be with child, shall be guilty of a misdemeanor, and being convicted thereof shall be liable ... to be kept in penal servitude.'

50 Section 17, Criminal Law Amendment Act 1935.

51 See the Dáil Debate on the Control of Importation, Sale and Manufacture of Contraceptives Bill, 1974: Second Stage (Resumed), Dáil Eireann Debate, vol. 274, no. 6. Avaialble at: http://oireachtasdebates.oireachtas.ie/debates% 20authoring/debateswebpack.nsf/takes/dail1974071100004?opendocument

52 See *The Irish Times*, 15 May 1981.

53 Eighth Amendment of the Constitution Bill 1982: Committee Stage (Resumed) and Final Stages, Dáil Eireann Debate, Vol. 341, No. 10.

54 Eighth Amendment of the Constitution Bill 1982: Second Stage (Resumed), Dáil Eireann Debate, vol. 341, no. 5.

55 See the Dáil debated on the Eighth Amendment of the Constitution Bill, 1982: Committee Stage, Seanad Éireann Debate, Vol. 100 No. 9.

CHAPTER 8

56 For an overview of abortion statistics of Irish women having abortion in the UK see https://www.gov.uk/government/uploads/system/uploads/attachment_data/file/211790/2012_Abortion_Statistics.pdf

57 Article 40.3.3 reads: 'The State acknowledges the right to life of the unborn and, with due regard to the equal right to life of the mother, guarantees in its laws to respect, and, as far as practicable, by its laws to defend and vindicate that right.'

58 The Protocol states: 'Nothing in the Treaty on European Union ... shall affect the application in Ireland of Article 40.3.3 of the Constitution of Ireland.'

59 See HSE press statement, 11 July 2013: 'Number of Irish women giving addresses at UK abortion clinics decreases', http://www.hse.ie/eng/services/news/newsarchive/2013archive/july2013/ukabortionclinics.html

60 See for example http://www.irishtimes.com/news/politics/legal-confusion-in-savita-case-shatter-1.1360821

61 See http://www.pila.ie/bulletin/november-2013/20-november/complaint-lodged-with-un-human-rights-committee-regarding-ireland-s-abortion-laws/ and the website of the Termination for Medical Reasons group at http://www.terminationformedicalreasons.com/

62 For information on opinion polls, see http://ifpa.ie/Hot-Topics/Abortion/Public-Opinion.

CHAPTER 11

63 I would like to thank the women of ESCORT for being there and for giving so generously of their time. Thanks also to Mary Ewert for transcription, research support and for sharing her thinking about activism on young women's reproductive rights. An earlier version of this draft benefited from the encouragement of Anne Quesney and of the editors of this collection; my thanks to them. This chapter draws on research into abortion support groups for a larger book project, research which was originally funded by the ESRC. I wanted to contribute an analysis of ESCORT to this collection as one way of acknowledging Ailbhe Smyth's immeasurable contribution to feminist theory and practice through *The Abortion Papers Ireland* (1992) and many other initiatives. The women of ESCORT and Ailbhe Smyth have motivated this feminist in ways she's still struggling to acknowledge appropriately.

64 For one account of the impact of neo-liberalism on feminist NGO engagement with women's policy agencies within the state, and how it has required a shift from a state feminist framework to one of market feminism, see Kantola and Squires, 2012.

65 *Women have abortions every day: It's just one choice*, available at: http://www.youtube.com/watch?v=R4SSHkgD73E&feature=share&list=UU_sAZ5fW2b9pbM6QoCYLnGg and see: http://blog.ansirh.org/2013/10/using-video-to-destigmatize-abortion/

66 http://shareyourabortionstory.tumblr.com

67 http://www.terminationformedicalreasons.com

68 http://www.bbc.co.uk/news/blogs-trending-26224885

CHAPTER 12

69 'Restrictive laws have much less impact on stopping women from ending an unwanted pregnancy than on forcing those who are determined to do so to seek out clandestine means' (Cohen, 2009 – no page number supplied).

70 The text of article 41.2 stipulates that:,
1° In particular the State recognises that by her life within the home, woman gives to the State support without which the common good cannot be achieved.
2° The State shall therefore endeavour to ensure that mothers shall not be obliged by economic necessity to engage in labour to the neglect of their duties in the home.

71 Mary McGee, mother of four with a heart condition which could have endangered her life should she fall pregnant again, took a constitutional case against the state's ban on contraception and won (Murphy-Lawless, 1993).

72 From 64 in 1968 to 4,000 in 1984.

73 PLAC included a wide array of members, such as the Society for the Protection of the Unborn Child (SPUC), the Catholics Doctors Guild, Family Solidarity, the Knights of Columbanus and Opus Dei, to cite but a few (Randall, 1986).

74 'The State acknowledges the right to life of the unborn, and, with due regard to the equal right to life of the mother, guarantees in its laws to respect, and as far as practicable, by its laws to defend and vindicate that right' (article 40.3.3).

75 The case was taken by three women, who travelled abroad for abortion services and argued that the criminalisation of abortion services in Ireland had jeopardised their health and wellbeing, in violation of a number of articles of the European Convention on Human Rights (IFPA).

76 As befittingly noted in the Dictionary of Feminist Theory: 'deviance concepts are used by those in power to "naturalise" their way of doing things as normal and to label other ways of action as deviant' (Humm, 1989).

CHAPTER 15

77 Based on the Irish Family Planning Association's 'Abortion in Ireland: A Legal Timeline', http://www.ifpa.ie/Hot-Topics/Abortion/Abortion-in-Ireland-Timeline, accessed 18 February 2013.

78 It is understood, however, that Ms X went to Britain where her pregnancy was terminated (Smyth, 1992a, p. 7).

79 Irish Family Planning Association, http://www.ifpa.ie/Hot-Topics/Abortion/Statistics, accessed 20 February 2013.

80 Even though the recession upturned the balance and brought about a return to emigration.

81 http://www.akidwa.ie, accessed 3 November 2013.

82 Criminal Justice (Female Genital Mutilation) Act 2012,
    http://www.irishstatutebook.ie/pdf/2012/en.act.2012. 011.pdf

CHAPTER 16

83 http://www.tallgirlshorts.net/

84 Pindyck created one such assemblage called projectvoice.org which she
    created from her home in Brooklyn, New York 'in an effort to deflate the stigma
    of abortion and to bring her own abortion experience into conversation with
    others' (2013, p. 46).

85 https://www.education.ie/en/Schools-Colleges/Information/Diversity-of-
    Patronage/Diversity-of-Patronage-Survey-of-Parents.html

86 http://www.theguardian.com/world/2012/mar/23/abortion-what-children-schools

87 http://www.independent.ie/irish-news/school-principal-deeply-sorry-over-
    abortion-leaflets-29368569.html

88 http://clericalwhispers.blogspot.ie/2013/06/school-chair-resigns-in-anti-
    abortion.html

89 http://www.theliberal.ie/abortion-in-ireland-not-so-much-debate-as-debacle/

CHAPTER 17

90 First published (with emendations) in *The Independent*, 4 May 2013.
    Original version posted on libranwriter.wordpress.com, 7 May 2013.

CHAPTER 18

91 It is notable that the GP element of the scheme alone costs €17 million
    per annum (Dáil Éireann, 2014, HSE Primary Care Division, Reply to Clare
    Daly TD, PQ 18692-14), which makes it far more costly than equivalent
    midwife-led care schemes.

92 The deaths of these women, all of whom died in Irish maternity units between
    2007 and 2012, have been widely reported in the national press. The death of
    Tania McCabe is especially significant for the HSE report following her death,
    which contained recommendations about maternity units which were not acted
    upon, as became evident in the published investigations following the death of
    Savita Halappanavar. See HSE (2008) 'Report into maternal and child death at
    Our Lady of Lourdes hospital' and HIQA (2013) 'Investigation into the safety,
    quality and standards of services provided by the Health Service Executive to
    patients, including pregnant women, at risk of clinical deterioration, including
    those provided in University Hospital Galway, and as reflected in the care and
    treatment provided to Savita Halappanavar'.

CHAPTER 19

93 I am grateful to colleagues in the IFPA who have shared their expertise and
    insights during the writing of this chapter, in particular Evelyn Geraghty,

Director of Counselling, Dr Caitriona Henchion, Medical Director, Niall Behan, Chief Executive Officer and Denise Ryan, Communications Officer. Any factual errors are entirely my responsibility.

94 See [1973] IESC 2; [1974] IR 284 (19 December 1973).

95 United Nations Human Rights Committee. Concluding observations on the fourth periodic report of Ireland. July 2014. UN Doc CCPR/C/IRL/CO/2014.

96 Regulation of Information (Services Outside the State For Termination of Pregnancies) Act, 1995.

97 The IFPA owes the term 'conscientious commitment' to the work of Rebecca Cook and Bernard Dickens, see Dickens and Cook (2012).

98 See the Irish Human Rights Commission, Observations on the Protection of Life During Pregnancy Bill 2013.

99 Department of Health (2014) Implementation of the Protection of Life During Pregnancy Act. http://health.gov.ie/wp-content/ uploads/2014/09/Guidance-Document-Final-September-2014.pdf. Accessed July 6th 2015

CHAPTER 24

100 The Exchange was a charity, co-operative and collective arts centre in Temple Bar, Dublin. It provided a free space for people to express and develop their creative projects and talents, as well as to host meetings. It was closed down by Dublin City Council and the Temple Bar Cultural Trust on 29 January 2014, who chose to revoke its licence amid controversy and community outcry. Over 5,000 people have subsequently signed an online petition to lobby for its licence to be returned.

101 Seomra Spraoi is a social centre located in Dublin. It is run by a non-hierarchical, anti-capitalist collective on a not-for-profit basis. It hosts, among other things, workshops, gigs, political meetings, language lessons and bike repair workshops. The centre seeks to be a hub of positive resistance in a city and society where public spaces have been eaten away by consumerism and property speculation.

102 RAG (Revolutionary Anarcha-feminist Group) is a Dublin-based anarcha-feminist collective. Founded in 2006, RAG publish a magazine called *The Rag*, of which there have been six issues to date.

CHAPTER 25

103 See the Irish state's celebration of its human rights record during its membership of the UN Human Rights Council for the term 2013–2015: 'Ireland's Membership of the UN Human Rights Council 2013–2015'. Available at https://www.dfa.ie/our-role-policies/international-priorities/human-rights/ireland-and-the-human-rights-council/

104 For an overview of Irish abortion statistics see the Irish Family Planning Association http://www.ifpa.ie/Hot-Topics/Abortion/Statistics.

105 For an overview of opinion polls (2011–15) on support for Irish abortion reform see http://www.ifpa.ie/Hot-Topics/Abortion/Public-Opinion.

BIBLIOGRAPHY

Abortion Support Network (ASN), https://www.abortionsupport.org.uk/about/faqs/#4, accessed 1 April 2014

Abortion Support Network (2014), Newsletter, March 2014, https://www.abortion support.org.uk/newsletters/asn-march-2014-newsletter, accessed 1 April 2014

Adelman, L., Middleton, S. and Ashworth, K. *Britain's Poorest Children: severe and persistent poverty and social exclusion* (London: Save the Children, 2003)

Agamben, G. *Homo Sacer: sovereign power and bare life* (Stanford, CA: Stanford University Press, 1995)

Agamben, G., *State of Exception* (Chicago: Chicago University Press, 2005)

Ahmed, S., *The Cultural Politics of Emotion* (Edinburgh: Edinburgh University Press, 2004)

AIMS, 'New HSE birth statistics show a continuing high level of interventions including C-sections, instrumental deliveries and episiotomies'. Retrieved from http://aimsireland.ie/new-hse-birth-statistics-show-a-continuing-high-level-of-interventions-including-c-sections-instrumental-deliveries-and-episiotomies, accessed 5 August 2014

All Party Committee on the Constitution, *Report of the All-Party Committee on the Constitution (Fifth Progress Report)* (Dublin: Government Publications, 2000)

Anonymous a (a medical practitioner), 'Contraception and Controversy', *Irish Times*, 22 October 1965

Anonymous b, 'Pope Renews Birth Control Opposition', *Irish Times*, 26 January 1971

Anonymous c, 'Repeal of Law on Contraceptives Urged', *Irish Times*, 1 March 1971

Anonymous d, 'Alteration of Law Would Be "a Curse upon Our Country"' (McQuaid's Pastoral), *Irish Times*, 29 March 1971

Anonymous e, 'Hierarchy Enters the Contraceptive Controversy: state not bound by Church's moral law, say bishops', *Irish Times*, 26 November 1973

Anonymous f, 'Right To Life Cannot Be Selective, Says Bishop,' *Irish Times*, 11 April 1983

Anonymous g, 'Poll an Opportunity – Archbishop', *Irish Times*, 20 August 1983

Anonymous h, 'Opposition by Chief Rabbi', *Irish Times*, 5 September 1983

Appiah, K.A., *The Honor Code: how moral revolutions happen* (New York: W.W. Norton & Company, 2010)

Apple, M.W., *Education and Power* (London: Routledge & Kegan Paul, 1982)

Armstrong, F., *Spaced Out: policy, difference and the challenge of inclusive education* (Dordecht: Kluwer Academic Publishers, 2003)

Arnold, M. and Kirby, P., *The Abortion Referendum: the case against* (Dublin: Anti-Amendment Campaign, 1982)

Asian Communities for Reproductive Justice, A New Vision for Advancing our Movement for Reproductive Health, Reproductive Rights, and Reproductive Justice, http://forwardtogether.org/assets/docs/ACRJ-A-New-Vision.pdf, accessed 05 July 2015

Atwood, M., *The Handmaid's Tale* (London: Vintage, 1996)

Bacchi, C.L., *Women, Policy and Politics: the construction of policy problems* (London: Sage, 1999)

Bacik, I., *Kicking and Screaming: dragging Ireland into the 21st century* (Dublin: The O'Brien Press, 2004)

Badinter, E., *The Myth of Motherhood: an historical view of the maternal instinct* (Paris: Flammarion, 1981)

Baker, J., Lynch, K., Cantillon, S. and Walsh, J., *Equality from Theory to Action* (Basingstoke: Palgrave Macmillan, 2004)

Balibar, E., 'Racism and Crisis', in E. Balibar and I. Wallerstein (eds), *Race, Nation, Class: ambiguous identities* (London: Verso, 1991)

Barr, J., *Liberating Knowledge: research, feminism and adult education* (Leicester: NIACE, 1999)

Barron, D., 'The Practice of Illegal Abortion', *Irish Medical News*, 16 November 2009

Barry, U., 'Abortion in the Republic of Ireland', *Feminist Review*, 29 May 1988, pp. 57–63

Barry, U. 'Movement, Change and Reaction: the struggle over reproductive rights in Ireland', in A. Smyth (ed.), *The Abortion Papers Ireland* (Dublin: Attic Press, 1992), pp. 107–18

Barry, U. (ed.), *Where Are We Now? New feminist perspectives on women in contemporary Ireland* (Dublin: New Island Press, 2008)

Begley, C., Devane, D., Clarke, M., McCann, C., Hughes, P., Reilly, M. and Doyle, M., 'Comparison of Midwife-led and Consultant-led Care of Healthy Women at Low Risk of Childbirth Complications in the Republic of Ireland: a randomised trial', *BMC Pregnancy and Childbirth*, vol. 11, no. 1, 2011, p. 85

Belfast Telegraph, 'Creationist Bible Group and its Web of Influence at Stormont', 1 September 2010, http://www.belfasttelegraph.co.uk/news/politics/creationist-bible-group-and-its-web-of-influence-at-stormont-28787760.html [2010a], accessed 4 August 2014

Belfast Telegraph, 'Why Good Book Could Be Bad News for DUP', 7 June 2010, http://www.belfasttelegraph.co.uk/opinion/why-good-book-could-be-bad-news-for-dup-28540057.html [2010b] accessed 4 August 2014.

Berer, M., 'Termination of Pregnancy as Emergency Obstetric Care: the interpretation of Catholic health policy and the consequences for pregnant women – an analysis of the death of Savita Halappanavar in Ireland and similar cases', *Reproductive Health Matters*, vol. 21, no. 41, 2013, pp. 9–17

Bettinger-López, C. and Sturm, S.P., 'International Union, *UAW v. Johnson Controls*: history of litigation alliances and mobilization to challenge fetal protection policies', in M.E. Gilles and R.L. Goluboff (eds), *Civil Rights Stories* (New York: Foundation Press, 2007), http://papers.ssrn.com/sol3/papers.cfm?abstract_id=982252, accessed 5 July 2015

Binchy, W., 'Ethical Issues in Reproductive Medicine: a legal perspective', in M. Reidy (ed.), *Ethical Issues in Reproductive Medicine* (Dublin: Gill & Macmillan, 1982), pp. 95–117

Bloomer, F., and Fegan, E., 'Critiquing Recent Abortion Law and Policy in Northern Ireland', *Critical Social Policy*, vol. 34, 2014, pp. 109–20

Blunt, A., 'Geography and the Humanities Tradition', in S.L. Holloway, S.P. Rice and G. Valentine (eds), *Key Concepts in Geography* (London: SAGE, 2007), pp. 73–91

Boland, C., 'Bishop Says Abortion Wrong in Every Case', *Irish Times*, 4 June 1982

Bolton, G., 'Narrative writing: reflective enquiry into professional practice', *Educational Action Research*, vol. 14, no. 2, 2006, pp. 203–18

Boonstra, H.D., 'The Heart of the Matter: public funding of abortion for poor women in the United States', *Guttmacher Policy Review*, vol. 10, no. 1, 2007, pp. 12–16

Bourdieu, P., *Outline of a Theory of Practice*, translated by Richard Nice (Cambridge: Cambridge University Press, 1977)

Bourdieu, P., *The Logic of Practice* (Cambridge: Polity Press, 1990)

Boyle, M. *Re-thinking Abortion: psychology, gender, power and the law* (London: Routledge, 1997)

Breen, C., 'The Policy of Direct Provision in Ireland: A Violation of Asylum Seekers' Right to an Adequate Standard of Housing'. *International Journal of Refugee Law*, vol. 20, no. 4, 2008, pp. 611–636

Brewis, G., *Social History of Student Volunteering: Britain and beyond, 1880–1980* (Basingstoke: Palgrave Macmillan, 2014)

Brick, A. and Layte, R. 'Exploring Trends in the Rate of Caesarean Section in Ireland, 1999–2007', *The Economic and Social Review*, vol. 42, no. 4, 2011, pp. 383–406

Bristow, J. *Abortion Review*, 22 January 2013, http://www.reproductivereview.org/index.php/site/article/1315, accessed 1 April 2014

British Pregnancy Advisory Service (BPAS) 'Abortion Law Reformers, Pioneers of Change: interviews with people who made the 1967 Abortion Act possible', https://www.bpas.org/js/filemanager/files/abortion_pioneers.pdf, accessed 5 July 2015

Brocklehurst, P., 'Perinatal and Maternal Outcomes by Planned Place of Birth for Healthy Women with Low-Risk Pregnancies: the birthplace in England national prospective cohort study', *British Medical Journal* (BMJ), vol. 343, 2011

Brookfield, S.D., *The Power of Critical Theory for Adult Learning and Teaching* (Berkshire: Open University Press, 2005)

Brown, C., 'Claire Ordered Drugs Online and Had an Abortion at Home: this is her story', *Irish Examiner*, 30 January 2013

Buckley, Bishop John, Right to Life pastoral letter, http://www.catholicbishops.ie /2012/12/08/life-pastoral-letter-bishop-john-buckley, accessed 10 March 2015

Burke, P.J., *Accessing Education: effectively widening participation* (Stoke on Trent: Trentham Books, 2002)

Burke, P.J. and Jackson, S., *Reconceptualising Lifelong Learning: feminist interventions* (London: Routledge, 2007)

Burke, S., 'Irish Figures on Maternal Mortality: not "the best in the world"', *Medical Independent*, December 2012, http://www.medicalindependent.ie/20844/ not_ the_best_in_the_world (requires registration and is only available to medical personnel). Journal Date: 13 December 2012. URL, accessed 20 August 2014

Buttenweiser, S. and Levine, R., 'Breaking Silences: a post-abortion support model', in M.G. Fried (ed.), *From Abortion to Reproductive Freedom: transforming a movement* (Boston: South End Press, 1990)

Byrne, A. and Leonard, M. (eds), *Women and Irish Society: a sociological reader* (Belfast: Beyond the Pale Publications, 1997)

Cahill, A., 'UN: Irish abortion law treats women as "vessels"', *Irish Examiner*, 16 July 2014

Campbell, A., 'Obstetric Violence as Violence against Women', unpublished dissertation, University College Dublin, 2014

Catechism of the Catholic Church, http://www.vatican.va/archive/ccc_css/archive/ catechism/p3s2c2a5.htm, accessed 8 May 2105

Catholic Press and Information Office (CPIO), Dublin, *The Catholic Church and Abortion* (Dublin: Veritas, 1994)

Center for Reproductive Rights, US, 'Whose Right to Life? Women's rights and prenatal protection under human rights comparative law', http://www.reproductiverights.org/document/whose-right-to-life-womens- rights-and-prenatal-protections-under-human-rights-and-comparati, accessed 18 August 2014

Chancer, L., 'Abortion Without Apology', in M.G. Fried (ed.), *From Abortion to Reproductive Freedom: transforming a movement* (Boston: South End Press, 1990)

Choice Ireland, http://choiceireland.org

Cisler, L., 'Unfinished Business: birth control and women's liberation', in R. Morgan (ed.), *Sisterhood is Powerful* (New York: Vintage, 1970)

Clancy, M., 'Aspects of Women's Contribution to the Oireachtas Debate in the Irish Free State, 1922–1937', in M. Luddy and C. Murphy (eds), *Women Surviving: studies in Irish women's history in the 19th and 20th centuries* (Dublin: Poolbeg, 1990)

Clancy, S., 'Women, This Country Hates Us', *Irish Left Review*, http://www.irishleft review.org/2014/08/21/women-state-hates/#sthash.79OH1jBq.dpuf, accessed 10 March 2015

Clear, C., 'The Women Cannot Be Blamed', in M. O'Dowd and S. Wichert (eds), *Chattel, Servant or Citizen: women's status in church, state and society* (Belfast: Institute of Irish Studies, QUB, 1995)

Clements, C. 'Review of *The Ages of Voluntarism: how we got to the big society*', http://www.history.ac.uk/reviews/review/1226, accessed 1 April 2014

Clements, S. and Ingham, R., *Improving Knowledge Regarding Abortions Performed on Irish Women in the UK*, Report 19 (Dublin: Crisis Pregnancy Agency, 2007)

Cloud, D.L., '"To Veil the Threat of Terror": Afghan women and the clash of civilizations in the imagery of the US war on terrorism', *Quarterly Journal of Speech*, vol. 90, no. 3, 2004, pp. 285–306

CMACE, 'Saving Mothers' Lives: reviewing maternal deaths to make motherhood safer, 2006–2008. The eighth report of the confidential enquiries into maternal deaths in the United Kingdom', *BJOG*, vol. 118, no. 1, 2011, pp. 1–203

Coghlan, D., 'Customs Officers at Dublin Rail Station Knew What Hit Them!', *Irish Times*, 24 May 1971

Cohen, S., 'Facts and Consequences: legality, incidence and safety of abortion worldwide', *Guttmacher Policy Review*, vol. 12, no. 4, 2009

Coliver, S. (ed.), *The Right to Know: human rights and access to reproductive health information* (London: Article 19, 1995)

Commission on Emigration and other Population Problems, 1948-1954: reports. (Dublin: Stationery Office, 1954)

Commission on the Status of Women, *Report to Minister for Finance* (Dublin: Stationery Office, 1972)

Commission to Inquire into Child Abuse, *Report, Volume IV* (Dublin: Stationery Office, 2009)

Conlon, C., *Concealed Pregnancy: a case study from an Irish setting* (Dublin: Crisis Pregnancy Agency, 2006)

Conlon, C., *Concealed Pregnancy Guidelines* (Dublin: Crisis Pregnancy Agency, 2009)

Conlon, C., *Concealed Pregnancy: a case study from an Irish setting* (Dublin: Crisis Pregnancy Agency, 2009)

Conlon, D. and Carvalho, M. *Spaces of Motherhood*, http://reconstruction.eserver.org/ Issues/031/conlon.htm, accessed 20 August 2014

Connolly, L., 'From Revolution to Devolution: mapping the contemporary women's movement in Ireland', in A. Byrne and M. Leonard (eds), *Women and Irish Society: a sociological reader* (Belfast: Beyond the Pale Publications, 1997)

Connolly, L., *The Irish Women's Movement: from revolution to devolution* (Dublin: The Lilliput Press, 2003)

Connolly, L. and O'Toole, T., *Documenting Irish Feminisms: the second wave* (Dublin: Woodfield Press, 2005)

Conrad, P., 'Medicalization and Social Control', *Annual Review of Sociology*, vol. 18, 1992, pp. 209–32

Conroy Jackson, P., 'Women's Movement and Abortion: the criminalization of Irish women', in D. Dahlerup (ed.), *The New Women's Movement: feminism and political power in Europe and the US* (London: Sage Publications, 1986)

Conroy Jackson, P., 'Outside the Jurisdiction: Irish women seeking abortion', in A. Smyth (ed.), *The Abortion Papers Ireland* (Dublin: Attic Press, 1992)

Conroy, P., 'Lone Mothers: the case of Ireland', in J. Lewis (ed.), *Lone Mothers in European Welfare Regimes: shifting policy logics* (London: Jessica Kingsley Publishers, 1997)

Conroy, P., 'Ireland: rape and incest not grounds for abortion', *Reproductive Laws for the 21st Century Papers*, Center for Women Policy Studies, Washington, January 2012, www.centerwomenpolicy.org, accessed 1 April 2014

Conroy, P., 'Constance Markievicz: Social and Personal', communications to the Countess Markievicz School, Liberty Hall Theatre, Dublin, 18 May 2013 (unpublished)

Constitution Review Group, *Report of the Constitution Review Group* (Dublin: Government Publications, 1996)

Control of Importation, Sale and Manufacture of Contraceptives Bill, 1974

Coogan, T.P., *De Valera: Long Fellow, Long Shadow* (London: Hutchinson, 1993)

Cook, R.J. and Dickens, B.M., 'Human Rights Dynamics of Abortion Law Reform', *Human Rights Quarterly*, University of Toronto, Canada, vol. 25, no. 1, 2003, pp. 1–59

Cousin, G., 'Positioning Positionality: the reflexive turn', in M. Savin-Baden and C. Howell Major (eds), *New Approaches to Qualitative Research: wisdom and uncertainty* (London: Routledge, 2010)

Coulter Smyth, S., 'Address to Joint Committee on Health and Children, 8 January 2013', http://oireachtasdebates.oireachtas.ie/debates%20authoring/DebatesWebPack.nsf/committeetakes/HEJ2013010800033?opendocument, accessed 5 August 2014

Crang, M. and Thrift, N. (eds), *Thinking Space* (London: Routledge, 2003)

Cresswell, T., *Place: a short introduction* (Oxford: Blackwell, 2004)

Cullen Owens, R., *A Social History of Women in Ireland, 1870–1970* (Dublin: Gill & Macmillan, 2005)

Cullen, P., 'News Report', *Irish Times*, 22 November 2012

Cullen, P. and Holland, K., '"Horrendous, Barbaric, Inhumane": Savita's husband gives his verdict', *Irish Times*, 20 April 2013 [2013a]

Cullen, P. and Holland, K., 'Maternity Care Concerns Raised in Savita Report', *Irish Times*, 10 October 2013 [2013b]

Dáil debates. Reilly, James (2012). 19 December 2012. 57136/12 https://www.kildarestreet.com/debates/?id=2012-12-19a.352, accessed 7th July 2015Dáil Éireann Debate, *Nurses and Midwives Bill, 2010: Report Stage (Resumed)*, vol. 730, no. 6, 21 April 2011

Dáil Éireann Debate, *Medical Treatment (Termination of Pregnancy in Case of Risk to Life of Pregnant Woman) (No. 2) Bill 2012: Second Stage [Private Members] (Continued)*, vol. 784, no. 2, 27 November 2012

Dáil Éireann Debate, *Leader's Questions (Continued)*, 12 June 2013

Daly, M., 'Feminist Research Methodology: the case of Ireland', in A. Byrne and R. Lentin (eds), *(Re)searching Women* (Dublin: Institute of Public Administration, 2000), pp. 60–72

de Silva, E., *Good Enough Mothering? feminist perspectives on lone motherhood* (London: Routledge, 1996)

DeBarra, D., Letter to the Editor, *Irish Times*, Tuesday, 8 May 2007, 'Abortion Case and Miss D.', http://safeandlegal.blogspot.ie/2007/05/deirdre-de-barras-letter-in-irish-times_07.html, accessed 10 August 2014

Department of Health (2014) Implementation of the Protection of Life During Pregnancy Act. http://health.gov.ie/wp-content/uploads/2014/09/Guidance-Document-Final-September-2014.pdf, accessed July 6th 2015

Department of Health UK, *Changing Childbirth (England and Wales)* (London: HMSO, 1993)

Department of Health UK, *Abortion Statistics, England and Wales 2012: summary of information from the abortion notification forms returned to the Chief Medical Officers of England and Wales* (London: HMSO, 2013)

Department of Health UK , *Abortion Statistics: England and Wales 2012* (London: UK Department of Health, 2013), www.gov.uk/dh, accessed 1 April 2014

Devane, D., Brennan, M., Begley, C., Clarke, M., Walsh, D., Sandall, J. and Normand, C., *Socioeconomic Value of the Midwife: a systematic review, meta-synthesis and economic analysis of midwife-led models of care* (London: Royal College of Midwives, 2010)

Devane, D., Lalor, J., Daly, S., McGuire, W. and Smith, V., 'Cardiotocography Versus Intermittent Auscultation of Fetal Heart on Admission to Labour Ward for Assessment of Fetal Wellbeing (2012), *Cochrane Database Systematic Review*, vol. 2, CD005122, doi: 10.1002/14651858.CD005122.pub4

Devane, D., Murphy-Lawless, J. and Begley, C.M., 'Childbirth Policies and Practices in Ireland and the Journey towards Midwifery-led Care', *Midwifery*, vol. 23, no. 1, 2007, pp. 92–101

Dhaliwal, S. and Yuval-Davis, N. (eds), *Women against Fundamentalism* (London: Lawrence and Wishart, 2014)

DHSSPS, *The Limited Circumstances for a Lawful Termination of Pregnancy in Northern Ireland* (Belfast: DHSSPS, 2013)

Dickens, B.M. and Cook, R.J., 'Conscientious Commitment to Women's Health', *International Journal of Gynecology and Obstetrics*, vol. 113, 2011, pp. 163–6

Donnellan, E., 'Pregnant Woman Turned Away from Monaghan Has Baby in Ambulance', *Irish Times*, 4 July 2003

Donnellan, E., 'Mother Dies after Giving Birth in Drogheda', *Irish Times*, 28 April 2011

Doran, K. (Bishop of Elphin), *Breakfast*, Newstalk 106, 9 March 2015, http://www.newstalk.com/Bishop-of-Elphin-Kevin-Doran-gay-marriage-Newstalk-Breakfast-same-sex-marriage, accessed 1 April 2014

Doucet, A. and Mauthner, N.S., 'What Can Be Known and How? Narrated subjects and the listening guide', *Qualitative Research*, vol. 8, no. 2, 2008, pp. 399–423

Duden, B., *Disembodying Women: perspectives on pregnancy and the unborn* (Cambridge, MA: Harvard University Press, 1993)

Eaton, P. and Warnick, M., *Marie Stopes: a checklist of her writings* (London: Croom Helm Ltd, 1977)

Engeli, I., Green-Pedersen, C. and Larsen, L.T. *Morality Politics in Western Europe: parties, agendas and policy choices* (Basingstoke: Palgrave Macmillan, 2012)

Enright, M., 'Finding the Hidden Constitution: explaining Ireland's abortion law', http://criticallegalthinking.com/2014/08/20/finding-hidden-constitution-explaining-irelands-abortion-law, accessed 31 July 2014 [2014a]

Enright, M., 'Abortion Secrecy/Abortion Privacy', http://humanrights.ie/uncategorized/abortion-secrecyabortion-privacy, accessed 31 July 2014 [2014b]

Ertlelt, S., 'Cardinal O'Malley to Boycott Boston College Graduation's Pro-Abortion Speaker', http://www.lifenews.com/2013/05/10/cardinal-omalley-to-boycott-boston-college-graduations-pro-abortion-speaker, accessed 10 May 2013

ESRI, *Perinatal Statistics Report 2011* (Dublin: Health Research and Information Division, ESRI, 2012)

Expert Group (Department of Health and Children), *Report of the Expert Group on the Judgment in A, B and C v Ireland* (Dublin: Department of Health and Children, 2012))

Faludi, S., *Backlash: the undeclared war against women* (London: Chatto & Windus, 1992)

Family Planning Association (FPA), *Factsheet – Contraception: past, present and future*, http://www.fpa.org.uk/sites/default/files/contraception-past-present-and-future-factsheet-november-2010.pdf, accessed 1 April 2014

Farry, D., 'Pro-life Campaigners Threaten To Burn Minister and His Family out of Home', *The Irish Mirror*, 19 June 2013

Ferree, M.M., 'Resonance and Radicalism: feminist framing in the abortion debates of the United States and Germany', *American Journal of Sociology*, vol. 109, no. 2, 2003, pp. 304–44

Ferree, M.M., Gamson, W.A., Gerhards, J. and Rucht, D., *Shaping Abortion Discourse: democracy and the public sphere in Germany and the United States* (Cambridge: Cambridge University Press, 2002)

Ferriter, D., *The Transformation of Ireland, 1900–2000* (London: Profile Books, 2004)

Ferriter, D., *Occasions of Sin: sex and society in modern Ireland* (London: Profile Books, 2012)

Fine-Davis, M., *Psychological Effects of Abortion on Women: A Review of the Literature* (Dublin: Crisis Pregnancy Agency, 2007)

Fletcher, R., 'Silences: Irish women and abortion', *Feminist Review*, vol. 50, 1995, pp. 44–66

Fletcher, R., 'Pro-Life Absolutes, Feminist Challenges: the fundamentalist narrative of Irish abortion law, 1986–1992', *Osgoode Hall LJ*, vol. 36, no. 1, 1998

Fletcher, R., 'National Crisis, Supranational Opportunity: the Irish construction of abortion as a European service', *Reproductive Health Matters*, vol. 8, no. 16, 2000, pp. 35–44

Fletcher, R., 'Reproducing Irishness: race, gender and abortion law', *Canadian Journal of Women and the Law*, vol. 17, no. 2, 2005, pp. 365–404

Fletcher, R., *Submission to the Health Committee on the General Scheme of the Protection of Life During Pregnancy Bill 2013*. Published Online, May 2013. Volume 1. 31/HHCN/012 http://www.oireachtas.ie/parliament/media/committees/healthandchildren/Volume1.pdf, accessed 04 July 2015

Fortin, N.M., 'Gender Role Attitudes and the Labour Market Outcomes of Women across OECD Countries', *Oxford Review of Economic Policy*, vol. 21, no. 3, 2005, pp. 416–38

Foucault, M., *Discipline and Punish: the birth of the prison* (London: Penguin, 1991)

Foucault, M., 'Fearless Speech', in J. Pearson (ed.), *Fearless Speech* (Los Angeles: Semiotext(e), 2001)

Foucault, M., *Society Must Be Defended: lectures at the Collège de France, 1975–1976* (London: Allen Lane, 2003)

Francome, C., *Abortion in the USA and the UK* (Aldershot: Ashgate, 2004)

Freire, P., *Pedagogy of the Oppressed*, translated by M.B. Ramos (London: Sheed & Ward, 1979)

Fried, M.G. (ed.), *From Abortion to Reproductive Freedom: transforming a movement* (Boston: South End Press, 1990)

Fried, M.G., Ross, L., Solinger, R., Bond-Leonard, T.M. and Danforth, J., 'Understanding Reproductive Justice: a response to O'Brien', *RH Reality Check*, 8 May 2013, http://rhrealitycheck.org/article/2013/05/08/understanding-reproductive-justice-a-response-to-obrien, accessed 1 April 2014

Fuller, L., *Irish Catholicism since 1950: the undoing of a culture* (Dublin: Gill & Macmillan, 2004)

Furedi, A., 'Open Letter on the Importance of Reproductive Choice', *RH Reality Check*, 5 June 2013, http://rhrealitycheck.org/article/2013/06/05/an-open-letter-on-the-importance-of-reproductive-choice, accessed 1 April 2014

Gartland, F., 'Fall in Seizures of Drugs that Induce Abortion', *Irish Times*, 27 May 2013

Gearty, C., 'The Politics of Abortion', *Journal of Law and Society*, vol. 19, no. 4, 1992, pp. 441–53

Ging, D., 'All-Consuming Images: new gender formations in post-Celtic-Tiger Ireland', in D. Ging, M. Cronin and P. Kirby (eds), *Transforming Ireland: challenges, critiques, resources* (Manchester: Manchester University Press, 2009), pp. 52–70

Ginsburg, F.D., *Contested Lives: the abortion debate in an American community* (Berkeley, CA: University of California Press, 1989)

Girvin, B., 'The Referendums on Abortion 1992', *Irish Political Studies*, vol. 8, no. 1, 1993, pp. 118–24

Goldberg, D.T., *The Racial State* (Oxford: Blackwell, 2002)

Gomperts, R., 'Women on Waves: where next for the abortion boat?' *Reproductive Health Matters*, vol. 10, no. 19, 2002, pp. 180–3

Government of Ireland, *Bunreacht na hÉireann (Constitution of Ireland)* (Dublin: Government Publications Office, 1937)

Government of Ireland, *General Scheme of the Protection of Life During Pregnancy Bill 2013* (Dublin: Government Publications Office, 2013)

Government of Ireland, *Green Paper on Abortion* (Dublin: Government Publications, 1999)

Grace, A. P., & Hill, R. 'Positioning Queer in Adult Education: Intervening in politics and practice in North America'. *Studies in the Education of Adults*, vol. 36, no.2, 2004, pp.167-189

Gray, B. and Ryan, L., '(Dis)Locating "Woman" and Women in Representations of Irish Nationality', in A. Byrne and M. Leonard (eds), *Women and Irish Society. a sociological reader* (Belfast: Beyond the Pale Publications, 1997)

Greene, M., 'Teaching in a Moment of Crisis: the spaces of imagination', *The New Educator*, vol. 1, 2005, pp. 77–80

Greene, M., 'Teaching as Possibility: a light in dark times', in S. Macrine (ed.), *Critical Pedagogy in Uncertain Times: hope and possibilities* (New York: Palgrave Macmillan, 2009)

Greer, G., *The Whole Woman* (New York: Alfred A. Knopf, 1999)

Grewal, I. and Kaplan, C., *Scattered Hegemonies: postmodernity and transnational feminist practices* (Minneapolis: University of Minnesota Press, 1994)

Griffin, D., 'Symphysiotomy Group Urges Government to Support Redress Bill, *Irish Times*, 9 April 2013

Gruenewald, D.A., 'Foundations of Place: a multidisciplinary framework for place-conscious education', *American Educational Research Journal*, vol. 40, no. 3, 2003, pp. 619–54

Gwynn Morgan, D., *A Judgment Too Far? judicial activism and the Constitution* (Cork: Cork University Press, 2001)

Hadley, J., *Abortion: between freedom and necessity* (London: Virago Press, 1996)

Halfmann, D., *Doctors and Demonstrators: how political institutions shape abortion law in the United States, Britain and Canada* (Chicago: Chicago University Press, 2011)

Hall, S., *The Hard Road to Renewal: Thatcherism and the crisis of the Left* (London: Verso, 1998)

Hansard, *Northern Ireland Assembly Business, Monday, 22 October 2007*, http://archive.niassembly.gov.uk/record/reports2007/071022.htm, accessed 1 April 2014

Hansard, *Official Report – Committee for Health, Social Services and Public Safety, Guidance on Termination of Pregnancy in Northern Ireland: DHSSPS briefing*, http://www.niassembly.gov.uk/assembly-business/official-report/committee-minutes-of-evidence/session-2013-2014/october-2013/guidance-on-termination-of-pregnancy-in-northern-ireland-dhssps-briefing, accessed 1 April 2014 (Hansard 2013a)

Hansard, *Official Report Northern Ireland Assembly, 12 March 2013*, http://www.niassembly.gov.uk/assembly-business/official-report/reports-12-13/12-march-2013, accessed 1 April 2014 (Hansard 2013b)

Hartman, B., *Reproductive Rights and Wrongs: the global politics of population control and contraceptive choice* (New York: Harper & Row Publishers, 1987)

Haughey, N., 'Matrons Tell Martin about "Debilitating Haemorrhage" of Midwives', *Irish Times*, 11 August 2001

Hayes, A. and Urquhart, D. (eds), *The Irish Women's History Reader* (London: Routledge, 2001)

Henshaw, S.K., Singh, S. and Haas, T. 'The Incidence of Abortion Worldwide', *International Family Planning Perspectives*, vol. 25, 1999, pp. 30–8

Hesketh, T., *The Second Partitioning of Ireland* (Dublin: Brandsma Books, 1990)

Hewson, B., 'Ireland's Miss D: a "bizarre dispute"', *Abortion Review*, 24 May 2007, http://www.abortionreview.org/index.php/site/article/186, accessed 1 April 2014

Hilton, M. and McKay, J., *The Ages of Voluntarism: how we got to the big society* (Oxford: Oxford University Press, 2011)

Himmelweit, S., 'More Than "A Woman's Right to Choose"?', *Feminist Review*, vol. 29, 1998, pp. 38–56

HIQA, *Patient Safety Investigation report into services University Hospital Galway (UHG) and as reflected in the care provided to Savita Halappanavar* Dublin: HIQA, 2013)

Hodnett, E., Gates, S., Hofmeyr, G., Sakala, C. and Weston, J., 'Continuous Support for Women during Childbirth', http://www.cochrane.org/CD003766/PREG_continuous-support-for-women-during-childbirth, accessed 1 April 2014

Hogan, L., 'Maternity Chief Warns of Overstretched Services, *Irish Independent*, 27 June 2011, http://www.independent.ie/national-news/maternity-chief-warns-of-overstretched-services-2806473.html, accessed 1 April 2014

Hoggart, L., 'Feminist Principles Meet Political Reality: the case of the National Abortion Campaign', http://www.prochoiceforum.org.uk/al6.php, accessed 1 April 2014

Holland, K., 'Reasons for Women Not To Be Cheerful', *Irish Times*, 29 December 2012

Holland, K., *Savita: the tragedy that shook the nation* (London: Transworld Ireland, 2013) [2013a]

Holland, K., 'Savita Death Report Finds Foetus, Not Mother, Was Main Focus', *Irish Times*, 2 April 2013 [2013b]

Holland, K., 'Savita Inquest Recalls Midwife and Doctor to Resolve Disparity in their Testimonies, *Irish Times*, 17 April 2013 [2013c]

Holland, K., 'Maternity Care Concerns Raised in Savita Report', *Irish Times*, 10 October 2013 [2013d]

Holland, K., 'UN Human Rights Committee and Ireland', *Irish Times*, 15 July 2014 [2014a]

Holland, K, 'Ireland in Breach of Human Rights Law on Abortion', *Irish Times*, 16 July 2014 [2014b]

Holland, K., 'Women Sought Abortion at Eight Weeks', *Irish Times*, 23 August 2014 [2014c]

Holloway, L. and Hubbard, P., *People and Place: the extraordinary geographies of everyday life* (Essex: Pearson Education Limited, 2001)

Hollway, W., 'Gender Difference and the Production of Subjectivity', in J. Henriques, W. Hollway, C. Urwin, C. Venn and V. Walkeraine (eds), *Changing the Subject* (London: Methuen, 1984)

Hollway, W., 'Gender Difference and the Production of Subjectivity', in S. Jackson and S. Scott (eds), *Feminism and Sexuality: a reader* (Edinburgh: Edinburgh University Press, 1996)

hooks, b., *Feminism is for Everybody* (London: Pluto Press, 2000)

Horgan, G. and Monteith, M., *A Child Rights Impact Assessment of the Impact of Welfare Reform on Children in Northern Ireland* (Belfast: Northern Ireland Commissioner for Children and Young People (NICCY), 2012)

Horgan, G. and O'Connor, J.S., 'Abortion and Citizenship Rights in a Devolved Region of the UK', *Social Policy and Society*, vol. 13, no. 1, 2013

Horgan, J., 'Church Not in Favour of Law Changes' (Bishops' statement), *Irish Times*, 12 March 1971 [1971a]

Horgan, J., 'Church of Ireland Backs Birth Control Bill', *Irish Times*, 13 May 1971 [1971b]

Horgan, J., *Sean Lemass: the enigmatic patriot* (Dublin: Gill & Macmillan, 1999)

House of Commons, *Maternity Services, Second Report, Vol. 1. Report together with appendices and the proceedings of the Committee* (London: HMSO, 1992)

Houston, M., 'Death as a Result of Infection during Miscarriage Rare', *Irish Times*, 14 November 2012

HSE, CMO, *Midland Regional Hospital, Portlaoise Perinatal Deaths (2006–date), Report to the Minister for Health, February 2014* (Dublin: HSE)

HSE, *Report into maternal and child death at Our Lady of Lourdes hospital* (HSE: Dublin, 2008)

Hubbard, P., Kitchin, R., Bartley, B. and Fuller, D., *Thinking Geographically: space, theory and contemporary human geography* (London: Continuum, 2005)

Hug, C., *The Politics of Sexual Morality in Ireland* (New York: St Martin's Press, 1999)

Human Rights Watch, 'A State of Isolation: access to abortion for women in Ireland', http://www.hrw.org/reports/2010/01/28/state-isolation-0, accessed 1 April 2014

Humm, M., *The Dictionary of Feminist Theory* (London: Harvester Wheatsheaf, 1989)

Humphreys, J., 'Abortion Text Seen as Timebomb', *Irish Times*, 28 December 2102

IFPA (Irish Family Planning Association). *IFPA annual report 2010: Access, choice & advocacy.* (Dublin: IFPA, 2011)

Independent.ie., 'Grotto Death January 31, 1984', http://www.independent.ie/lifestyle/grotto-death-january-31-1984-26789174.html, accessed 1 April 2014

Inglis T., *Truth, Power and Lies: Irish society and the case of the Kerry babies* (Dublin: UCD Press, 2003)

Inglis, T., *Lessons in Irish Sexuality* (Dublin: UCD Press, 1998) [1998a]

Inglis, T., *Moral Monopoly: the rise of the Catholic Church in modern Ireland* (Dublin: UCD Press, 1998) [1998b]

Innes, C.L., *Women and Nation in Irish Literature and Society, 1880–1935* (Athens, GA: University of Georgia Press, 1993)

Irish Bishops' Conference, 'An Opportunity Not to Be Lost', Statement of 12 December 2001, http://www.catholicbishops.ie/2002/03/08/an-opportunity-not-to-be-lost-plain-text, accessed 1 April 2014

Irish Central, 'Top Bishops Clash over Excommunication of Catholics Who Support New Abortion Bill', http://www.irishcentral.com/news/top-bishops-clash-over-excommunication-of-catholics-who-support-new-abortion-bill-208277631-237590991.html, accessed 21 May 2013

Irish Family Planning Association (IFPA), *The Irish Journey: Women's Stories of Abortion.* (Dublin: IFPA, 2000)

Irish Family Planning Association (IFPA), ABC v Ireland (Dublin: IFPA, 2010)

Irish Family Planning Association (IFPA), 'Ireland's Sexual and Reproductive History', www.ifpa.ie/Media-Info/History-of-Sexual-Health-in-Ireland, accessed 1 April 2014

Irish Family Planning Association (IFPA), 'Release of UK Abortion Statistics 2013', http://www.ifpa.ie/node/569, accessed 1 April 2014 [2013a]

Irish Family Planning Association (IFPA), 'Abortion in Ireland: a legal timeline, https://www.ifpa.ie/Hot-Topics/Abortion/Abortion-in-Ireland-Timeline, accessed 20 February 2013 [2013b]

Irish Human Rights Commission *Observations on the Protection of Life During Pregnancy Bill 2013*. (Irish Human Rights Commission, Dublin: 2013)

Irish Times, 'News Report of Morning Ireland National Radio Show on 19th December 2012', *Irish Times*, 19 December 2012 [2012b]

Irish Times, 'MRBI Opinion Poll on Attitudes towards Abortion in Ireland', *Irish Times*, 13 June 2013

Irish Times, 'News Report of News at One National Radio Show on 2 May 2013', *Irish Times*, 2 May 2013

Irish Times, 'A Cruel and Pitiless Ireland', Editorial, *Irish Times*, 20 February 2013

Irish Times, Editorial, 'Lobbying on Abortion', 28 August 2012 [2012a]

Irish Women's Abortion Support, Group, 'Across the Water', *Feminist Review*, (1988) vol. 29, pp. 64–71

Jackson, N., 'Family Law: fertility and parenthood', in A. Connolly (ed.), *Gender and the Law in Ireland* (Dublin: Oak Tree Press, 1993)

Jackson-Conroy, P. and O'Reilly, B., *The Deadly Solution to an Irish Problem: back street abortion* (pamphlet) (Dublin: Women's Right to Choose Campaign, 1983)

Joint Oireachtas Committee on Health and Children, *Report on Protection of Life During Pregnancy Bill (Heads of), May 2013* (Dublin: Stationery Office, 2013)

Joint Oireachtas Committee on Health and Children, *Report on Public Hearing on the Implementation of the Government Decision Following the Publication of the Expert Group Report on A, B and C v Ireland, January 2013* (Dublin: Stationery Office, 2013)

Jones, J., 'Time To Cut through the Red Tape for a Better Maternity Service, *Irish Times*, 29 October 2013

Jones, M., *These Obstreperous Lassies: a history of the Irish Women Workers' Union* (Dublin: Gill & Macmillan, 1988)

Kamp, S. and Squires, J., *Feminisms* (Oxford: Oxford University Press, 1997)

Kantola, J. and Squires, J., 'From State Feminism to Market Feminism', *International Political Science Review*, vol. 33, 2012, pp. 382–400

Katz Rothman, B., *Recreating Motherhood: ideology and technology in a patriarchal society* (London: W.W. Norton & Company, 1987)

Kavanagh, R., *Mamie Cadden: backstreet abortionist* (Cork: Mercier Press, 2005)

Kennedy, P., *Maternity in Ireland: a woman-centred perspective* (Dublin: The Liffey Press, 2002)

Kennedy, S., 'Abortion in an Era of Neoliberal Choice', *Socialist Review*, no. 400, March 2015, pp. 8–10, http://socialistreview.org.uk/400/abortion-era-neoliberal-choice, accessed 27 June 2015

Kennelly, B. and Ward, E., 'The Abortion Referendums', in M. Gallagher and M. Laver (eds), *How Ireland Voted, 1992* (Dublin: PSAI Press & Folens, 1993), pp. 115–34

Kerrigan, G., 'The Moral Civil War', *Magill Magazine*, September 1983

Kimport, K., Perrucci, A. and Weitz, T.A., 'Addressing the Silence in the Noise: how abortion support talklines meet some women's needs for non-political discussion of their experiences', *Women and Health*, vol. 52, no. 1, 2012, pp. 88–100

Kingston, J., Whelan, A., and Bacik, I., *Abortion and the Law* (Dublin: Round Hall Sweet and Maxwell, 1997)

Knirk, J., *Women of the Dáil: gender, republicanism and the Anglo-Irish Treaty* (Dublin: Irish Academic Press, 2006)

KPMG, *Independent Review of Maternity and Gynaecology Services in the Greater Dublin Area* (Dublin: HSE, 2009)

Kumar, A., Hessini, L. and Mitchell, E.M., 'Conceptualising Abortion Stigma', *Culture, Health and Sexuality*, vol. 11, no. 6, pp. 625–39

Leahy, Bishop Brendan, 'Homily Notes for Vigil for Life – Saint John's Cathedral, Limerick', http://www.catholicbishops.ie/2013/07/09/homily-notes-bishop-brendan-leahy-vigil-life-saint-johns-cathedral-limerick, accessed 27 June 2015

Lee, E., *Abortion, Motherhood and Mental Health: medicalizing reproduction in the United States and Great Britain* (New York: Transaction Publishers, 2003)

Lees, S., *Sugar and Spice* (London: Routledge, 1993)

Lefebvre, H., *The Production of Space* (Oxford: Blackwell Publications, 1991)

Lentin, R., 'Strangers and Strollers: feminist notes on researching migrant m/others', *Women's Studies International Forum*, vol. 27, no. 4, 2004, pp. 301–14

Lentin, R. and McVeigh, R., *After Optimism? Ireland, racism and globalisation* (Dublin: Metro Éireann Publications, 2006)

Luibhéid, E., 'Childbearing against the State? Asylum seeker women in the Irish Republic', *Women's Studies International Forum*, vol. 27, no. 4, 2004, pp. 335–50

Luibhéid, E., 'Sexual Regimes and Migration Controls: reproducing the Irish nation-state in transnational contexts', *Feminist Review*, vol. 83, 2006, pp. 60–78

Luibhéid, E., *Pregnant on Arrival: making the illegal immigrant* (Minneapolis: University of Minnesota Press, 2013)

Luker, K., *Abortion and the Politics of Motherhood* (Berkeley, CA: University of California Press, 1984)

Luna, Z.T., 'Marching toward Reproductive Justice: coalitional (re) framing of the March for Women's Lives', *Sociological Inquirer*, vol. 80, no. 4, 2010, pp. 554–78

Lutomski, J., Murphy, M., Devane, D., Meaney, S. and Greene, R., 'Private Health Care Coverage and Increased Risk of Obstetric Intervention', *BMC Pregnancy and Childbirth*, vol. 14, no. 1, 2014, p. 13

Luttrell, W., *School Smart and Mother Wise: working-class women's identity and schooling* (Routledge: New York, 1997)

Lynch, K., 'Equality studies, the academy and the role of research in emancipatory social change.' *Economic and Social Review*, vol. 30, 1999, pp 41–70

MacCurtain, M. and Ó Corráin, D., *Women in Irish Society: the historical dimension* (Dublin: Arlen House/The Women's Press, 1978)

MacDonald, S., 'Bishops to Challenge Legislation in Court', *Irish Independent*, 9 July 2013

MacKinnon, C. '*Roe v. Wade*: a study in male ideology', in J. Garfield and P. Hennessey (eds), *Abortion: moral and legal perspectives* (Amherst: University of Massachusetts, 1984), pp. 52–3

Maguire, M.J., *Precarious Childhood in Post-Independence Ireland* (Manchester: Manchester University Press, 2009)

Maher, M., 'A Short History of the Pill in Ireland', *Irish Times*, 14 March 1968

Mahon, E., Conlon, C. and Dillon, L., *Women and Crisis Pregnancy: a report presented to the Department of Health and Children* (Dublin: The Stationery Office, 1998)

Mander, R. and Murphy-Lawless, J., *The Politics of Maternity* (London: Routledge, 2013)

Mander, R., Murphy-Lawless, J. and Edwards, N., 'Reflecting on Good Birthing: an innovative approach to culture change (Part 1)', *MIDIRS International Midwifery Digest*, vol. 19, no. 4, 2009, pp. 481–6

Massey, D., *Space, Place and Gender* (Cambridge: Polity, 2004)

Mayock, P., Kitching, K., and Morgan, M. *Relationships and sexuality education (RSE) in the context of social, personal and health education (SPHE): an assessment of the challenges to full implementation of the programme in post-primary schools.* (Dublin: Crisis Pregnancy Agency, 2007)

McArdle, D., *The Irish Republic* (Dublin: The Irish Press Ltd, 1937)

McAvoy, S., 'From Anti-amendment Campaigns to Demanding Reproductive Justice: the changing landscape of abortion rights activism in Ireland, 1983–2008', in J. Schweppe (ed.), *The Unborn Child, Article 40.3.3 and Abortion in Ireland: twenty-five years of protection* (Dublin: The Liffey Press, 2008), pp. 15–45

McAvoy, S., "Bring Forth Abundantly in the Earth and Multiply Therein" (Genesis 9:7): aspects of Irish discourse on contraception (1837–1908)', in M. Leane and E. Kiely (eds), *Sexualities and Irish Society: a reader* (Dublin: Orpen Press, 2014), pp. 3–23

McCafferty, N., *A Woman to Blame: the Kerry babies case* (Dublin: Attic Press, 2004)

McCoole, S., *No Ordinary Women: Irish female activists in the revolutionary years, 1900–1923* (Dublin: The O'Brien Press, 2004)

McDonald, H., 'Ireland and UN Human Rights Committee', *The Guardian*, 24 July 2014

McDonald, H., 'Pregnant Women Face Abortion Ban in Ireland Even if They're a Suicide Risk, *The Guardian*, 7 August 2014

McDonogh, M., 'Widower Says Inquest into Wife's Death "a Cover-up"', *Irish Times*, 16 July 2014, http://www.irishtimes.com/news/crime-and-law/courts/widower-says-inquest-into-wife-s-death-a-cover-up-1.1868178

McDowell, L., *Gender, Identity and Place: understanding feminist geographies* (Cambridge: Polity Press, 1999)

McGorrian, C., Frazer, K., Daly, L., Moore, R. G., Turner, J., Sweeney, M. R., and Kelleher, C. C., 'The health care experiences of Travellers compared to the general population: the All-Ireland Traveller Health Study.' *Journal of health services research & policy*, vol. 17, no. 3, 2012, pp 173–180

McKittrick, K. and Peake, L., 'What Difference Does Difference Make to Geography?', in N. Castree, A. Rogers and D. Sherman (eds), *Questioning Geography: fundamental debates* (Oxford: Blackwell, 2005), pp. 39–54

McNay, L., *Gender and Agency: reconfiguring the subject in feminist and social theory* (Cambridge: Polity Press, 2000)

MDE, *Confidential Maternal Death Enquiry in Ireland, Report for Triennium 2009–2011* (Cork: Maternal Death Enquiry Ireland, 2012)

Meaney, G., 'Sex and Nation: women in Irish culture and politics', in A. Smyth (ed.), *Irish Women's Studies Reader* (Dublin: Attic Press, 1993)

Meaney, G., 'Migrant Bodies: maternity and the construction of white identities in Ireland', Paper presented at the Double Vision: Liminal Irish Identities Conference, University College Dublin, 18–20 March 2005

Milotte, M., *Banished Babies: the secret history of Ireland's baby export business* (Dublin: New Island Books, 2011)

Morgan, K.P., 'Contested Bodies, Contested Knowledges: women, health and the politics of medicalization', in S. Sherwin (ed.), *Agency, Autonomy and Politics in Women's Health* (Philadelphia: Temple University Press, 1998), pp. 83–121

Morrissey, J., 'An Examination of the Relationship between the Catholic Church and the Medical Profession in Ireland in the Period 1922–1992 with Particular Emphasis on the Impact of this Relationship in the Field of Reproductive Medicine', unpublished PhD thesis, University College Dublin, 2004

Mullally, S., 'Debating Reproductive Rights in Ireland', *Human Rights Quarterly*, vol. 27, no. 1, 2005, pp. 78–104

Murphy, A., 'To Decriminalise Abortion is a Contradiction of the Most Fundamental Principle of the Legal System' (an interview with Cardinal Raymond Burke), *Catholic Voice*, 1 February 2013

Murphy, C. and O'Herlihy, C., 'Maternal Mortality Statistics in Ireland: should they carry a health warning?', *Irish Medical Journal*, vol. 100, no. 8, 2007

Murphy, D.J. and Fahey, T., 'A Retrospective Cohort Study of Mode of Delivery among Public and Private Patients in an Integrated Maternity Hospital Setting, *BMJ Open*, vol. 3, no. 11, 2013

Murphy-Lawless, J., 'The Obstetric View of Feminine Identity: a case history of the use of forceps on unmarried women in 19th-century Ireland', in A. Smyth (ed.), *The Abortion Papers: Ireland* (Dublin: Attic Press, 1992)

Murphy-Lawless, J., 'Fertility, Bodies and Politics: the Irish case', *Reproductive Health Matters*, vol. 1, no. 2, 1993, pp. 53–64

Murphy-Lawless, J., 'Bodies Coming and Going: women's perspectives on childbearing in Ireland', in C. Douglass (ed.), *Barren States: the population implosion in Europe* (Oxford: Berg, 2005)

Murphy-Lawless, J., '"The Ceiling Caves In": the current state of maternity services in Ireland', *MIDIRS International Midwifery Digest*, vol. 21, no. 4, 2011, pp. 446–51.

Murphy-Lawless, J., 'A Brief Glimpse into Hell', *AIMS*, vol. 26, no. 1, 2014, pp. 6–10

Naughton, G., 'Woman Suffered Fatal Cardiac Arrest after Induced Labour, Inquest Told', *Irish Times*, 19 April 2013

National Archives of Ireland, Dept. of the Taoiseach file, 2003/16/34 , Copy of Teheran Resolution (2003)

National Archives of Ireland, Dept. of the Taoiseach file, 2003/16/34, Copy of the Bishops' Statement Attached to Memorandum for Government, Dated 19 Aibreán 1971

National Archives of Ireland, Dept. of the Taoiseach file, 2003/16/34, Department of Justice Memoranda Dated 23 Aibreán 1971, 21 Bealtaine 1971 and 30 Bealtaine 1972

National Archives UK, 'Offences Against the Person Act 1861, Article 58', http://www.legislation.gov.uk/ukpga/Vict/24-25/100/section/58, accessed 1 April 2014

Negra, D., 'On Not Watching Oprah in Post-Celtic Tiger Ireland', *Celebrity Studies*, vol. 3, no. 1, 2012, pp. 112–15

Neustatter, A. and Newson, G., *Mixed Feelings: the experience of abortion* (London: Pluto Press, 1986)

Nie, J.-B., *Behind the Silence: Chinese voices on abortion* (Oxford: Rowman & Littlefield Publishers, 2005)

NISRA, *Births in Northern Ireland 2012* (Belfast: Northern Ireland Statistics and Research Agency, 2012)

Noonan, J.T. (ed.), *The Morality of Abortion: legal and historical perspectives* (Cambridge, MA: Harvard University Press, 1970)

Oaks, L., '"Abortion Is Part of the Irish Experience, It Is Part of What We Are": the transformation of public discourses on Irish abortion policy', *Women's Studies International Forum*, vol. 25, no. 3, 2002, pp. 315–33

O'Brien, C., 'HSE Managers Warned of Risks to Patients from Funding Cuts and Understaffing', *Irish Times*, 20 August 2013, http://www.irishtimes.com/news/politics/hse-managers-warned-of-risks-to-patients-from-funding-cuts-and-understaffing-1.1490023, accessed 1 April 2014

O'Brien, E., *Down by the River* (London: Penguin, 1997)

O'Brien, J., 'Why We Are and Must Remain "Pro-Choice"', *RH Reality Check*, 25 April 2013, http://rhrealitycheck.org/article/2013/04/25/why-we-are-and-must-remain-for-choice, accessed 1 April 2014

O'Carroll, J., 'Bishops, Knights – and Pawns? Traditional thought and the Irish abortion referendum debate of 1983', *Irish Political Studies*, vol. 6, no. 1, 1991, pp. 53–71

O'Connor, M., 'Too Few Midwives, Too Many Babies', *Irish Times*, 6 May 2002

O'Connor, P., *Emerging Voices: women in contemporary Irish society* (Dublin: Institute of Public Administration, 1998)

O'Connor, P., 'Ireland: a man's world?', *The Economic and Social Review*, vol. 31, no. 1 January 2000

Oliver, M., 'Defining Impairment and Disability: issues at stake', in C. Barnes and G. Mercer (eds), *Exploring the Divide* (Leeds: The Disability Press, 1996), pp. 29–54

O'Regan, E., 'Stretched Services "Put Lives of Mothers and Babies at Risk"', *Irish Independent*, 12 December 2007, http://www.independent.ie/national-news/stretched-services-put-lives-of-mothers-and-babies-at-risk-1244689.html, accessed 1 April 2014

O'Regan, E., 'Former Victims of Michael Neary Accuse Health Minister of Breaking Compensation Promise', *Irish Independent*, 21 March 2013

O'Regan, E., 'Lives at Risk as Midwife Ratio in Our Maternity Units "Unsafe"', *Irish Independent*, 7 March 2014, http://www.independent.ie/lifestyle/health/lives-at-risk-as-midwife-ratio-in-our-maternity-units-unsafe-30071002.html, accessed 1 April 2014

O'Regan, M., 'Abortion Legislation about Protecting Mother's Life – Reilly', *Irish Times*, 15 July 2013

O'Reilly, E., *Masterminds of the Right* (Dublin: Attic Press, 1992)

O'Shea, S., 'Asylum Seekers in Limerick on Hunger Strike', *Irish Times*, 18 August 2014

O'Sullivan, D., *Cultural Politics and Irish Education since the 1950s: policy paradigms and power* (Dublin: Institute of Public Administration, 2005)

O'Sullivan, E. and O'Donnell, I. (eds), *Coercive Confinement in Ireland: patients, prisoners and penitents* (Manchester: Manchester University Press, 2012)

O'Toole, F., 'Lessons in the Power of the Church', *Irish Times*, 6 June 2009

O'Toole, F., 'Repression Shaped Our Passive Society', *Irish Times*, 26 February 2013

Peillon, M., *Contemporary Irish Society: an introduction* (Dublin: Gill & Macmillan, 1982)

Petchesky, R.P., *Abortion and Woman's Choice: the state, sexuality and reproductive freedom* (Boston: Northeastern University Press, 1984)

Petchesky, R.P., 'Fetal Images: the power of visual culture in the politics of reproduction', *Feminist Studies*, vol. 13, no. 2, 1987, pp. 263–92

Petchesky, R.P., 'Fetal Images: the power of visual culture in the politics of reproduction', in M. Stanworth (ed.), *Reproductive Technologies: gender, motherhood and medicine* (Cambridge: Polity Press, 1987), pp. 57–80

Petchesky, R.P. and Judd, K., *Negotiating Reproductive Rights* (London: Zed Press, 1998)

Philo, C., 'Foucault's Geography', in M. Crang and N. Thrift (eds), *Thinking Space* (London: Routledge, 2003), pp. 205–38

Pinar, W., *What Is Curriculum Theory?* (New Jersey: Lawrence Erlbaum Associates, 2004)

Pindyck, M., 'Towards a Side-spreading of the Subject of Abortion in Schools', *Sex Education*, vol. 13, no. 1, 2013, pp. S45–S55

Pollitt, K., 'Remember Savita Halappanavar', *The Nation*, 20 November 2012, http://www.thenation.com/article/171398/remember-savita-halappanavar#, accessed 1 April 2014

Pollitt, K., *Pro: reclaiming abortion rights* (New York: Picador, 2014)

Pope John Paul II, *Evangelium Vitae* (Rome: The Vatican, 1995)

Pope Paul VI, *Humane Vitae* (Rome: The Vatican, 1968)

Precious Life, http://www.preciouslife.com/resources, accessed 27 June 2015

Protection of Life During Pregnancy Bill 2013, http://www.irishstatutebook.ie/pdf/2013/en.act.2013.0035.pdf, accessed 1 April 2014

Price, K., 'What Is Reproductive Justice? How women of color activists are redefining the pro-choice paradigm', *Meridians: feminism, race, transnationalism*, vol. 10, no. 2, 2010, pp. 42–65

Qadir, Z., 'Ireland's Abortion Debate', *The Lancet*, vol. 381, no. 9878, 2013, p. 1614

Quesney, A., 'Speaking Up, Speaking Out: abortion in Ireland, exploring women's voices and pro-choice activism', unpublished MSc dissertation, Birkbeck College, University of London, 2012

Randall, V., 'Politics of Abortion in Ireland', in J. Lovenduski and J. Outshoorn (eds), *The New Politics of Abortion* (London: Sage Publishing Ltd, 1986)

Rapp, R., *Testing Women, Testing the Fetus: the social impact of amniocentesis in America* (New York: Routledge, 1999)

Rattigan, C., *What Else Could I Do? Single mothers and infanticide: Ireland, 1900–1950* (Dublin: Irish Academic Press, 2012)

Reilly, C., 'They Told Me She Was Exaggerating – Now She's Gone: Rotunda neglected care of Bimbo Onanuga, says partner', *Metro Éireann*, June 2011

Rhus, M., *Managing the Immigration and Employment of Non-EU Nationals in Ireland* (Dublin: The Policy Institute, Trinity College Dublin in association with COMPAS, 2005)

Rich, A. 'Notes Toward a Politics of Location' (1984). In C. R. McCann & S.-K. Kim (Eds.), *Feminist Theory Reader: Local and Global Perspectives*. (New York: Routledge, 2003)

Rich, A., *Of Woman Born: motherhood as experience and institution* (New York: Norton, 1976)

Riessman, C.K., *Narrative Methods for the Human Sciences* (Thousand Oaks, CA: Sage, 2008)

Riegal, R., 'AG Warned of "Time Bomb" of Pro-life Amendment', *Irish Independent*, 28 December 2012

Rossiter, A., *Ireland's Hidden Diaspora: the 'abortion trail' and the making of a London-Irish underground, 1980–2000* (London: Iasc Publishing, 2009)

Rothman, B.K. *Recreating Motherhood* (New Brunswick: Rutgers University Press, 2000)

Rowbotham, S., Segal, L. and Wainwright, H., *Beyond the Fragments: Feminism and the Making of Socialism* (London: Merlin Press, 2013), https://forworkerspower.wordpress.com/2013/04/16/beyond-the-fragments-feminism-and-the-making-of-socialism, accessed 1 April 2014

RTÉ, 'Midwife confirms she told Sanita Halappanavar Ireland a 'catholic country', 11 April 2013 (b). http://www.rte.ie/news/health/2013/0410/380613-savita-halappanavar-inquest/panavar-inquest/accessed 1 April 2014.

RTÉ, *Nine O'Clock News*, 'Ireland Wins Seat on the UN Human Rights Council' (13 November 2012) http://www.rte.ie/news/2012/1112/345326-ireland-wins-seat-on-un-human-rights-council/

RTÉ, *Prime Time*, 3 May 2013

RTÉ, 'HIQA Report into Savita Halappanavar's Death' (2013), http://www.rte.ie/news/player/2013/1010/20453023-hiqa-report-into-savita halappanavars-death, accessed 1 April 2014

Ruane, M., *The Irish Journey: women's stories of abortion* (Dublin: IFPA, 2000), available for download from www.ifpa.ie

Rúdólfsdóttir, A.G., 'I Am Not a Patient and I Am Not a Child': the institutionalization and experience of pregnancy', *Feminism and Psychology*, vol. 10, no. 3, 2000, pp. 337–50

Rukeyser, M., 'Kathe Kollwitz', in *The Collected Poems of Muriel Rukeyser* (Pittsburgh, Pittsburgh University Press, 2005)

Sandall, J., Soltani, H., Gates, S., Shennan, A. and Devane, D., 'Midwife-led Continuity Models Versus Other Models of Care for Childbearing Women', *Cochrane Database of Systematic Reviews*, No. 8, 2013

Sanger, M., *Margaret Sanger: an autobiography* (New York: Dover Publications Inc., 1971)

Savin-Baden, M., *Learning Spaces: creating opportunities for knowledge creation in academic life* (Berkshire: McGraw Hill, 2008)

Scannell, Y., 'The Constitution and the Role of Women', in B. Farrell (ed.), *De Valera's Constitution and Ours* (Dublin: RTÉ, 1987), pp. 123–36

Scheff, T.J., 'Shame and the Social Bond: a sociological theory', *Sociological Theory*, vol. 18, no. 1, 2000, pp. 84–99

Schweppe, J. (ed.), *The Unborn Child, Article 40.3.3 and Abortion in Ireland: twenty-five years of protection* (Dublin: Liffey Press, 2008)

Sedgh, G., Singh, S., Shah, I.H., Ahman, E., Henshaw, S.K. and Bankole, A., 'Induced Abortion: incidence and trends worldwide from 1995 to 2008', *The Lancet*, vol. 379, no. 9816, 2008, pp. 625–632

Segar, J., *The State of Women in the World Atlas* (London: Penguin, 2001)

Sethna, C., Palmer, B., Ackerman, K. and Janovicek, N., 'Choice, Interrupted: travel and inequality of access to abortion services since the 1960s', *Labour/Le Travail*, vol. 71, no. 1, 2013, pp. 29–48

Shannon, J., 'Maternal Death: into the great unknown', *Medical Independent*, 5 June 2010, http://www.medicalindependent.ie/1389/maternal_death_%E2%80%93_into_the_great_unknown, accessed 1 April 2014

Sheehan, F. and Hand, L., '1980s Abortion Referendum Was One of My Biggest Mistakes, Garret FitzGerald Admitted', *Irish Independent*, 17 December 2012

Sheldon, S., *Beyond Control: medical power and abortion law* (London: Pluto Press, 1997)

Sheridan, K., 'Stories of Abortion by People Who Have Been Through It', *Irish Times*, 24 March 2012

Sherlock, L., *Literature review and policy analysis on the cost of contraception.* (Unpublished report, Dublin: Crisis Pregnancy Agency, 2008)

Sherlock, L,. 'Sociopolitical influences on sexuality education in Sweden and Ireland.' *Sex Education*, vol, 12, no. 4, 2012, pp. 383-396

Siggins, L., 'Pregnant Women Fare Better Under Midwife-led Care – Study', *Irish Times*, 21 August 2013

Silliman, J., Fried, M.G., Ross, L. and Gutierrez, E., *Undivided Rights: women of color organizing for reproductive justice* (Boston: South End Press, 2004)

Silvers, A., 'On Not Iterating Women's Disability: a crossover perspective on genetic dilemmas', in A. Donchin and L. Purdy (eds), *Embodying Bioethics* (Lanham: Rowman & Littlefield, 1999), pp. 177–202

Skeggs, B., *Formations of Class and Gender: Becoming Respectable* (London: Sage, 1997)

Smet, S., '*A, B and C v. Ireland*: abortion and the margin of appreciation', http://strasbourgobservers.com/2010/12/17/a-b-and-c-v-ireland-abortion-and-the-margin-of-appreciation, accessed 1 April 2014

Smith, A., 'Beyond Pro-Choice Versus Pro-Life: women of color and reproductive justice', *NWSA Journal*, vol. 17, no. 1, 2005, pp. 119–40

Smyth, A. (ed), *The Abortion Papers Ireland* (Dublin: Attic Press, 1992)

Smyth, A., 'A Sadistic Farce', in A. Smyth (ed.), *The Abortion Papers Ireland* (Dublin: Attic Press, 1992) [1992a]

Smyth, A., 'The Politics of Abortion in a Police State', in A. Smyth (ed.), *The Abortion Papers Ireland* (Dublin: Attic Press, 1992) [1992b]

Smyth, A., 'An Interview with Ailbhe Smyth', http://www.tallgirlshorts.net/mary mary/ailbhe.html, accessed 1 April 2014

Smyth, L., 'Narratives of Irishness and the Problem of Abortion: the X case, 1992', *Feminist Review*, vol. 60, no. 1, 1998, pp. 61–83

Smyth, L., *Abortion and Nation: the politics of reproduction in contemporary Ireland* (Aldershot: Ashgate, 2005)

Smyth, L., 'From Rights to Compassion: the D case and contemporary abortion politics', in J. Schweppe (ed.), *The Unborn Child, Article 40.3.3 and Abortion in Ireland: twenty-five years of protection* (Dublin: The Liffey Press, 2008), pp. 47–64

Smyth, L., *The Demands of Motherhood* (Basingstoke: Palgrave Macmillan, 2012)

Solinger, R., *Beggars and Choosers* (New York: Hill & Wang, 2001)

Solomons, M., *Pro Life? The Irish question* (Dublin: The Lilliput Press, 1992)

Solomon, R., *True To Our Feelings: what our emotions are really telling us* (Oxford: Oxford University Press, 2007)

Sosa, G., 'The Midwife Manager', in R. Mander and V. Fleming (eds), *Becoming a Midwife* (London: Routledge, 2009)

Southall Black Sisters, *A Celebration of Survival and Struggle: Southall Black Sisters, 1979–1989* (London: Southall Black Sisters, 1990)

Squires, J., *Gender in Political Theory* (Cambridge: Polity Press, 1999)

Sterling, A.M., 'The European Union and Abortion Tourism: liberalizing Ireland's abortion law', *Boston College International and Comparative Law Review*, vol. 20, no. 2, 1997, pp. 385–406

Teman, E., 'Embodying Surrogate Motherhood: pregnancy as a dyadic body-project', *Body and Society*, vol. 15, no. 3, 2009, pp. 47–69

Termination for Medical Reasons (TFMR), http://www.terminationformedica lreasons.com, accessed 27 June 2015

Thapar-Björkert, S. and Ryan, L., 'Mother India/Mother Ireland: comparative gendered dialogues of colonialism and nationalism in the early 20th century', *Women's Studies International Forum*, vol. 25, no. 3, 2002, pp. 301–13

The Lancet, 'Ireland's Abortion Law: a start but not enough', vol. 382, no. 9888, p. 182, accessed July 2015

Tobin, C., Murphy-Lawless, J. and Beck, C.T., 'Childbirth in Exile: asylum-seeking women's experience of childbirth in Ireland', *Midwifery*, vol. 30, no. 7, 2014, pp. 831–8

Tran, L., 'Legal Rights and the Maternal-Fetal Conflict', *Science Creative Quarterly*, vol. 2, no. 8, January 2006, http://www.scq.ubc.ca/legal-rights-and-the-natural-foetal-conflict, accessed 18 August 2015

Threlfall, M. (ed.), *Mapping the Women's Movement: feminist politics and social transformation in the North* (Mappings Series) (London: Verso, 1996)

Tuan, L.-F., *Space and Place: the perspective of experience* (Minneapolis: University of Minnesota Press, 2007)

Turner, M., 'The introduction of internment in Ireland ... for 14-year-old-girls' (cartoon), *Irish Times*, 17 February 1992

Uí Chonnachtaigh, S., 'Confessions of a Closeted Cared-for', http://revaluingcare.net/ confessions-of-a-closeted-cared-for-by-sorcha-ui-chonnachtaigh, accessed 1 April 2014

United Nations, 'World Abortion Policies 2013', http://www.un.org/en/development/ desa/population/publications/policy/world-abortion-policies-2013.shtml, accessed 1 April 2014

Valentine, G., *Social Geographies: society and space* (Harlow: Longman, 2001)

Valiulis, M.G., 'Defining Their Role in the New State: Irishwomen's protest against the Juries Act of 1927', *The Canadian Journal of Irish Studies*, vol. 18, no. 1, 1992, pp. 43–60

Valiulis, M.G., 'Power, Gender and Identity in the Irish Free State', in J. Hoff and M. Coulter (eds), *Irish Women's Voices Past and Present* (Bloomington, IN: Indiana University Press, 1995)

Wainwright, H., 'Introduction', in S. Rowbotham, L. Segal and H. Wainwright, *Beyond the Fragments: feminism and the case for socialism* (London: Routledge, 2002), https://forworkerspower.wordpress.com/2013/01/20/beyond-the-fragments-feminism-and-the-making-of-socialism-introduction-by-hilary-wainwright, accessed 1 April 2014

Walsh, D., 'Medical and Social Characteristics of Irish Residents Whose Pregnancies Were Terminated under the 1967 Abortion Act in 1971 and 1972', *Journal of the Irish Medical Association*, vol. 68, no. 6, 1975, pp. 143–9

Walters, W., 'Acts of Demonstration: mapping the territory of (non) citizenship', in E. Isin and G. Nielsen (eds), *Acts of Citizenship* (London: Zed Books, 2008)

Ward, M., *Unmanageable Revolutionaries: women and Irish nationalism* (London: Pluto Press, 1983)

Weeks, J., *The World We Have Won: the remaking of erotic and intimate life* (London: Routledge, 2007)

West, R., 'From Choice to Reproductive Justice: de-constitutionalizing abortion rights', *The Yale Law Journal*, 2009, pp. 1394–1432

Whitaker, R. and Horgan, G., 'Abortion Governance in the New Northern Ireland', in L. Anton, S. DeZordo and J. Mishtal (eds), *A Right that Isn't? Abortion governance and associated protest logistics in postwar Europe* (New York: Berghahn, forthcoming)

Wiegman, R., *Object Lessons* (Durham: Duke University Press, 2004, 2012)

Wiley, M. and Merriman, B., *Women and Health Care in Ireland: knowledge, attitudes and behaviour* (Dublin: Oak Tree Press, 1996)

Wittig, M., *The Straight Mind and Other Essays.* (Boston: Beacon Press, 1982)

Workers Solidarity Movement, 'The Train that Crashed through the Anti-condom Law', *Workers Solidarity,* no. 101, January–February 2008

World Health Organisation (WHO), *Maternal Mortality in 2005: estimates developed by WHO/UNICEF/UNFPA and the World Bank* (Geneva: World Bank, 2007)

Youdell, D., *Impossible Bodies, Impossible Selves: exclusions and student subjectivities* (Dordecht: Springer, 2006)

Young, I.M., *Justice and the Politics of Difference* (Princeton, NJ: Princeton University Press, 1990)

Yuval-Davis, N., *Gender and Nation* (London: Sage Publications, 1997)

COURT CASES

Attorney General v. X and Others, High Court, No 847P (Costello J), 17 February 1992, Supreme Court, No 47 (Finlay, CJ, Hederman, McCarthy, O'Flaherty and Egan, JJ), 5 March 1992, ILRM 401

R v. Bourne, I KB 687 (1939)

Roe v. Wade, 410 US 113 (US Supreme Court 1973)

Doe v. Bolton, 410 179, 1973 (US Supreme Court 1973)

McGee v. Attorney General, IR 284 (1974)

Attorney General (SPUC) v. Open Door Counselling Ltd, ILRM 477 (1987)

R v. Morgantaler, 44 D.L.R. (4th) SCC (Supreme Court of Canada 1988)

SPUC v. Grogan (No. 2) Case 159/90, 3 CMLR 849 (1991)

Attorney General v. X, IR 1 (1992)

Open Door No. 2 (15 EHRR 244 1993)

Winnipeg Child and Family Services (Northwest Area) v. G. (D.F.) Supreme Court Judgments [1997] 3 SCR 925

A and B v. Eastern Health Board and C, ILRM 464 (1998)

Charatan, F US BMJ 319, 1220 (US Supreme Court 1999)

VO v. France (European Court of Human Rights 2004)

D v. Ireland, Application No. 26499/02 (ECHR, 28 June 2006)

D v. District Judge Brennan, HSE and Ireland, IEHC (2007)

A, B and C v. Ireland, Application No. 25579/054 (ECHR, 16 December 2010)

Appeal Decision re A, B and C v. Ireland (European Court of Human Rights 2012)

PP v. Health Service Executive, IEHC 622 (2014)

INDEX